PARISH MASS BOOK

YEAR B – Volume 2

McCRIMMONS
Great Wakering Essex UK

This edition first published in 2012
Published by McCrimmon Publishing Co Ltd
10–12 High Street, Great Wakering, Essex, SS3 0EQ, UK
Telephone (01702) 218 956   Fax (01702) 216082
info@mccrimmons.com   www.mccrimmons.com

Compilation and layout
© Copyright 2012, McCrimmon Publishing Co Ltd

ISBN 978-0-85597-716-0   A5 Standard edition
ISBN 978-0-85597-717-7   A4 Large-print edition

Concordat cum Originali   Jane Porter

Nihil obstat   Rt Rev Mgr David Manson
                            Censor Deputatus, 2012

Imprimatur   + Rt Rev Thomas McMahon
                            Bishop of Brentwood

Approved for use in the dioceses of England and Wales.
Permission granted for distribution in the dioceses of Scotland and Ireland.

Acknowledgements

Excerpts from the English translation and chants of *The Roman Missal* © 2010, International Commission on English in the Liturgy Corporation (ICEL); the English translation of *General Introduction from Lectionary for Mass* © 1969, 1981, 1997, ICEL; excerpts from the English translation of *Holy Communion & Worship of the Eucharist outside Mass* © 1974, ICEL; excerpts from the English translation of *Rite of Christian Initiation of Adults* © 1985, ICEL; excerpts from the English translation of *Ceremonial of Bishops* © 1989, ICEL. All rights reserved.

Further copyright acknowledgements are found on page 4.

Project management and typesetting: Patrick Geary.

The publishers wish to express their thanks to the following for their help in the preparation of this volume: Patrick Geary, Martin Foster and Jane Porter.

Cover design: Nick Snode.

Cover illustration by The Benedictine Sisters of Turvey Abbey. The four letters of this Christogram represent a traditional abbreviation of the Greek words for 'Jesus Christ' (i.e., the first and last letters of each of the words – 'IHCOYC XPICTOC' (Iesùs Christòs).

Typeset in ITC Stone Serif and ITC Stone Sans
Printed and bound by Permanent Printing Ltd., Hong Kong.   B/AE/40

CONTENTS

MUSIC

Some music is printed in the *Order of Mass* and in the propers. A fuller set of chants for the *Order of Mass* is found in the section *Music for the Order of Mass*. Cross-references to these chants are provided in the *Order of Mass*.

Consistent with the approach used in the Altar edition of *The Roman Missal*, the music of the chants is notated in order to avoid the use of key signatures. This does not preclude the chants being sung at a different pitch. Indeed, a pitch should be chosen which is comfortable for the Priest, Deacon, reader, cantor and assembly, in order to aid full participation in the liturgy.

ORDER OF MASS

In celebrating the Eucharist, the people of God assemble as the body of Christ to fulfil the Lord's command: 'do this in memory of me' (Luke 22:19).

At the Last Supper the Lord gathered his disciples, he spoke to them, took bread and wine, broke the bread, and gave them the Bread of life and the Cup of eternal salvation. In the Eucharist the Church to this day makes Christ's memorial and celebrates his presence in the same sequence of actions: we gather in Christ's name, in the Liturgy of the Word we listen as the word of God is proclaimed and explained, in the Liturgy of the Eucharist, we take bread and wine, give thanks, and receive the Body and Blood of Christ.

Christ is always present in his Church, particularly in its liturgical celebrations. In the celebration of Mass, Christ is really present in the very liturgical assembly gathered in his name, in the person of the minister who acts in the person of Christ, in the proclamation of his word and under the Eucharistic species. This presence of Christ under the appearance of bread and wine is called real, not to exclude other ways in which Christ is present, but because it is real *par excellence*.

cf Celebrating the Mass nn 18–19, 22;
General Instruction of the Roman Missal n 27;
Holy Communion and the Worship of the Eucharist
Outside Mass n 6.

OUTLINE OF THE ORDER OF MASS

INTRODUCTORY RITES
Opening Song
Greeting
Penitential Act
Gloria (omitted during Advent and Lent)
Opening Prayer

LITURGY OF THE WORD
First Reading
Responsorial Psalm
Second Reading
Gospel Acclamation
Gospel
Homily
Profession of Faith
Prayer of the Faithful

LITURGY OF THE EUCHARIST
Preparation of Gifts
Prayer over the Gifts
EUCHARISTIC PRAYER

COMMUNION RITE
The Lord's Prayer
Rite of Peace
Lamb of God
Holy Communion
Prayer after Communion

CONCLUDING RITES
Blessing
Dismissal

INTRODUCTORY RITES

> *Where two or three are gathered in my name,*
> *there am I in their midst.*
> *(Matthew 18:20)*
>
> The Introductory Rites help the faithful come together as one, to establish communion and to prepare themselves properly to listen to the word of God and to celebrate the Eucharist worthily.

ENTRANCE SONG
ALL STAND

While the Entrance Song is sung, the Priest approaches the altar with the ministers and venerates it.

SIGN OF THE CROSS
▷ *Music p 207*

All make the Sign of the Cross as the Priest says

Priest: In the name of the Father, and of the Son, and of the Holy Spirit.
People: **Amen.**

GREETING

Priest: The grace of our Lord Jesus Christ,
           and the love of God,
           and the communion of the Holy Spirit
           be with you all.

or

Priest: Grace to you and peace from God our Father
           and the Lord Jesus Christ.

or

Priest: The Lord be with you.
People: **And with your spirit.**

A Bishop will say:

Bishop: Peace be with you
People: **And with your spirit.**

The Priest, or a Deacon, or another minister, may very briefly introduce the faithful to the Mass of the day.

PENITENTIAL ACT

Because of its emphasis on Easter and Baptism, the Blessing and Sprinkling of Water (page 50) may take place on Sundays, especially in Easter Time. When it is used it replaces the Penitential Act.

Otherwise, one of the following three forms of the Penitential Act is used. Each Penitential Act begins with the invitation to the faithful by the Priest:

        Brethren (brothers and sisters), let us acknowledge our sins,
        and so prepare ourselves to celebrate the sacred mysteries.

A brief pause for silence follows.

On certain days during the Church's year, for example Palm Sunday and the Easter Vigil, and during certain other celebrations, for example a Funeral Mass, Rite of Acceptance into the Order of Catechumens, the Introductory Rites take a different form.

Penitential Act A

All: I confess to almighty God
            and to you, my brothers and sisters,
            that I have greatly sinned,
            in my thoughts and in my words,
            in what I have done and in what I have failed to do,

All strike their breast.

            through my fault, through my fault,
            through my most grievous fault;
            therefore I ask blessed Mary ever-Virgin,
            all the Angels and Saints,
            and you, my brothers and sisters,
            to pray for me to the Lord our God.

Penitential Act B   ▷ Music p 208

Priest: Have mercy on us, O Lord.
People: **For we have sinned against you.**

Priest: Show us, O Lord, your mercy.
People: **And grant us your salvation.**

Penitential Act C   ▷ Music p 208

After the silence the Priest or another minister invokes the gracious works of the Lord
to which he invites the Kyrie eleison invocations, in sequence, as in the example below:

Priest or minister: You were sent to heal the contrite of heart:
                      Lord, have mercy.   *or*   Kyrie, eleison.
People: **Lord, have mercy.**   *or*   **Kyrie, eleison.**

Priest or minister: You came to call sinners:
                      Christ, have mercy.   *or*   Christe, eleison.
People: **Christ, have mercy.** *or*   **Christe, eleison.**

Priest or minister: You are seated at the right hand of the Father to intercede for us:
                      Lord, have mercy.   *or*   Kyrie, eleison.
People: **Lord, have mercy.**   *or*   **Kyrie, eleison.**

The absolution by the Priest follows all of the options above

Priest: May almighty God have mercy on us,   ▷ Music p 209
            forgive us our sins,
            and bring us to everlasting life.
All: **Amen.**

ORDER

KYRIE

▷ Music p 209

The Kyrie, eleison (Lord, have mercy) invocations may follow:

Lord, have mercy.	Kyrie, eleison.
Lord, have mercy.	**Kyrie, eleison.**

Christ, have mercy.	*or*	Christe, eleison.
Christ, have mercy.		**Christe, eleison.**

Lord, have mercy.	Kyrie, eleison.
Lord, have mercy.	**Kyrie, eleison.**

GLORIA

▷ Music p 210

When indicated this hymn is sung or said:

All: **Glory to God in the highest,
and on earth peace to people of good will.
We praise you,
we bless you,
we adore you,
we glorify you,
we give you thanks for your great glory,
Lord God, heavenly King,
O God, almighty Father.**

**Lord Jesus Christ, Only Begotten Son,
Lord God, Lamb of God, Son of the Father,
you take away the sins of the world,
      have mercy on us;
you take away the sins of the world,
      receive our prayer;
you are seated at the right hand of the Father,
      have mercy on us.**

**For you alone are the Holy One,
you alone are the Lord,
you alone are the Most High,
Jesus Christ,
with the Holy Spirit,
in the glory of God the Father.
Amen.**

COLLECT

▷ Proper

Priest: Let us pray.

All pray in silence for a while. Then the Priest says the Collect, to which the people respond:

People: **Amen.**

ALL SIT

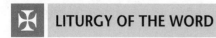 LITURGY OF THE WORD

> *Did not our hearts burn within us as he spoke to us*
> *and explained the Scriptures to us?*
> *(cf Luke 24:32)*
>
> In the Liturgy of the Word the assembly listens with hearts burning as the Lord speaks to it again and it responds with words of praise and petition.
>
> By hearing the word proclaimed in worship, the faithful again enter into the unending dialogue between God and the covenant people, a dialogue sealed in the sharing of the Eucharistic food and drink. The proclamation of the word is thus integral to the Mass and at its very centre.
>
> *Celebrating the Mass nn 19, 152*

FIRST READING   ▷ *Proper*

The reader goes to the ambo and proclaims the First Reading, while all sit and listen.

To indicate the end of the reading, the reader acclaims:

Reader: The word of the Lord.   ▷ *Music p 211*
All: **Thanks be to God.**

Following this reading, and the other readings it is appropriate to have a brief time of quiet as those present take the word of God to heart and begin to prepare a prayerful response to what they have heard.

RESPONSORIAL PSALM

The psalmist or cantor sings or says the Psalm, with the people making the response.

SECOND READING

On Sundays and certain other days there is a second reading.

To indicate the end of the reading, the reader acclaims:

Reader: The word of the Lord.   ▷ *Music p 211*
All: **Thanks be to God.**

GOSPEL ACCLAMATION   **ALL STAND**

The assembly stands for the Gospel Acclamation to welcome the Gospel.
The Gospel Acclamation may not be omitted where there is more than one reading before the Gospel.

The Gospel Acclamation is

Alleluia

GOSPEL

The assembly remains standing in honour of the Gospel reading,
the high point of the Liturgy of the Word.

At the ambo the Deacon, or the Priest, sings or says:

Deacon or Priest: The Lord be with you.   ▷ *Music p 211*
All: **And with your spirit.**

Deacon or Priest: A reading from the holy Gospel according to N.

The Deacon or Priest makes the Sign of the Cross on the book and, together with the people,
on his forehead, lips, and breast.

All: **Glory to you, O Lord.**

At the end of the Gospel, the Deacon, or the Priest, acclaims:

Deacon or Priest: The Gospel of the Lord.
All: **Praise to you, Lord Jesus Christ.**

ALL SIT

HOMILY

The Homily is preached by a Priest or Deacon on all Sundays and Holydays of Obligation.
On other days, it is recommended.

At the end of the Homily it is appropriate for there to be a brief silence for recollection.

ALL STAND

PROFESSION OF FAITH

On Sundays and Solemnities, the Profession of Faith will follow.

In Masses that include acceptance into the order of catechumens and in ritual Masses for the election
or enrolment of names or for the Scrutinies, the Profession of Faith may be omitted.

On most occasions the form used is that of the Niceno-Constantinopolitan Creed.
However, especially during Lent and Easter Time, the Apostles' Creed (page 12) may be used.

If the Profession of Faith is not said, the Prayer of the Faithful follows.

Niceno-Constantinopolitan Creed   ▷ *Music p 212*

I believe in one God,
the Father almighty,
maker of heaven and earth,
of all things visible and invisible.

I believe in one Lord Jesus Christ,
the Only Begotten Son of God,
born of the Father before all ages.
God from God, Light from Light,
true God from true God,
begotten, not made, consubstantial with the Father;

through him all things were made.
For us men and for our salvation
he came down from heaven,

At the words that follow, up to and including 'and became man', all bow.

and by the Holy Spirit was incarnate of the Virgin Mary,
and became man.

For our sake he was crucified under Pontius Pilate,
he suffered death and was buried,
and rose again on the third day
in accordance with the Scriptures.
He ascended into heaven
and is seated at the right hand of the Father.
He will come again in glory
to judge the living and the dead
and his kingdom will have no end.

I believe in the Holy Spirit, the Lord, the giver of life,
who proceeds from the Father and the Son,
who with the Father and the Son is adored and glorified,
who has spoken through the prophets.

I believe in one, holy, catholic and apostolic Church.
I confess one Baptism for the forgiveness of sins
and I look forward to the resurrection of the dead
and the life of the world to come. Amen.

THE APOSTLES' CREED

Instead of the Niceno-Constantinopolitan Creed, the Apostles' Creed, may be used.

I believe in God,
the Father almighty
Creator of heaven and earth,
and in Jesus Christ, his only Son, our Lord,

At the words that follow, up to and including 'the Virgin Mary', all bow.

who was conceived by the Holy Spirit,
born of the Virgin Mary,
suffered under Pontius Pilate,
was crucified, died and was buried;
he descended into hell;
on the third day he rose again from the dead;
he ascended into heaven,
and is seated at the right hand of God the Father almighty;
from there he will come to judge the living and the dead.

I believe in the Holy Spirit,
the holy catholic Church,
the communion of saints,
the forgiveness of sins,
the resurrection of the body,
and life everlasting. Amen.

PRAYER OF THE FAITHFUL

*Enlightened and moved by God's word, the assembly exercises its priestly function
by interceding for all humanity.*

Priest's Introduction

The Priest calls the assembly to prayer.

Intentions

As a rule the series of intentions is:

1   for the needs of the Church
2   for public authorities and the salvation of the whole world
3   for those burdened with any kind of difficulty
4   for the local community

*Nevertheless, in particular celebrations such as Confirmation, Marriage, or a Funeral, the series of
intentions may reflect more closely the particular occasion.*

The Deacon, or a Reader, announces short intentions for prayer to the assembly.

*After each intention there is a significant pause while the assembly prays,
then the response is sung or said.*

Example responses:

Deacon or Reader: We pray to the Lord.
All: **Lord, hear our prayer.**

or

Deacon or Reader: Let us pray to the Lord,
All: **Grant this, almighty God.**

or

Deacon or Reader: Let us pray to the Lord,
All: **Christ, hear us.**   *or*   **Christ, graciously hear us.**

or

Deacon or Reader: Let us pray to the Lord,
All: **Lord, have mercy.**   *or*   **Kyrie, eleison.**

After the final intention and response, there may be a period of silent prayer.

Priest's Prayer

Then the Priest says a concluding prayer to which all reply:

All: **Amen.**

ALL SIT

✠ LITURGY OF THE EUCHARIST

> *Their eyes were opened and they recognised him in the breaking of bread.*
> *(cf Luke 24:30–31)*
>
> At the Last Supper, Christ instituted the Sacrifice and Paschal meal that make the Sacrifice of the cross present in the Church. From the days of the Apostles the Church has celebrated that Sacrifice by carrying out what the Lord did and handed over to his disciples to do in his memory. Like him, the Church has taken bread and wine, given thanks to God over them, broken the bread, and shared the bread and cup of blessing as the Body and Blood of Christ (cf 1 Corinthians 10:16).
> *Celebrating the Mass n 174*

PREPARATION OF THE GIFTS

A hymn or song may be sung, or instrumental music played during the collection, the procession, and the presentation of the gifts. If there is no music, the Priest may speak the following words aloud and the people acclaim the response at the end of each prayer.

Priest: Blessed are you, Lord God of all creation,
for through your goodness we have received
the bread we offer you:
fruit of the earth and work of human hands,
it will become for us the bread of life.

People: **Blessed be God for ever.**

Priest: Blessed are you, Lord God of all creation,
for through your goodness we have received
the wine we offer you:
fruit of the vine and work of human hands,
it will become our spiritual drink.

People: **Blessed be God for ever.**

ALL STAND

The Priest completes additional personal preparatory rites, and the people rise as he says:

Priest: Pray, brethren (brothers and sisters),   ▷ *Music p 214*
that my sacrifice and yours
may be acceptable to God,
the almighty Father.

People: **May the Lord accept the sacrifice at your hands
for the praise and glory of his name,
for our good
and the good of all his holy Church.**

PRAYER OVER THE OFFERINGS   ▷ *Proper*

Then the Priest says the Prayer over the Offerings, at the end of which the people acclaim:

People: **Amen.**

EUCHARISTIC PRAYER

The Eucharistic Prayer, the centre and summit of the entire celebration, sums up what it means for the Church to celebrate the Eucharist. It is a memorial proclamation of praise and thanksgiving for God's work of salvation, a proclamation in which the Body and Blood of Christ are made present by the power of the Holy Spirit and the people are joined to Christ in offering his Sacrifice to the Father. The Eucharistic Prayer is proclaimed by the Priest celebrant in the name of Christ and on behalf of the whole assembly, which professes its faith and gives its assent through dialogue, acclamations, and the Amen. Since the Eucharistic Prayer is the summit of the Mass, it is appropriate for its solemn nature and importance to be enhanced by being sung.

Celebrating the Mass n 186

Eucharistic Prayers I to IV are the principal prayers and are for use throughout the liturgical year. Eucharistic Prayer IV has a fixed preface and so may only be used when a Mass has no preface of its own and on Sundays in Ordinary Time. Eucharistic Prayers I to IV and Eucharistic Prayers for Reconciliation I and II are printed in full, beginning on page 18.

PREFACE DIALOGUE

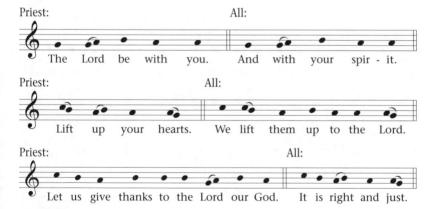

Priest: The Lord be with you.
All: And with your spirit.

Priest: Lift up your hearts.
All: We lift them up to the Lord.

Priest: Let us give thanks to the Lord our God.
All: It is right and just.

Priest: The Lord be with you.
People: **And with your spirit.**

Priest: Lift up your hearts.
People: **We lift them up to the Lord.**

Priest: Let us give thanks to the Lord our God.
People: **It is right and just.**

PREFACE

The Priest continues with the Preface.

▷ *Prefaces p 66*

SANCTUS

The Priest concludes the Preface with the people, singing or saying aloud:

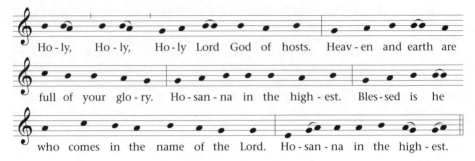

Ho-ly, Ho-ly, Ho-ly Lord God of hosts. Heav-en and earth are
full of your glo-ry. Ho-san-na in the high-est. Bles-sed is he
who comes in the name of the Lord. Ho-san-na in the high-est.

All: **Holy, Holy, Holy Lord God of hosts.**
Heaven and earth are full of your glory.
Hosanna in the highest.
Blessed is he who comes in the name of the Lord.
Hosanna in the highest.

or

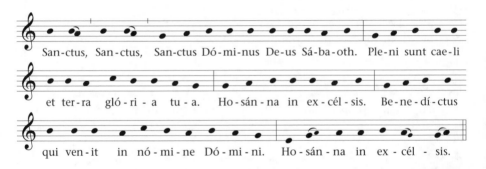

San-ctus, San-ctus, San-ctus Dó-mi-nus De-us Sá-ba-oth. Ple-ni sunt cae-li
et ter-ra gló-ri-a tu-a. Ho-sán-na in ex-cél-sis. Be-ne-dí-ctus
qui ven-it in nó-mi-ne Dó-mi-ni. Ho-sán-na in ex-cél-sis.

ALL KNEEL

Texts for Eucharistic Prayers I to IV and Eucharistic Prayers for Reconciliation I and II follow on page 18.

MEMORIAL ACCLAMATION

The Memorial Acclamation follows the words of Institution and the elevation of the host and chalice.

The Priest sings:

The mys-ter-y of faith.

And the people continue with one of the following acclamations.

ORDER

Memorial Acclamation A

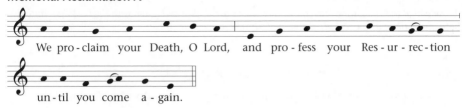

We pro - claim your Death, O Lord, and pro - fess your Res - ur - rec - tion

un - til you come a - gain.

Memorial Acclamation B

When we eat this Bread and drink this Cup, we pro - claim your

Death, O Lord, un - til you come a - gain.

Memorial Acclamation C

Save us, Sav - iour of the world, for by your Cross

and Res - ur - rec - tion you have set us free.

Memorial Acclamation D *for Ireland only*

My Lord and my God.

Priest: The mystery of faith.

People: **We proclaim your Death, O Lord,
and profess your Resurrection
until you come again.**

or

People: **When we eat this Bread and drink this Cup,
we proclaim your Death, O Lord,
until you come again.**

or

People: **Save us, Saviour of the world,
for by your Cross and Resurrection
you have set us free.**

or for Ireland only:

People: **My Lord and my God.**

DOXOLOGY AND GREAT AMEN

At the end of the Eucharistic Prayer, the Priest takes the chalice and paten with the host and, raising both, he alone sings (or says) the Doxology. The people acclaim 'Amen'.

Priest:

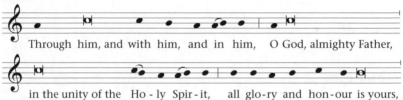

Through him, and with him, and in him,   O God, almighty Father,

in the unity of the   Ho - ly Spir - it,   all glo-ry and hon-our is yours,

People:

for ev - er   and   ev - er.   A - men.

Priest: Through him, and with him, and in him,
           O God, almighty Father,
           in the unity of the Holy Spirit,
           all glory and honour is yours,
           for ever and ever.
People: **Amen.**   ▷ *page 57*

EUCHARISTIC PRAYERS

EUCHARISTIC PRAYER I

THE ROMAN CANON

On certain occasions, special forms of parts of the Eucharistic Prayer may be used.

Priest: To you, therefore, most merciful Father,
           we make humble prayer and petition
           through Jesus Christ, your Son, our Lord:
           that you accept
           and bless ✠ these gifts, these offerings,
           these holy and unblemished sacrifices,
           which we offer you firstly
           for your holy catholic Church.
           Be pleased to grant her peace,
           to guard, unite and govern her
           throughout the whole world,
           together with your servant N. our Pope
           and N. our Bishop,*
           and all those who, holding to the truth,
           hand on the catholic and apostolic faith.

---

* Mention may be made here of the Coadjutor Bishop, or Auxiliary Bishops

ORDER

Commemoration of the Living

Remember, Lord, your servants N. and N.
and all gathered here,
whose faith and devotion are known to you.
For them, we offer you this sacrifice of praise
or they offer it for themselves
and all who are dear to them:
for the redemption of their souls,
in hope of health and well-being,
and paying their homage to you,
the eternal God, living and true.

Communicantes

In communion with those whose memory we venerate,
especially the glorious ever-Virgin Mary,
Mother of our God and Lord, Jesus Christ,
and blessed Joseph, her Spouse,
your blessed Apostles and Martyrs,
Peter and Paul, Andrew,
(James, John,
Thomas, James, Philip,
Bartholomew, Matthew,
Simon and Jude;
Linus, Cletus, Clement, Sixtus,
Cornelius, Cyprian,
Lawrence, Chrysogonus,
John and Paul,
Cosmas and Damian)
and all your Saints;
we ask that through their merits and prayers,
in all things we may be defended
by your protecting help.
(Through Christ our Lord. Amen.)

Hanc Igitur

Therefore, Lord, we pray:
graciously accept this oblation of our service,
that of your whole family;
order our days in your peace,
and command that we be delivered from eternal damnation
and counted among the flock of those you have chosen.
(Through Christ our Lord. Amen.)

Be pleased, O God, we pray,
to bless, acknowledge,
and approve this offering in every respect;
make it spiritual and acceptable,
so that it may become for us
the Body and Blood of your most beloved Son,
our Lord Jesus Christ.

On the day before he was to suffer,
he took bread in his holy and venerable hands,
and with eyes raised to heaven
to you, O God, his almighty Father,
giving you thanks, he said the blessing,
broke the bread
and gave it to his disciples, saying:

Take this, all of you, and eat of it,
for this is my Body,
which will be given up for you.

In a similar way, when supper was ended,
he took this precious chalice
in his holy and venerable hands,
and once more giving you thanks, he said the blessing
and gave the chalice to his disciples, saying:

Take this, all of you, and drink from it,
for this is the chalice of my Blood,
the Blood of the new and eternal covenant,
which will be poured out for you and for many
for the forgiveness of sins.

Do this in memory of me.

Memorial Acclamation

The Priest sings:

The mys - ter - y of faith.

And the people continue with one of the following acclamations:

ORDER

Memorial Acclamation A

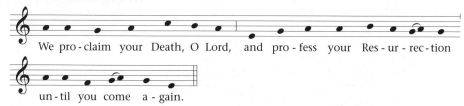

We pro-claim your Death, O Lord, and pro-fess your Res-ur-rec-tion
un-til you come a-gain.

Memorial Acclamation B

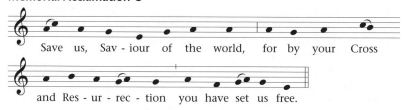

When we eat this Bread and drink this Cup, we pro-claim your
Death, O Lord, un-til you come a-gain.

Memorial Acclamation C

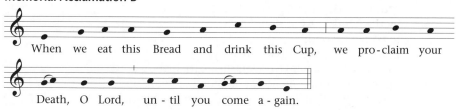

Save us, Sav-iour of the world, for by your Cross
and Res-ur-rec-tion you have set us free.

Memorial Acclamation D *for Ireland only*

My Lord and my God.

Priest: Therefore, O Lord,
as we celebrate the memorial of the blessed Passion,
the Resurrection from the dead,
and the glorious Ascension into heaven
of Christ, your Son, our Lord,
we, your servants and your holy people,
offer to your glorious majesty
from the gifts that you have given us,
this pure victim,
this holy victim,
this spotless victim,
the holy Bread of eternal life
and the Chalice of everlasting salvation.

Be pleased to look upon these offerings
with a serene and kindly countenance,
and to accept them,
as once you were pleased to accept
the gifts of your servant Abel the just,
the sacrifice of Abraham, our father in faith,
and the offering of your high priest Melchizedek,
a holy sacrifice, a spotless victim.

In humble prayer we ask you, almighty God:
command that these gifts be borne
by the hands of your holy Angel
to your altar on high
in the sight of your divine majesty,
so that all of us, who through this participation at the altar
receive the most holy Body and Blood of your Son,
may be filled with every grace and heavenly blessing.
(Through Christ our Lord. Amen.)

Commemoration of the Dead

Remember also, Lord, your servants N. and N.,
who have gone before us with the sign of faith
and rest in the sleep of peace.
Grant them, O Lord, we pray,
and all who sleep in Christ,
a place of refreshment, light and peace.
(Through Christ our Lord. Amen.)

To us, also, your servants, who, though sinners,
hope in your abundant mercies,
graciously grant some share
and fellowship with your holy Apostles and Martyrs:
with John the Baptist, Stephen,
Matthias, Barnabas,
(Ignatius, Alexander,
Marcellinus, Peter,
Felicity, Perpetua,
Agatha, Lucy,
Agnes, Cecilia, Anastasia)
and all your Saints;
admit us, we beseech you,
into their company,
not weighing our merits,
but granting us your pardon,
through Christ our Lord.

ORDER

Through whom
you continue to make all these good things, O Lord;
you sanctify them, fill them with life,
bless them, and bestow them upon us.

Doxology and Great Amen

At the end of the Eucharistic Prayer, the Priest takes the chalice and paten with the host and, raising both, he alone sings (or says) the Doxology. The people acclaim 'Amen'.

Priest: Through him, and with him, and in him,
            O God, almighty Father,
            in the unity of the Holy Spirit,
            all glory and honour is yours,
            for ever and ever.
People: **Amen.**

...for ev - er and ev - er.   A - men.

▷ *page 57*

EUCHARISTIC PRAYER II

This Eucharistic Prayer has its own Preface, but it may also be used with other Prefaces, especially those that present an overall view of the mystery of salvation.

On certain occasions, special forms of parts of the Eucharistic Prayer may be used.

Preface Dialogue

The Lord be with you.   And with your spir - it.

Lift up your hearts.   We lift them up to the Lord.

Let us give thanks to the Lord our God.   It is right and just.

Preface

Priest: It is truly right and just, our duty and our salvation,
           always and everywhere to give you thanks, Father most holy,
           through your beloved Son, Jesus Christ,
           your Word through whom you made all things,
           whom you sent as our Saviour and Redeemer,
           incarnate by the Holy Spirit and born of the Virgin.

           Fulfilling your will and gaining for you a holy people,
           he stretched out his hands as he endured his Passion,
           so as to break the bonds of death and manifest the resurrection.

           And so, with the Angels and all the Saints
           we declare your glory,
           as with one voice we acclaim:

Sanctus

All:

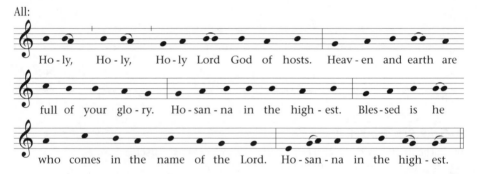

Ho-ly, Ho-ly, Ho-ly Lord God of hosts. Heav-en and earth are full of your glo-ry. Ho-san-na in the high-est. Bles-sed is he who comes in the name of the Lord. Ho-san-na in the high-est.

Priest: You are indeed Holy, O Lord,   **ALL KNEEL**
           the fount of all holiness.
           Make holy, therefore, these gifts, we pray,
           by sending down your Spirit upon them like the dewfall,
           so that they may become for us
           the Body and ✠ Blood of our Lord Jesus Christ.

           At the time he was betrayed
           and entered willingly into his Passion,
           he took bread and, giving thanks, broke it,
           and gave it to his disciples, saying:

           TAKE THIS, ALL OF YOU, AND EAT OF IT,
           FOR THIS IS MY BODY,
           WHICH WILL BE GIVEN UP FOR YOU.

           In a similar way, when supper was ended,
           he took the chalice
           and, once more giving thanks,
           he gave it to his disciples, saying:

ORDER

Tᴀᴋᴇ ᴛʜɪs, ᴀʟʟ ᴏꜰ ʏᴏᴜ, ᴀɴᴅ ᴅʀɪɴᴋ ꜰʀᴏᴍ ɪᴛ,
ꜰᴏʀ ᴛʜɪs ɪs ᴛʜᴇ ᴄʜᴀʟɪᴄᴇ ᴏꜰ ᴍʏ Bʟᴏᴏᴅ,
ᴛʜᴇ Bʟᴏᴏᴅ ᴏꜰ ᴛʜᴇ ɴᴇᴡ ᴀɴᴅ ᴇᴛᴇʀɴᴀʟ ᴄᴏᴠᴇɴᴀɴᴛ,
ᴡʜɪᴄʜ ᴡɪʟʟ ʙᴇ ᴘᴏᴜʀᴇᴅ ᴏᴜᴛ ꜰᴏʀ ʏᴏᴜ ᴀɴᴅ ꜰᴏʀ ᴍᴀɴʏ
ꜰᴏʀ ᴛʜᴇ ꜰᴏʀɢɪᴠᴇɴᴇss ᴏꜰ sɪɴs.

Dᴏ ᴛʜɪs ɪɴ ᴍᴇᴍᴏʀʏ ᴏꜰ ᴍᴇ.

Memorial Acclamation

The Priest sings:

The mys - ter - y of faith.

And the people continue with one of the following acclamations:

Memorial Acclamation A

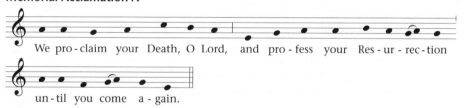

We pro - claim your Death, O Lord, and pro - fess your Res - ur - rec - tion un - til you come a - gain.

Memorial Acclamation B

When we eat this Bread and drink this Cup, we pro - claim your Death, O Lord, un - til you come a - gain.

Memorial Acclamation C

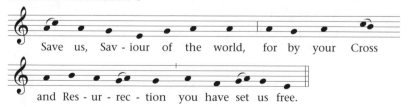

Save us, Sav - iour of the world, for by your Cross and Res - ur - rec - tion you have set us free.

Memorial Acclamation D   *for Ireland only*

My Lord and my God.

Priest: Therefore, as we celebrate
            the memorial of his Death and Resurrection,
            we offer you, Lord,
            the Bread of life and the Chalice of salvation,
            giving thanks that you have held us worthy
            to be in your presence and minister to you.

            Humbly we pray
            that, partaking of the Body and Blood of Christ,
            we may be gathered into one by the Holy Spirit.

            Remember, Lord, your Church,
            spread throughout the world,
            and bring her to the fullness of charity,
            together with N. our Pope and N. our Bishop *
            and all the clergy.

In Masses for the Dead, the following may be added:
            Remember your servant N.,
            whom you have called (today)
            from this world to yourself.
            Grant that he (she) who was united with your Son in a death like his,
            may also be one with him in his Resurrection.

            Remember also our brothers and sisters
            who have fallen asleep in the hope of the resurrection,
            and all who have died in your mercy:
            welcome them into the light of your face.
            Have mercy on us all, we pray,
            that with the Blessed Virgin Mary, Mother of God,
            with blessed Joseph, her Spouse,
            with the blessed Apostles,
            and all the Saints who have pleased you throughout the ages,
            we may merit to be coheirs to eternal life,
            and may praise and glorify you
            through your Son, Jesus Christ.

---

* Mention may be made here of the Coadjutor Bishop, or Auxiliary Bishops

Doxology and Great Amen

At the end of the Eucharistic Prayer, the Priest takes the chalice and paten with the host and, raising both, he alone sings (or says) the Doxology. The people acclaim 'Amen'.

Priest: Through him, and with him, and in him,
          O God, almighty Father,
          in the unity of the Holy Spirit,
          all glory and honour is yours,
          for ever and ever.

People: **Amen.**

Priest: People:

...for ev - er and ev - er.   A-men.

▷ *page 57*

EUCHARISTIC PRAYER III

On certain occasions, special forms of parts of the Eucharistic Prayer may be used.

Priest: You are indeed Holy, O Lord,
          and all you have created
          rightly gives you praise,
          for through your Son our Lord Jesus Christ,
          by the power and working of the Holy Spirit,
          you give life to all things and make them holy,
          and you never cease to gather a people to yourself,
          so that from the rising of the sun to its setting
          a pure sacrifice may be offered to your name.

          Therefore, O Lord, we humbly implore you:
          by the same Spirit graciously make holy
          these gifts we have brought to you for consecration,
          that they may become the Body and ✠ Blood
          of your Son our Lord Jesus Christ,
          at whose command we celebrate these mysteries.

          For on the night he was betrayed
          he himself took bread,
          and, giving you thanks, he said the blessing,
          broke the bread and gave it to his disciples, saying:

          TAKE THIS, ALL OF YOU, AND EAT OF IT,
          FOR THIS IS MY BODY,
          WHICH WILL BE GIVEN UP FOR YOU.

ORDER

In a similar way, when supper was ended,
he took the chalice,
and, giving you thanks, he said the blessing,
and gave the chalice to his disciples, saying:

TAKE THIS, ALL OF YOU, AND DRINK FROM IT,
FOR THIS IS THE CHALICE OF MY BLOOD,
THE BLOOD OF THE NEW AND ETERNAL COVENANT,
WHICH WILL BE POURED OUT FOR YOU AND FOR MANY
FOR THE FORGIVENESS OF SINS.

DO THIS IN MEMORY OF ME.

Memorial Acclamation

The Priest sings:

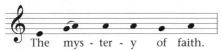

The mys - ter - y of faith.

And the people continue with one of the following acclamations:

Memorial Acclamation A

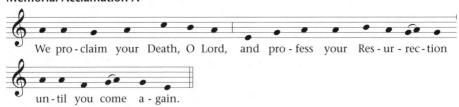

We pro - claim your Death, O Lord, and pro - fess your Res - ur - rec - tion

un - til you come a - gain.

Memorial Acclamation B

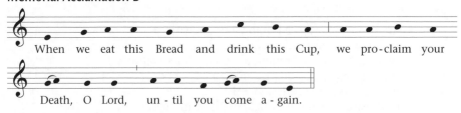

When we eat this Bread and drink this Cup, we pro - claim your

Death, O Lord, un - til you come a - gain.

Memorial Acclamation C

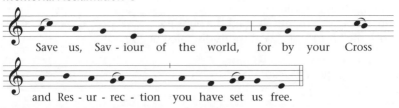

Save us, Sav - iour of the world, for by your Cross

and Res - ur - rec - tion you have set us free.

ORDER

Memorial Acclamation D   *for Ireland only*

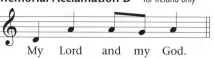

My   Lord   and   my   God.

Priest: Therefore, O Lord, as we celebrate the memorial
of the saving Passion of your Son,
his wondrous Resurrection
and Ascension into heaven,
and as we look forward to his second coming,
we offer you in thanksgiving
this holy and living sacrifice.

Look, we pray, upon the oblation of your Church
and, recognizing the sacrificial Victim by whose death
you willed to reconcile us to yourself,
grant that we, who are nourished
by the Body and Blood of your Son
and filled with his Holy Spirit,
may become one body, one spirit in Christ.

May he make of us
an eternal offering to you,
so that we may obtain an inheritance with your elect,
especially with the most Blessed Virgin Mary, Mother of God,
with blessed Joseph, her Spouse,
with your blessed Apostles and glorious Martyrs
(with Saint N.: *the Saint of the day or Patron Saint*)
and with all the Saints,
on whose constant intercession in your presence
we rely for unfailing help.

May this Sacrifice of our reconciliation,
we pray, O Lord,
advance the peace and salvation of all the world.
Be pleased to confirm in faith and charity
your pilgrim Church on earth,
with your servant N. our Pope and N. our Bishop,*
the Order of Bishops, all the clergy,
and the entire people you have gained for your own.

Listen graciously to the prayers of this family,
whom you have summoned before you:
in your compassion, O merciful Father,
gather to yourself all your children
scattered throughout the world.

* Mention may be made here of the Coadjutor Bishop, or Auxiliary Bishops

† To our departed brothers and sisters
and to all who were pleasing to you
at their passing from this life,
give kind admittance to your kingdom.
There we hope to enjoy for ever the fullness of your glory
through Christ our Lord,
through whom you bestow on the world all that is good. †

In Masses for the Dead, the following may be said:
† Remember your servant N.
whom you have called (today)
from this world to yourself.
Grant that he (she) who was united with your Son in a death like his,
may also be one with him in his Resurrection,
when from the earth
he will raise up in the flesh those who have died,
and transform our lowly body
after the pattern of his own glorious body.
To our departed brothers and sisters, too,
and to all who were pleasing to you
at their passing from this life,
give kind admittance to your kingdom.
There we hope to enjoy for ever the fullness of your glory,
when you will wipe away every tear from our eyes.
For seeing you, our God, as you are,
we shall be like you for all the ages
and praise you without end,
through Christ our Lord,
through whom you bestow on the world all that is good. †

Doxology and Great Amen
At the end of the Eucharistic Prayer, the Priest takes the chalice and paten with the host and, raising both, he alone sings (or says) the Doxology. The people acclaim 'Amen'.

Priest: Through him, and with him, and in him,
          O God, almighty Father,
          in the unity of the Holy Spirit,
          all glory and honour is yours,
          for ever and ever.
People: **Amen.**

Priest: People:

...for ev - er and ev - er.   A - men.

▷ *page 57*

ORDER

EUCHARISTIC PRAYER IV

This Eucharistic Prayer has its own Preface which may not be replaced by another, because of the
structure of the Prayer itself, which presents a summary of the history of salvation.
On certain occasions, special forms of parts of the Eucharistic Prayer may be used.

Preface Dialogue

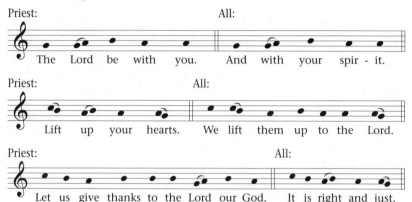

Priest: The Lord be with you.   All: And with your spir - it.

Priest: Lift up your hearts.   All: We lift them up to the Lord.

Priest: Let us give thanks to the Lord our God.   All: It is right and just.

Preface

Priest: It is truly right to give you thanks,
            truly just to give you glory, Father most holy,
            for you are the one God living and true,
            existing before all ages and abiding for all eternity,
            dwelling in unapproachable light;
            yet you, who alone are good, the source of life,
            have made all that is,
            so that you might fill your creatures with blessings
            and bring joy to many of them by the glory of your light.

            And so, in your presence are countless hosts of Angels,
            who serve you day and night
            and, gazing upon the glory of your face,
            glorify you without ceasing.

            With them we, too, confess your name in exultation,
            giving voice to every creature under heaven,
            as we acclaim:

Sanctus   *(see over)*

Sanctus

All:

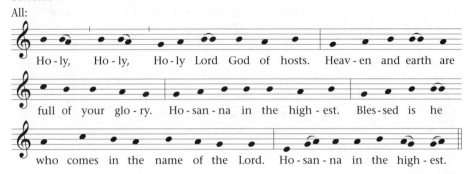

Ho-ly, Ho-ly, Ho-ly Lord God of hosts. Heav-en and earth are full of your glo-ry. Ho-san-na in the high-est. Bles-sed is he who comes in the name of the Lord. Ho-san-na in the high-est.

ALL KNEEL

Priest: We give you praise, Father most holy,
for you are great
and you have fashioned all your works
in wisdom and in love.
You formed man in your own image
and entrusted the whole world to his care,
so that in serving you alone, the Creator,
he might have dominion over all creatures.
And when through disobedience he had lost your friendship,
you did not abandon him to the domain of death.
For you came in mercy to the aid of all,
so that those who seek might find you.
Time and again you offered them covenants
and through the prophets
taught them to look forward to salvation.

And you so loved the world, Father most holy,
that in the fullness of time
you sent your Only Begotten Son to be our Saviour.
Made incarnate by the Holy Spirit
and born of the Virgin Mary,
he shared our human nature
in all things but sin.
To the poor he proclaimed the good news of salvation,
to prisoners, freedom,
and to the sorrowful of heart, joy.
To accomplish your plan,
he gave himself up to death,
and, rising from the dead,
he destroyed death and restored life.

And that we might live no longer for ourselves
but for him who died and rose again for us,
he sent the Holy Spirit from you, Father,
as the first fruits for those who believe,
so that, bringing to perfection his work in the world,
he might sanctify creation to the full.

Therefore, O Lord, we pray:
may this same Holy Spirit
graciously sanctify these offerings,
that they may become
the Body and ✠ Blood of our Lord Jesus Christ
for the celebration of this great mystery,
which he himself left us
as an eternal covenant.

For when the hour had come
for him to be glorified by you, Father most holy,
having loved his own who were in the world,
he loved them to the end:
and while they were at supper,
he took bread, blessed and broke it,
and gave it to his disciples, saying:

TAKE THIS, ALL OF YOU, AND EAT OF IT,
FOR THIS IS MY BODY,
WHICH WILL BE GIVEN UP FOR YOU.

In a similar way,
taking the chalice filled with the fruit of the vine,
he gave thanks,
and gave the chalice to his disciples, saying:

TAKE THIS, ALL OF YOU, AND DRINK FROM IT,
FOR THIS IS THE CHALICE OF MY BLOOD,
THE BLOOD OF THE NEW AND ETERNAL COVENANT,
WHICH WILL BE POURED OUT FOR YOU AND FOR MANY
FOR THE FORGIVENESS OF SINS.

DO THIS IN MEMORY OF ME.

Memorial Acclamation

The Priest sings:

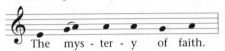

The mys - ter - y of faith.

And the people continue with one of the following acclamations:

Memorial Acclamation A

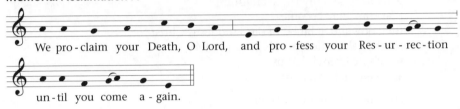

We pro - claim your Death, O Lord, and pro - fess your Res - ur - rec - tion un - til you come a - gain.

Memorial Acclamation B

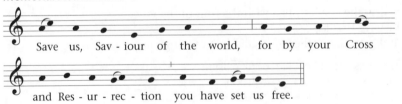

When we eat this Bread and drink this Cup, we pro - claim your Death, O Lord, un - til you come a - gain.

Memorial Acclamation C

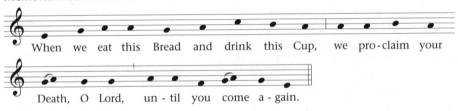

Save us, Sav - iour of the world, for by your Cross and Res - ur - rec - tion you have set us free.

Memorial Acclamation D   *for Ireland only*

My Lord and my God.

Priest: Therefore, O Lord,
as we now celebrate the memorial of our redemption,
we remember Christ's Death
and his descent to the realm of the dead,
we proclaim his Resurrection
and his Ascension to your right hand,
and as we await his coming in glory,
we offer you his Body and Blood,
the sacrifice acceptable to you
which brings salvation to the whole world.

Look, O Lord, upon the Sacrifice
which you yourself have provided for your Church,
and grant in your loving kindness
to all who partake of this one Bread and one Chalice
that, gathered into one body by the Holy Spirit,
they may truly become a living sacrifice in Christ
to the praise of your glory.

Therefore, Lord, remember now
all for whom we offer this sacrifice:
especially your servant N. our Pope,
N. our Bishop,* and the whole Order of Bishops,
all the clergy,
those who take part in this offering,
those gathered here before you,
your entire people,
and all who seek you with a sincere heart.

Remember also
those who have died in the peace of your Christ
and all the dead,
whose faith you alone have known.

To all of us, your children,
grant, O merciful Father,
that we may enter into a heavenly inheritance
with the Blessed Virgin Mary, Mother of God,
with blessed Joseph, her Spouse,
and with your Apostles and Saints in your kingdom.
There, with the whole of creation,
freed from the corruption of sin and death,
may we glorify you through Christ our Lord,
through whom you bestow on the world all that is good.

---

* Mention may be made here of the Coadjutor Bishop, or Auxiliary Bishops

Doxology and Great Amen

At the end of the Eucharistic Prayer, the Priest takes the chalice and paten with the host and, raising both, he alone sings (or says) the Doxology. The people acclaim 'Amen'.

Priest: Through him, and with him, and in him,
            O God, almighty Father,
            in the unity of the Holy Spirit,
            all glory and honour is yours,
            for ever and ever.

People: **Amen.**

Priest: People:

...for   ev - er   and   ev - er.   A-men.

▷ *page 57*

EUCHARISTIC PRAYER FOR RECONCILIATION I

The Eucharistic Prayers for Reconciliation may be used in Masses in which the mystery of reconciliation is conveyed to the faithful in a special way, including Masses during Lent.

Although these Eucharistic Prayers have been provided with a proper Preface, they may also be used with other Prefaces that refer to penance and conversion, as, for example, the Prefaces of Lent.

Priest: The Lord be with you.   ▷ *Music p 15*
People: **And with your spirit.**

Priest: Lift up your hearts.
People: **We lift them up to the Lord.**

Priest: Let us give thanks to the Lord our God.
People: **It is right and just.**

Priest: It is truly right and just
            that we should always give you thanks,
            Lord, holy Father, almighty and eternal God.

            For you do not cease to spur us on
            to possess a more abundant life
            and, being rich in mercy,
            you constantly offer pardon
            and call on sinners
            to trust in your forgiveness alone.

            Never did you turn away from us,
            and, though time and again we have broken your covenant,
            you have bound the human family to yourself
            through Jesus your Son, our Redeemer,
            with a new bond of love so tight
            that it can never be undone.

Even now you set before your people
a time of grace and reconciliation,
and, as they turn back to you in spirit,
you grant them hope in Christ Jesus
and a desire to be of service to all,
while they entrust themselves
more fully to the Holy Spirit.

And so, filled with wonder,
we extol the power of your love,
and, proclaiming our joy
at the salvation that comes from you,
we join in the heavenly hymn of countless hosts,
as without end we acclaim:

All: **Holy, Holy, Holy Lord God of hosts.**
       Heaven and earth are full of your glory.
       Hosanna in the highest.
       Blessed is he who comes in the name of the Lord.
       Hosanna in the highest.

▷ Music p 16

Priest: You are indeed Holy, O Lord,
          and from the world's beginning
          are ceaselessly at work,
          so that the human race may become holy,
          just as you yourself are holy.

ALL KNEEL

Look, we pray, upon your people's offerings
and pour out on them the power of your Spirit,
that they may become the Body and ✠ Blood
of your beloved Son, Jesus Christ,
in whom we, too, are your sons and daughters.

Indeed, though we once were lost
and could not approach you,
you loved us with the greatest love:
for your Son, who alone is just,
handed himself over to death,
and did not disdain to be nailed for our sake
to the wood of the Cross.

But before his arms were outstretched between heaven and earth,
to become the lasting sign of your covenant,
he desired to celebrate the Passover with his disciples.

As he ate with them,
he took bread
and, giving you thanks, he said the blessing,
broke the bread and gave it to them, saying:

TAKE THIS, ALL OF YOU, AND EAT OF IT,
FOR THIS IS MY BODY,
WHICH WILL BE GIVEN UP FOR YOU.

In a similar way, when supper was ended,
knowing that he was about to reconcile all things in himself
through his Blood to be shed on the Cross,
he took the chalice, filled with the fruit of the vine,
and once more giving you thanks,
handed the chalice to his disciples, saying:

TAKE THIS, ALL OF YOU, AND DRINK FROM IT,
FOR THIS IS THE CHALICE OF MY BLOOD,
THE BLOOD OF THE NEW AND ETERNAL COVENANT,
WHICH WILL BE POURED OUT FOR YOU AND FOR MANY
FOR THE FORGIVENESS OF SINS.

DO THIS IN MEMORY OF ME.

Priest: The mystery of faith.   ▷ Music p 17
People: **We proclaim your Death, O Lord,**
           and profess your Resurrection
           until you come again.
or
People: **When we eat this Bread and drink this Cup,**
           we proclaim your Death, O Lord,
           until you come again.
or
People: **Save us, Saviour of the world,**
           for by your Cross and Resurrection
           you have set us free.

or for Ireland only:
People: **My Lord and my God.**

Priest: Therefore, as we celebrate
           the memorial of your Son Jesus Christ,
           who is our Passover and our surest peace,
           we celebrate his Death and Resurrection from the dead,
           and looking forward to his blessed Coming,
           we offer you, who are our faithful and merciful God,
           this sacrificial Victim
           who reconciles to you the human race.

           Look kindly, most compassionate Father,
           on those you unite to yourself
           by the Sacrifice of your Son,
           and grant that, by the power of the Holy Spirit,
           as they partake of this one Bread and one Chalice,

they may be gathered into one Body in Christ,
who heals every division.

Be pleased to keep us always
in communion of mind and heart,
together with N. our Pope and N. our Bishop.*
Help us to work together
for the coming of your Kingdom,
until the hour when we stand before you,
Saints among the Saints in the halls of heaven,
with the Blessed Virgin Mary, Mother of God,
the blessed Apostles and all the Saints,
and with our deceased brothers and sisters,
whom we humbly commend to your mercy.

Then, freed at last from the wound of corruption
and made fully into a new creation,
we shall sing to you with gladness
the thanksgiving of Christ,
who lives for all eternity.

Priest: Through him, and with him, and in him,   ▷ *Music p 18*
            O God, almighty Father,
            in the unity of the Holy Spirit,
            all glory and honour is yours,
            for ever and ever.
People: **Amen.**

▷ *page 57*

EUCHARISTIC PRAYER FOR RECONCILIATION II

The Eucharistic Prayers for Reconciliation may be used in Masses in which the mystery of reconciliation is conveyed to the faithful in a special way, including Masses during Lent.

Although these Eucharistic Prayers have been provided with a proper Preface, they may also be used with other Prefaces that refer to penance and conversion, as, for example, the Prefaces of Lent.

Preface
Priest: The Lord be with you.   ▷ *Music p 15*
People: **And with your spirit.**

Priest: Lift up your hearts.
People: **We lift them up to the Lord.**

Priest: Let us give thanks to the Lord our God.
People: **It is right and just.**

Priest: It is truly right and just
            that we should give you thanks and praise,
            O God, almighty Father,

* Mention may be made here of the Coadjutor Bishop, or Auxiliary Bishops

for all you do in this world,
through our Lord Jesus Christ.

For though the human race
is divided by dissension and discord,
yet we know that by testing us
you change our hearts
to prepare them for reconciliation.

Even more, by your Spirit you move human hearts
that enemies may speak to each other again,
adversaries may join hands,
and peoples seek to meet together.

By the working of your power
it comes about, O Lord,
that hatred is overcome by love,
revenge gives way to forgiveness,
and discord is changed to mutual respect.

Therefore, as we give you ceaseless thanks
with the choirs of heaven,
we cry out to your majesty on earth,
and without end we acclaim:

All: **Holy, Holy, Holy Lord God of hosts.**   ▷ *Music p 16*
         Heaven and earth are full of your glory.
         Hosanna in the highest.
         Blessed is he who comes in the name of the Lord.
         Hosanna in the highest.

ALL KNEEL

Priest: You, therefore, almighty Father,
         we bless through Jesus Christ your Son,
         who comes in your name.
         He himself is the Word that brings salvation,
         the hand you extend to sinners,
         the way by which your peace is offered to us.
         When we ourselves had turned away from you
         on account of our sins,
         you brought us back to be reconciled, O Lord,
         so that, converted at last to you,
         we might love one another
         through your Son,
         whom for our sake you handed over to death.

         And now, celebrating the reconciliation
         Christ has brought us,
         we entreat you:
         sanctify these gifts by the outpouring of your Spirit,

ORDER

that they may become the Body and ✠ Blood of your Son,
whose command we fulfil
when we celebrate these mysteries.

For when about to give his life to set us free,
as he reclined at supper,
he himself took bread into his hands,
and, giving you thanks, he said the blessing,
broke the bread and gave it to his disciples, saying:

TAKE THIS, ALL OF YOU, AND EAT OF IT,
FOR THIS IS MY BODY,
WHICH WILL BE GIVEN UP FOR YOU.

In a similar way, on that same evening,
he took the chalice of blessing in his hands,
confessing your mercy,
and gave the chalice to his disciples, saying:

TAKE THIS, ALL OF YOU, AND DRINK FROM IT,
FOR THIS IS THE CHALICE OF MY BLOOD,
THE BLOOD OF THE NEW AND ETERNAL COVENANT,
WHICH WILL BE POURED OUT FOR YOU AND FOR MANY
FOR THE FORGIVENESS OF SINS.

DO THIS IN MEMORY OF ME.

Priest: The mystery of faith.   ▷ Music p 17
People: **We proclaim your Death, O Lord,**
          and profess your Resurrection
          until you come again.
or
People: **When we eat this Bread and drink this Cup,**
          we proclaim your Death, O Lord,
          until you come again.
or
People: **Save us, Saviour of the world,**
          for by your Cross and Resurrection
          you have set us free.
or for Ireland only:
People: **My Lord and my God.**

Priest: Celebrating, therefore, the memorial
          of the Death and Resurrection of your Son,
          who left us this pledge of his love,
          we offer you what you have bestowed on us,
          the Sacrifice of perfect reconciliation.

Holy Father, we humbly beseech you
to accept us also, together with your Son,
and in this saving banquet
graciously to endow us with his very Spirit,
who takes away everything
that estranges us from one another.

May he make your Church a sign of unity
and an instrument of your peace among all people
and may he keep us in communion
with N. our Pope and N. our Bishop *
and all the Bishops
and your entire people.

Just as you have gathered us now at the table of your Son,
so also bring us together,
with the glorious Virgin Mary, Mother of God,
with your blessed Apostles and all the Saints,
with our brothers and sisters
and those of every race and tongue
who have died in your friendship.
Bring us to share with them the unending banquet of unity
in a new heaven and a new earth,
where the fullness of your peace will shine forth
in Christ Jesus our Lord.

Priest: Through him, and with him, and in him,   ▷ *Music p 18*
O God, almighty Father,
in the unity of the Holy Spirit,
all glory and honour is yours,
for ever and ever.

People: **Amen.**

---

* Mention may be made here of the Coadjutor Bishop, or Auxiliary Bishops

ORDER

EUCHARISTIC PRAYERS FOR USE IN MASSES FOR VARIOUS NEEDS

These Eucharistic Prayers have their own Prefaces which may not be replaced by another, because of the structure of the Prayers themselves.

I   THE CHURCH ON THE PATH OF UNITY

Priest: The Lord be with you. ▷ *Music p 15*
People: **And with your spirit.**

Priest: Lift up your hearts.
People: **We lift them up to the Lord.**

Priest: Let us give thanks to the Lord our God.
People: **It is right and just.**

Priest: It is truly right and just to give you thanks
and raise to you a hymn of glory and praise,
O Lord, Father of infinite goodness.

For by the word of your Son's Gospel
you have brought together one Church
from every people, tongue, and nation,
and, having filled her with life by the power of your Spirit,
you never cease through her
to gather the whole human race into one.

Manifesting the covenant of your love,
she dispenses without ceasing
the blessed hope of your Kingdom
and shines bright as the sign of your faithfulness,
which in Christ Jesus our Lord
you promised would last for eternity.

And so, with all the Powers of heaven,
we worship you constantly on earth,
while, with all the Church,
as one voice we acclaim:

All: **Holy, Holy, Holy Lord God of hosts.** ▷ *Music p 16*
Heaven and earth are full of your glory.
Hosanna in the highest.
Blessed is he who comes in the name of the Lord.
Hosanna in the highest.

ALL KNEEL

You are indeed Holy and to be glorified, O God,
who love the human race
and who always walk with us on the journey of life.
Blessed indeed is your Son,
present in our midst
when we are gathered by his love,
and when, as once for the disciples, so now for us,
he opens the Scriptures and breaks the bread.

Therefore, Father most merciful,
we ask that you send forth your Holy Spirit
to sanctify these gifts of bread and wine,
that they may become for us
the Body and ✠ Blood
of our Lord Jesus Christ.

On the day before he was to suffer,
on the night of the Last Supper,
he took bread and said the blessing,
broke the bread and gave it to his disciples, saying:

TAKE THIS, ALL OF YOU, AND EAT OF IT,
FOR THIS IS MY BODY,
WHICH WILL BE GIVEN UP FOR YOU.

In a similar way, when supper was ended,
he took the chalice, gave you thanks
and gave the chalice to his disciples, saying:

TAKE THIS, ALL OF YOU, AND DRINK FROM IT,
FOR THIS IS THE CHALICE OF MY BLOOD,
THE BLOOD OF THE NEW AND ETERNAL COVENANT,
WHICH WILL BE POURED OUT FOR YOU AND FOR MANY
FOR THE FORGIVENESS OF SINS.

DO THIS IN MEMORY OF ME.

Priest: The mystery of faith.   ▷ *Music p 17*
People: **We proclaim your Death, O Lord,
and profess your Resurrection
until you come again.**

or

People: **When we eat this Bread and drink this Cup,
we proclaim your Death, O Lord,
until you come again.**

or

People: **Save us, Saviour of the world,
for by your Cross and Resurrection
you have set us free.**

ORDER

or   *for Ireland only:*

People: **My Lord and my God.**

Therefore, holy Father,
as we celebrate the memorial of Christ your Son, our Saviour,
whom you led through his Passion and Death on the Cross
to the glory of the Resurrection,
and whom you have seated at your right hand,
we proclaim the work of your love until he comes again
and we offer you the Bread of life
and the Chalice of blessing.

Look with favour on the oblation of your Church,
in which we show forth
the paschal Sacrifice of Christ that has been handed on to us,
and grant that, by the power of the Spirit of your love,
we may be counted now and until the day of eternity
among the members of your Son,
in whose Body and Blood we have communion.

Lord, renew your Church (which is in N.)
by the light of the Gospel.
Strengthen the bond of unity
between the faithful and the pastors of your people,
together with N. our Pope, N. our Bishop,*
and the whole Order of Bishops,
that in a world torn by strife
your people may shine forth
as a prophetic sign of unity and concord.

Remember our brothers and sisters (N. and N.),
who have fallen asleep in the peace of your Christ,
and all the dead, whose faith you alone have known.
Admit them to rejoice in the light of your face,
and in the resurrection give them the fullness of life.

Grant also to us,
when our earthly pilgrimage is done,
that we may come to an eternal dwelling place
and live with you for ever;
there, in communion with the Blessed Virgin Mary, Mother of God,
with the Apostles and Martyrs,
(with Saint N.: *the Saint of the day or Patron*)
and with all the Saints,
we shall praise and exalt you
through Jesus Christ, your Son.

---

* Mention may be made here of the Coadjutor Bishop, or Auxiliary Bishops

Priest: Through him, and with him, and in him,   ▷ Music p 18
O God, almighty Father,
in the unity of the Holy Spirit,
all glory and honour is yours,
for ever and ever.

People: **Amen.**

▷ page 70

II GOD GUIDES HIS CHURCH ALONG THE WAY OF SALVATION

Priest: The Lord be with you.   ▷ Music p 15
People: **And with your spirit.**

Priest: Lift up your hearts.
People: **We lift them up to the Lord.**

Priest: Let us give thanks to the Lord our God.
People: **It is right and just.**

It is truly right and just, our duty and our salvation,
always and everywhere to give you thanks,
Lord, holy Father,
creator of the world and source of all life.

For you never forsake the works of your wisdom,
but by your providence are even now at work in our midst.
With mighty hand and outstretched arm
you led your people Israel through the desert.
Now, as your Church makes her pilgrim journey in the world,
you always accompany her
by the power of the Holy Spirit
and lead her along the paths of time
to the eternal joy of your Kingdom,
through Christ our Lord.

And so, with the Angels and Saints,
we, too, sing the hymn of your glory,
as without end we acclaim:

All: **Holy, Holy, Holy Lord God of hosts.**   ▷ Music p 16
Heaven and earth are full of your glory.
Hosanna in the highest.
Blessed is he who comes in the name of the Lord.
Hosanna in the highest.

ALL KNEEL

Priest: You are indeed Holy and to be glorified, O God,
who love the human race
and who always walk with us on the journey of life.

Blessed indeed is your Son,
present in our midst
when we are gathered by his love
and when, as once for the disciples, so now for us,
he opens the Scriptures and breaks the bread.

Therefore, Father most merciful,
we ask that you send forth your Holy Spirit
to sanctify these gifts of bread and wine,
that they may become for us
the Body and ✠ Blood
of our Lord Jesus Christ.

On the day before he was to suffer,
on the night of the Last Supper,
he took bread and said the blessing,
broke the bread and gave it to his disciples, saying:

TAKE THIS, ALL OF YOU, AND EAT OF IT,
FOR THIS IS MY BODY,
WHICH WILL BE GIVEN UP FOR YOU.

In a similar way, when supper was ended,
he took the chalice, gave you thanks
and gave the chalice to his disciples, saying:

TAKE THIS, ALL OF YOU, AND DRINK FROM IT,
FOR THIS IS THE CHALICE OF MY BLOOD,
THE BLOOD OF THE NEW AND ETERNAL COVENANT,
WHICH WILL BE POURED OUT FOR YOU AND FOR MANY
FOR THE FORGIVENESS OF SINS.

DO THIS IN MEMORY OF ME.

Priest: The mystery of faith.

▷ Music p 17

People: **We proclaim your Death, O Lord,
and profess your Resurrection
until you come again.**

or

People: **When we eat this Bread and drink this Cup,
we proclaim your Death, O Lord,
until you come again.**

or

People: **Save us, Saviour of the world,
for by your Cross and Resurrection
you have set us free.**

or *for Ireland only:*

People: **My Lord and my God.**

Priest: Therefore, holy Father,
as we celebrate the memorial of Christ your Son, our Saviour,
whom you led through his Passion and Death on the Cross
to the glory of the Resurrection,
and whom you have seated at your right hand,
we proclaim the work of your love until he comes again
and we offer you the Bread of life
and the Chalice of blessing.

Look with favour on the oblation of your Church,
in which we show forth
the paschal Sacrifice of Christ that has been handed on to us,
and grant that, by the power of the Spirit of your love,
we may be counted now and until the day of eternity
among the members of your Son,
in whose Body and Blood we have communion.

And so, having called us to your table, Lord,
confirm us in unity,
so that, together with N. our Pope and N. our Bishop,*
with all Bishops, Priests and Deacons,
and your entire people,
as we walk your ways with faith and hope,
we may strive to bring joy and trust into the world.

Remember our brothers and sisters (N. and N.),
who have fallen asleep in the peace of your Christ,
and all the dead, whose faith you alone have known.
Admit them to rejoice in the light of your face,
and in the resurrection give them the fullness of life.

Grant also to us,
when our earthly pilgrimage is done,
that we may come to an eternal dwelling place
and live with you for ever;
there, in communion with the Blessed Virgin Mary, Mother of God,
with the Apostles and Martyrs,
(with Saint N.: *the Saint of the day or Patron*)
and with all the Saints,
we shall praise and exalt you
through Jesus Christ, your Son.

---

* Mention may be made here of the Coadjutor Bishop, or Auxiliary Bishops

Priest: Through him, and with him, and in him,
        O God, almighty Father,
        in the unity of the Holy Spirit,
        all glory and honour is yours,
        for ever and ever.

▷ Music p 18

People: **Amen.**

▷ page 70

III JESUS, THE WAY TO THE FATHER

Priest: The Lord be with you.
People: **And with your spirit.**

▷ Music p 15

Priest: Lift up your hearts.
People: **We lift them up to the Lord.**

Priest: Let us give thanks to the Lord our God.
People: **It is right and just.**

Priest: It is truly right and just, our duty and our salvation,
        always and everywhere to give you thanks,
        holy Father, Lord of heaven and earth,
        through Christ our Lord.

        For by your Word you created the world
        and you govern all things in harmony.
        You gave us the same Word made flesh as Mediator,
        and he has spoken your words to us
        and called us to follow him.
        He is the way that leads us to you,
        the truth that sets us free,
        the life that fills us with gladness.

        Through your Son
        you gather men and women,
        whom you made for the glory of your name,
        into one family,
        redeemed by the Blood of his Cross
        and signed with the seal of the Spirit.

        Therefore, now and for ages unending,
        with all the Angels,
        we proclaim your glory,
        as in joyful celebration we acclaim:

All: **Holy, Holy, Holy Lord God of hosts.**
        Heaven and earth are full of your glory.
        Hosanna in the highest.
        Blessed is he who comes in the name of the Lord.
        Hosanna in the highest.

▷ Music p 16

ALL KNEEL

ORDER

Priest: You are indeed Holy and to be glorified, O God,
who love the human race
and who always walk with us on the journey of life.
Blessed indeed is your Son,
present in our midst
when we are gathered by his love
and when, as once for the disciples, so now for us,
he opens the Scriptures and breaks the bread.

Therefore, Father most merciful,
we ask that you send forth your Holy Spirit
to sanctify these gifts of bread and wine,
that they may become for us
the Body and ✠ Blood
of our Lord Jesus Christ.

On the day before he was to suffer,
on the night of the Last Supper,
he took bread and said the blessing,
broke the bread and gave it to his disciples, saying:

TAKE THIS, ALL OF YOU, AND EAT OF IT,
FOR THIS IS MY BODY,
WHICH WILL BE GIVEN UP FOR YOU.

In a similar way, when supper was ended,
he took the chalice, gave you thanks
and gave the chalice to his disciples, saying:

TAKE THIS, ALL OF YOU, AND DRINK FROM IT,
FOR THIS IS THE CHALICE OF MY BLOOD,
THE BLOOD OF THE NEW AND ETERNAL COVENANT,
WHICH WILL BE POURED OUT FOR YOU AND FOR MANY
FOR THE FORGIVENESS OF SINS.

DO THIS IN MEMORY OF ME.

Priest: The mystery of faith.   ▷ Music p 17
People: **We proclaim your Death, O Lord,
and profess your Resurrection
until you come again.**

or

People: **When we eat this Bread and drink this Cup,
we proclaim your Death, O Lord,
until you come again.**

or

People: **Save us, Saviour of the world,
for by your Cross and Resurrection
you have set us free.**

or   *for Ireland only:*

People: **My Lord and my God.**

Priest: Therefore, holy Father,
as we celebrate the memorial of Christ your Son, our Saviour,
whom you led through his Passion and Death on the Cross
to the glory of the Resurrection,
and whom you have seated at your right hand,
we proclaim the work of your love until he comes again
and we offer you the Bread of life
and the Chalice of blessing.

Look with favour on the oblation of your Church,
in which we show forth
the paschal Sacrifice of Christ that has been handed on to us,
and grant that, by the power of the Spirit of your love,
we may be counted now and until the day of eternity
among the members of your Son,
in whose Body and Blood we have communion.

By our partaking of this mystery, almighty Father,
give us life through your Spirit,
grant that we may be conformed to the image of your Son,
and confirm us in the bond of communion,
together with N. our Pope and N. our Bishop,*
with all other Bishops,
with Priests and Deacons,
and with your entire people.

Grant that all the faithful of the Church,
looking into the signs of the times by the light of faith,
may constantly devote themselves
to the service of the Gospel.
Keep us attentive to the needs of all
that, sharing their grief and pain,
their joy and hope,
we may faithfully bring them the good news of salvation
and go forward with them
along the way of your Kingdom.

Remember our brothers and sisters (N. and N.),
who have fallen asleep in the peace of your Christ,
and all the dead, whose faith you alone have known.
Admit them to rejoice in the light of your face,
and in the resurrection give them the fullness of life.

---

* Mention may be made here of the Coadjutor Bishop, or Auxiliary Bishops

Grant also to us,
when our earthly pilgrimage is done,
that we may come to an eternal dwelling place
and live with you for ever;
there, in communion with the Blessed Virgin Mary, Mother of God,
with the Apostles and Martyrs,
(with Saint N.: *the Saint of the day or Patron*)
and with all the Saints,
we shall praise and exalt you
through Jesus Christ, your Son.

Priest: Through him, and with him, and in him,   ▷ *Music p 18*
O God, almighty Father,
in the unity of the Holy Spirit,
all glory and honour is yours,
for ever and ever.

People: **Amen.**   ▷ *page 70*

IV   JESUS, WHO WENT ABOUT DOING GOOD

Priest: The Lord be with you.   ▷ *Music p 15*
People: **And with your spirit.**

Priest: Lift up your hearts.
People: **We lift them up to the Lord.**

Priest: Let us give thanks to the Lord our God.
People: **It is right and just.**

Priest: It is truly right and just, our duty and our salvation,
always and everywhere to give you thanks,
Father of mercies and faithful God.

For you have given us Jesus Christ, your Son,
as our Lord and Redeemer.

He always showed compassion
for children and for the poor,
for the sick and for sinners,
and he became a neighbour
to the oppressed and the afflicted.

By word and deed he announced to the world
that you are our Father
and that you care for all your sons and daughters.

And so, with all the Angels and Saints,
we exalt and bless your name
and sing the hymn of your glory,
as without end we acclaim:

All: **Holy, Holy, Holy Lord God of hosts.**
              Heaven and earth are full of your glory.
              Hosanna in the highest.
              Blessed is he who comes in the name of the Lord.
              Hosanna in the highest.

▷ Music p 16

ORDER

ALL KNEEL

Priest: You are indeed Holy and to be glorified, O God,
            who love the human race
            and who always walk with us on the journey of life.
            Blessed indeed is your Son,
            present in our midst
            when we are gathered by his love
            and when, as once for the disciples, so now for us,
            he opens the Scriptures and breaks the bread.

            Therefore, Father most merciful,
            we ask that you send forth your Holy Spirit
            to sanctify these gifts of bread and wine,
            that they may become for us
            the Body and ✠ Blood
            of our Lord Jesus Christ.

            On the day before he was to suffer,
            on the night of the Last Supper,
            he took bread and said the blessing,
            broke the bread and gave it to his disciples, saying:

            TAKE THIS, ALL OF YOU, AND EAT OF IT,
            FOR THIS IS MY BODY,
            WHICH WILL BE GIVEN UP FOR YOU.

            In a similar way, when supper was ended,
            he took the chalice, gave you thanks
            and gave the chalice to his disciples, saying:

            TAKE THIS, ALL OF YOU, AND DRINK FROM IT,
            FOR THIS IS THE CHALICE OF MY BLOOD,
            THE BLOOD OF THE NEW AND ETERNAL COVENANT,
            WHICH WILL BE POURED OUT FOR YOU AND FOR MANY
            FOR THE FORGIVENESS OF SINS.

            DO THIS IN MEMORY OF ME.

Priest: The mystery of faith.   ▷ *Music p 17*

People: **We proclaim your Death, O Lord,**
          and profess your Resurrection
          until you come again.

or

People: **When we eat this Bread and drink this Cup,**
          we proclaim your Death, O Lord,
          until you come again.

or

People: **Save us, Saviour of the world,**
          for by your Cross and Resurrection
          you have set us free.

or   *for Ireland only:*

People: **My Lord and my God.**

Priest: Therefore, holy Father,
          as we celebrate the memorial of Christ your Son, our Saviour,
          whom you led through his Passion and Death on the Cross
          to the glory of the Resurrection,
          and whom you have seated at your right hand,
          we proclaim the work of your love until he comes again
          and we offer you the Bread of life
          and the Chalice of blessing.

          Look with favour on the oblation of your Church,
          in which we show forth
          the paschal Sacrifice of Christ that has been handed on to us,
          and grant that, by the power of the Spirit of your love,
          we may be counted now and until the day of eternity
          among the members of your Son,
          in whose Body and Blood we have communion.

          Bring your Church, O Lord,
          to perfect faith and charity,
          together with N. our Pope and N. our Bishop,*
          with all Bishops, Priests and Deacons,
          and the entire people you have made your own.

          Open our eyes
          to the needs of our brothers and sisters;
          inspire in us words and actions
          to comfort those who labour and are burdened.
          Make us serve them truly,
          after the example of Christ and at his command.

---

* Mention may be made here of the Coadjutor Bishop, or Auxiliary Bishops

ORDER

And may your Church stand as a living witness
to truth and freedom,
to peace and justice,
that all people may be raised up to a new hope.

Remember our brothers and sisters (N. and N.),
who have fallen asleep in the peace of your Christ,
and all the dead, whose faith you alone have known.
Admit them to rejoice in the light of your face,
and in the resurrection give them the fullness of life.

Grant also to us,
when our earthly pilgrimage is done,
that we may come to an eternal dwelling place
and live with you for ever;
there, in communion with the Blessed Virgin Mary, Mother of God,
with the Apostles and Martyrs,
(with Saint N.: *the Saint of the day or Patron*)
and with all the Saints,
we shall praise and exalt you
through Jesus Christ, your Son.

Priest: Through him, and with him, and in him,   ▷ *Music p 18*
O God, almighty Father,
in the unity of the Holy Spirit,
all glory and honour is yours,
for ever and ever.
People: **Amen.**

▷ *page 70*

COMMUNION RITE

The eating and drinking together of the Lord's Body and Blood in a Paschal meal is the culmination of the Eucharist. The themes underlying these rites are the mutual love and reconciliation that are both the condition and the fruit of worthy communion and the unity of the many in the one.

Celebrating the Mass n 200

ORDER

ALL STAND

LORD'S PRAYER

Priest: At the Saviour's command
and formed by divine teaching,
we dare to say:

All: **Our Father, who art in heaven,**
hallowed be thy name;
thy kingdom come,
thy will be done
on earth as it is in heaven.
Give us this day our daily bread,
and forgive us our trespasses,
as we forgive those who trespass against us;
and lead us not into temptation,
but deliver us from evil.

⊳ *Music p 217*

Priest: Deliver us, Lord, we pray, from every evil,
graciously grant peace in our days,
that, by the help of your mercy,
we may be always free from sin
and safe from all distress,
as we await the blessed hope
and the coming of our Saviour, Jesus Christ.

All: **For the kingdom,**
the power and the glory are yours
now and for ever.

RITE OF PEACE

Priest: Lord Jesus Christ,
who said to your Apostles,
Peace I leave you, my peace I give you,
look not on our sins,
but on the faith of your Church,
and graciously grant her peace and unity
in accordance with your will.
Who live and reign for ever and ever.

All: **Amen.**

Priest: The peace of the Lord be with you always.

All: **And with your spirit.**

⊳ *Music p 217*

SIGN OF PEACE

The peace is always exchanged, though the invitation which introduces it is optional.

Deacon or Priest: Let us offer each other the sign of peace.

And all offer one another the customary sign of peace: a handclasp or handshake, which is an expression of peace, communion, and charity.

If commissioned ministers are to assist at Communion, it is desirable that they are in place on the sanctuary by the end of the exchange of peace. (Celebrating the Mass n 206)

BREAKING OF BREAD

The Priest takes the host, breaks it over the paten, and places a small piece into the chalice. Meanwhile the following is sung or said:

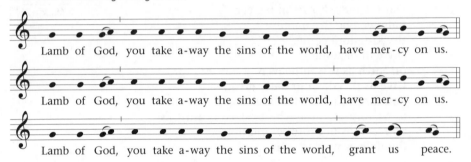

Lamb of God, you take a-way the sins of the world, have mer-cy on us.

Lamb of God, you take a-way the sins of the world, have mer-cy on us.

Lamb of God, you take a-way the sins of the world, grant us peace.

All: **Lamb of God, you take away the sins of the world, have mercy on us.**

Lamb of God, you take away the sins of the world, have mercy on us.

Lamb of God, you take away the sins of the world, grant us peace.

The invocation may be repeated several times if the Breaking of Bread is prolonged. The final time always ends 'grant us peace'.

ALL KNEEL

INVITATION TO COMMUNION

After his private prayers of preparation the Priest genuflects, takes the host and, holding it slightly raised above the paten or above the chalice says aloud:

Priest: Behold the Lamb of God,   ▷ *Music p 218*
behold him who takes away the sins of the world.
Blessed are those called to the supper of the Lamb.

All: **Lord, I am not worthy**
that you should enter under my roof,
but only say the word
and my soul shall be healed.

ORDER

HOLY COMMUNION

Communion Song

The communion song begins while the Priest is receiving the Body of Christ and normally continues until all communicants have received communion.

Distribution of Communion

By tradition the Deacon ministers the chalice. Beyond this, no distinctions are made in the assignment of consecrated elements to particular ministers for distribution. (Celebrating the Mass n 211)

The communicants come forward in reverent procession. Before receiving Holy Communion standing they make a preparatory act of reverence by bowing their heads in honour of Christ's presence in the Sacrament.

The Priest, Deacon or commissioned minister of Holy Communion raises a host slightly and shows it to each of the communicants, saying:

Priest, Deacon or minister: The Body of Christ.
Communicant: **Amen.**

And the communicant receives Holy Communion.

It is most desirable that the faithful share the Chalice. Drinking at the Eucharist is a sharing in the sign of the new covenant, a foretaste of the heavenly banquet and a sign of participation in the suffering Christ. (cf Celebrating the Mass n 209)

When Communion is ministered from the chalice, the minister offers it to each of the communicants, saying:

Priest, Deacon or minister: The Blood of Christ.
Communicant: **Amen.**

And the communicant receives Holy Communion.

Period of Silence or Song of Praise

After the distribution of Communion, if appropriate, a sacred silence may be observed for a while, or a psalm or other canticle of praise or a hymn may be sung.

PRAYER AFTER COMMUNION   `ALL STAND`

Priest: Let us pray.   `▷ Proper`

All pray in silence for a while, unless silence has just been observed.
Then the Priest says the Prayer after Communion, at the end of which the people acclaim:

All: **Amen.**

✠ CONCLUDING RITES

> ## Go, make disciples of all the nations.
> ## I am with you always; yes, to the end of time.
> ### (Matthew 28:19, 20)
>
> The purpose of the Concluding Rite is to send the people forth to put into effect in their daily lives the Paschal Mystery and the unity in Christ which they have celebrated. They are given a sense of abiding mission, which calls them to witness to Christ in the world and to bring the Gospel to the poor.
> *cf Celebrating the Mass n 217*

If they are necessary, any brief announcements to the people follow here.

BLESSING

Priest: The Lord be with you.   ▷ *Music p 219*

People: **And with your spirit.**

On certain occasions, the following blessing may be preceded by a solemn blessing or prayer over the people. Then the Priest blesses the people, singing or saying:

Priest: May almighty God bless you:

the Father, and the Son, ✠ and the Holy Spirit.

People: **Amen.**

In a Pontifical Mass, the celebrant receives the mitre and says:

Bishop: The Lord be with you.   ▷ *Music p 219*

All: **And with your spirit.**

Bishop: Blessed be the name of the Lord.

All: **Now and for ever.**

Bishop: Our help is in the name of the Lord.

All   **Who made heaven and earth.**

On certain occasions the following blessing may be preceded by a more solemn blessing or prayer over the people. Then the celebrant receives the pastoral staff, if he uses it, and says:

Bishop: May almighty God bless you:

making the Sign of the Cross over the people three times, he adds:

the Father, ✠ and the Son, ✠ and the Holy ✠ Spirit.

All: **Amen.**

If any liturgical action follows immediately, the rites of dismissal are omitted.

DISMISSAL

▷ *Music p 220*

Then the Deacon, or the Priest himself says the dismissal sentence.

Deacon or Priest: Go forth, the Mass is ended.
People: **Thanks be to God.**

or

Deacon or Priest: Go and announce the Gospel of the Lord.
People: **Thanks be to God.**

or

Deacon or Priest: Go in peace, glorifying the Lord by your life.
People: **Thanks be to God.**

or

Deacon or Priest: Go in peace.
People: **Thanks be to God.**

Then the Priest venerates the altar as at the beginning.
After making a profound bow with the ministers, he withdraws.

ORDER

APPENDIX TO THE ORDER OF MASS

RITE FOR THE BLESSING AND SPRINKLING OF WATER

BLESSING OF WATER

After the greeting, the Priest, with a vessel containing the water to be blessed before him, calls upon the people to pray in these or similar words:

Priest: Dear brethren (brothers and sisters),
let us humbly beseech the Lord our God
to bless this water he has created,
which will be sprinkled on us
as a memorial of our Baptism.
May he help us by his grace
to remain faithful to the Spirit we have received.

And after a brief pause for silence, he continues:

Priest: Almighty ever-living God,
who willed that through water,
the fountain of life and the source of purification,
even souls should be cleansed
and receive the gift of eternal life;
be pleased, we pray, to ✠ bless this water,
by which we seek protection on this your day, O Lord.
Renew the living spring of your grace within us
and grant that by this water we may be defended
from all ills of spirit and body,
and so approach you with hearts made clean
and worthily receive your salvation.
Through Christ our Lord.

All: **Amen.**

or

Priest: Almighty Lord and God,
who are the source and origin of all life,
whether of body or soul,
we ask you to ✠ bless this water,
which we use in confidence
to implore forgiveness for our sins
and to obtain the protection of your grace
against all illness and every snare of the enemy.
Grant, O Lord, in your mercy,
that living waters may always spring up for our salvation,
and so may we approach you with a pure heart
and avoid all danger to body and soul.
Through Christ our Lord.

All: **Amen.**

BLESSING OF SALT

Where the circumstances of the place or the custom of the people suggest that the mixing of salt be preserved in the blessing of water, the Priest may bless salt, saying:

Priest: We humbly ask you, almighty God:
be pleased in your faithful love to bless ✠ this salt
you have created,
for it was you who commanded the prophet Elisha
to cast salt into water,
that impure water might be purified.
Grant, O Lord, we pray,
that, wherever this mixture of salt and water is sprinkled,
every attack of the enemy may be repulsed
and your Holy Spirit may be present
to keep us safe at all times.
Through Christ our Lord.

All: **Amen.**

Then he pours the salt into the water.

SPRINKLING OF WATER

The Priest then sprinkles himself and the ministers, then the clergy and people, moving through the church, if appropriate.

Meanwhile, one of the following chants, or another appropriate song is sung.

ANTIPHON 1   *Psalm 50:9*

Sprinkle me with hyssop, O Lord, and I shall be cleansed;
wash me and I shall be whiter than snow.

ANTIPHON 2   *Ezekiel 36:25–26*

I will pour clean water upon you,
and you will be made clean of all your impurities,
and I shall give you a new spirit, says the Lord.

HYMN   *cf 1 Peter 1:3–5*

Blessed be the God and Father of our Lord Jesus Christ,
who in his great mercy has given us new birth into a living hope
through the Resurrection of Jesus Christ from the dead,
into an inheritance that will not perish,
preserved for us in heaven
for the salvation to be revealed in the last time!

PRAYER

When he returns to his chair and the singing is over, the Priest says:

Priest: May almighty God cleanse us of our sins,
and through the celebration of this Eucharist
make us worthy to share at the table of his Kingdom.

All: **Amen.**

The Mass continues with the Gloria.
If the Gloria is not indicated, the Mass continues with the Collect.

▷ page 9

✠ PREFACES

All the Prefaces within the scope of this volume are printed here, except those specific to a given Eucharistic Prayer (e.g. the Preface of Eucharistic Prayer II).

The Prefaces are printed in the order that the celebrations occur in the propers of this volume:

Proper of Time
Ordinary Time
- The Most Holy Trinity and Most Holy Body and Blood of Christ
- Sundays in Ordinary Time
- Our Lord Jesus Christ, King of the Universe

Proper of Saints

ORDINARY TIME — The Most Holy Trinity and Most Holy Body and Blood of Christ

The following Prefaces are said on specific occasions in Ordinary Time.

THE MYSTERY OF THE MOST HOLY TRINITY
This Preface is said on the Solemnity of The Most Holy Trinity.

It is truly right and just, our duty and our salvation,
always and everywhere to give you thanks,
Lord, holy Father, almighty and eternal God.

For with your Only Begotten Son and the Holy Spirit
you are one God, one Lord:
not in the unity of a single person,
but in a Trinity of one substance.

For what you have revealed to us of your glory
we believe equally of your Son
and of the Holy Spirit,
so that, in the confessing of the true and eternal Godhead,
you might be adored in what is proper to each Person,
their unity in substance,
and their equality in majesty.

For this is praised by Angels and Archangels,
Cherubim, too, and Seraphim,
who never cease to cry out each day,
as with one voice they acclaim:

Holy, Holy, Holy Lord God of hosts...

One of the Prefaces of the Most Holy Eucharist is said on the Solemnity of the Most Holy Body and Blood of Christ.

PREFACE I OF THE MOST HOLY EUCHARIST
THE SACRIFICE AND THE SACRAMENT OF CHRIST

It is truly right and just, our duty and our salvation,
always and everywhere to give you thanks,
Lord, holy Father, almighty and eternal God,
through Christ our Lord.

For he is the true and eternal Priest,
who instituted the pattern of an everlasting sacrifice
and was the first to offer himself as the saving Victim,
commanding us to make this offering as his memorial.
As we eat his flesh that was sacrificed for us,
we are made strong,
and, as we drink his Blood that was poured out for us,
we are washed clean.

And so, with Angels and Archangels,
with Thrones and Dominions,
and with all the hosts and Powers of heaven,
we sing the hymn of your glory,
as without end we acclaim:

Holy, Holy, Holy Lord God of hosts…

PREFACE II OF THE MOST HOLY EUCHARIST
THE FRUITS OF THE MOST HOLY EUCHARIST

It is truly right and just, our duty and our salvation,
always and everywhere to give you thanks,
Lord, holy Father, almighty and eternal God,
through Christ our Lord.

For at the Last Supper with his Apostles,
establishing for the ages to come the saving memorial of the Cross,
he offered himself to you as the unblemished Lamb,
the acceptable gift of perfect praise.

Nourishing your faithful by this sacred mystery,
you make them holy, so that the human race,
bounded by one world,
may be enlightened by one faith
and united by one bond of charity.

And so, we approach the table of this wondrous Sacrament,
so that, bathed in the sweetness of your grace,
we may pass over to the heavenly realities here foreshadowed.

Therefore, all creatures of heaven and earth
sing a new song in adoration,
and we, with all the host of Angels,
cry out, and without end we acclaim:

Holy, Holy, Holy Lord God of hosts…

APPENDIX

ORDINARY TIME — Sundays in Ordinary Time

The following Prefaces are said on Sundays in Ordinary Time which do not have a proper Preface.

PREFACE I
OF THE SUNDAYS IN ORDINARY TIME
THE PASCHAL MYSTERY
AND THE PEOPLE OF GOD

It is truly right and just,
    our duty and our salvation,
always and everywhere to give you thanks,
Lord, holy Father, almighty
    and eternal God,
through Christ our Lord.

For through his Paschal Mystery,
he accomplished the marvellous deed,
by which he has freed us
    from the yoke of sin and death,
summoning us to the glory
    of being now called
a chosen race, a royal priesthood,
a holy nation, a people
    for your own possession,
to proclaim everywhere your mighty works,
for you have called us out of darkness
into your own wonderful light.

And so, with Angels and Archangels,
with Thrones and Dominions,
and with all the hosts
    and Powers of heaven,
we sing the hymn of your glory,
as without end we acclaim:

Holy, Holy, Holy Lord God of hosts...

PREFACE II
OF THE SUNDAYS IN ORDINARY TIME
THE MYSTERY OF SALVATION

It is truly right and just,
    our duty and our salvation,
always and everywhere to give you thanks,
Lord, holy Father,
    almighty and eternal God,
through Christ our Lord.

For out of compassion for the waywardness
    that is ours,
he humbled himself
    and was born of the Virgin;
by the passion of the Cross
    he freed us from unending death,
and by rising from the dead
    he gave us life eternal.

And so, with Angels and Archangels,
with Thrones and Dominions,
and with all the hosts
    and Powers of heaven,
we sing the hymn of your glory,
as without end we acclaim:

Holy, Holy, Holy Lord God of hosts...

PREFACE III
OF THE SUNDAYS IN ORDINARY TIME
THE SALVATION OF MAN BY A MAN

It is truly right and just,
    our duty and our salvation,
always and everywhere to give you thanks,
Lord, holy Father,
    almighty and eternal God.

For we know it belongs
    to your boundless glory,
that you came to the aid of mortal beings
    with your divinity

and even fashioned for us
    a remedy out of mortality itself,
that the cause of our downfall
might become the means of our salvation,
through Christ our Lord.

Through him the host of Angels
    adores your majesty
and rejoices in your presence for ever.
May our voices, we pray, join with theirs
in one chorus of exultant praise,
    as we acclaim:

Holy, Holy, Holy Lord God of hosts...

PREFACE IV
OF THE SUNDAYS IN ORDINARY TIME
THE HISTORY OF SALVATION

It is truly right and just,
    our duty and our salvation,
always and everywhere to give you thanks,
Lord, holy Father,
    almighty and eternal God,
through Christ our Lord.

For by his birth he brought renewal
to humanity's fallen state,
and by his suffering cancelled out our sins;
by his rising from the dead
he has opened the way to eternal life,
and by ascending to you, O Father,
he has unlocked the gates of heaven.

And so, with the company
    of Angels and Saints,
we sing the hymn of your praise,
as without end we acclaim:

Holy, Holy, Holy Lord God of hosts...

PREFACE V
OF THE SUNDAYS IN ORDINARY TIME
CREATION

It is truly right and just,
    our duty and our salvation,
always and everywhere to give you thanks,
Lord, holy Father,
    almighty and eternal God.

For you laid the foundations of the world
and have arranged the changing
    of times and seasons;
you formed man in your own image
and set humanity over the whole world
    in all its wonder,
to rule in your name over all
    you have made
and for ever praise you
    in your mighty works,
through Christ our Lord.

And so, with all the Angels, we praise you,
as in joyful celebration we acclaim:

Holy, Holy, Holy Lord God of hosts...

PREFACE VI
OF THE SUNDAYS IN ORDINARY TIME
THE PLEDGE OF THE ETERNAL PASSOVER

It is truly right and just,
    our duty and our salvation,
always and everywhere to give you thanks,
Lord, holy Father,
    almighty and eternal God.

For in you we live and move
    and have our being,
and while in this body
we not only experience the daily effects
    of your care,
but even now possess the pledge
    of life eternal.

For, having received the first fruits
    of the Spirit,
through whom you raised up Jesus
    from the dead,
we hope for an everlasting share
    in the Paschal Mystery.

And so, with all the Angels, we praise you,
as in joyful celebration we acclaim:

Holy, Holy, Holy Lord God of hosts...

PREFACE VII
OF THE SUNDAYS IN ORDINARY TIME
SALVATION THROUGH
THE OBEDIENCE OF CHRIST

It is truly right and just,
    our duty and our salvation,
always and everywhere to give you thanks,
Lord, holy Father,
    almighty and eternal God.

For you so loved the world
that in your mercy you sent us the Redeemer,
to live like us in all things but sin,
so that you might love in us
    what you loved in your Son,
by whose obedience we have been restored
    to those gifts of yours
that, by sinning, we had lost
    in disobedience.

And so, Lord, with all the Angels and Saints,
we, too, give you thanks,
    as in exultation we acclaim:

Holy, Holy, Holy Lord God of hosts...

PREFACE VIII OF THE SUNDAYS IN ORDINARY TIME

THE CHURCH UNITED BY THE UNITY OF THE TRINITY

It is truly right and just,
our duty and our salvation,
always and everywhere to give you thanks,
Lord, holy Father,
almighty and eternal God.

For, when your children were scattered afar
by sin,
through the Blood of your Son
and the power of the Spirit,
you gathered them again to yourself,
that a people, formed as one
by the unity of the Trinity,

made the body of Christ
and the temple of the Holy Spirit,
might, to the praise
of your manifold wisdom,
be manifest as the Church.

And so, in company with
the choirs of Angels,
we praise you, and with joy we proclaim:

Holy, Holy, Holy Lord God of hosts...

ORDINARY TIME — Our Lord Jesus Christ, King of the Universe

CHRIST, KING OF THE UNIVERSE

This Preface is said on the Solemnity of Our Lord Jesus Christ, King of the Universe.

It is truly right and just, our duty and our salvation,
always and everywhere to give you thanks,
Lord, holy Father, almighty and eternal God.

For you anointed your Only Begotten Son,
our Lord Jesus Christ, with the oil of gladness
as eternal Priest and King of all creation,
so that, by offering himself on the altar of the Cross
as a spotless sacrifice to bring us peace,
he might accomplish the mysteries of human redemption
and, making all created things subject to his rule,
he might present to the immensity of your majesty
an eternal and universal kingdom,
a kingdom of truth and life,
a kingdom of holiness and grace,
a kingdom of justice, love and peace.

And so, with Angels and Archangels,
with Thrones and Dominions,
and with all the hosts and Powers of heaven,
we sing the hymn of your glory,
as without end we acclaim:

Holy, Holy, Holy Lord God of hosts...

PROPER OF SAINTS

These Prefaces are said in Masses from the Proper of Saints.

THE MISSION OF THE PRECURSOR

The following Preface is said on the Solemnity of the Nativity of John the Baptist (24 June).

It is truly right and just,
    our duty and our salvation,
always and everywhere to give you thanks,
Lord, holy Father,
    almighty and eternal God,
through Christ our Lord.

In his Precursor, Saint John the Baptist,
we praise your great glory,
for you consecrated him
    for a singular honour
among those born of women.

His birth brought great rejoicing;
even in the womb he leapt for joy
at the coming of human salvation.
He alone of all the prophets
pointed out the Lamb of redemption.

And to make holy the flowing waters,
he baptized the very author of Baptism
and was privileged to bear him
    supreme witness
by the shedding of his blood.

And so, with the Powers of heaven,
we worship you constantly on earth,
and before your majesty
without end we acclaim:

Holy, Holy, Holy Lord God of hosts...

THE TWOFOLD MISSION OF PETER AND PAUL IN THE CHURCH

The following Preface is said on the Solemnity of Saints Peter and Paul (29 June).

It is truly right and just,
    our duty and our salvation,
always and everywhere to give you thanks,
Lord, holy Father,
    almighty and eternal God.

For by your providence
the blessed Apostles Peter and Paul
    bring us joy:
Peter, foremost in confessing the faith,
Paul, its outstanding preacher,
Peter, who established the early Church
    from the remnant of Israel,
Paul, master and teacher of the Gentiles
    that you call.

And so, each in a different way
gathered together the one family of Christ;
and revered together throughout the world,
they share one Martyr's crown.

And therefore, with all the Angels
    and Saints,
we praise you, as without end we acclaim:

Holy, Holy, Holy Lord God of hosts...

THE MYSTERY OF THE TRANSFIGURATION

The following Preface is said on the Feast of the Transfiguration of the Lord (6 August).

It is truly right and just,
     our duty and our salvation,
always and everywhere to give you thanks,
Lord, holy Father,
     almighty and eternal God,
through Christ our Lord.

For he revealed his glory
     in the presence of chosen witnesses
and filled with the greatest splendour
     that bodily form
which he shares with all humanity,
that the scandal of the Cross
     might be removed from the hearts
          of his disciples
and that he might show
how in the Body of the whole Church
     is to be fulfilled
what so wonderfully shone forth
     first in its Head.

And so, with the Powers of heaven,
we worship you constantly on earth,
and before your majesty
without end we acclaim:

Holy, Holy, Holy Lord God of hosts...

THE GLORY OF MARY ASSUMED INTO HEAVEN

The following Preface is said on the Solemnity of The Assumption of the Blessed Virgin Mary (15 August).

It is truly right and just,
     our duty and our salvation,
always and everywhere to give you thanks,
Lord, holy Father,
     almighty and eternal God,
through Christ our Lord.

For today the Virgin Mother of God
was assumed into heaven
as the beginning and image
of your Church's coming to perfection
and a sign of sure hope and comfort
     to your pilgrim people;
rightly you would not allow her
to see the corruption of the tomb
since from her own body
     she marvellously brought forth
your incarnate Son, the Author of all life.

And so, in company
     with the choirs of Angels,
we praise you, and with joy we proclaim:

Holy, Holy, Holy Lord God of hosts...

Either of the following two Prefaces may be said on the Feast of the Exaltation of the Holy Cross (14 September).

THE VICTORY OF THE GLORIOUS CROSS

It is truly right and just,
     our duty and our salvation,
always and everywhere to give you thanks,
Lord, holy Father,
     almighty and eternal God.

For you placed the salvation of
     the human race
on the wood of the Cross,
so that, where death arose,
life might again spring forth
and the evil one, who conquered on a tree,
might likewise on a tree be conquered,
through Christ our Lord.

Through him the Angels
     praise your majesty,
Dominions adore and Powers
     tremble before you.
Heaven and the Virtues of heaven
     and the blessed Seraphim
worship together with exultation.

May our voices, we pray, join with theirs
in humble praise, as we acclaim:

Holy, Holy, Holy Lord God of hosts...

PREFACE I
OF THE PASSION OF THE LORD

THE POWER OF THE CROSS

It is truly right and just,
> our duty and our salvation,
always and everywhere to give you thanks,
Lord, holy Father,
> almighty and eternal God.

For through the saving Passion of your Son
the whole world has received a heart
to confess the infinite power
> of your majesty,

since by the wondrous power of the Cross
your judgement on the world
> is now revealed
and the authority of Christ crucified.

And so, Lord, with all the Angels and Saints,
we, too, give you thanks,
> as in exultation we acclaim:

Holy, Holy, Holy Lord God of hosts...

THE GLORY OF JERUSALEM, OUR MOTHER

This Preface is said on the Solemnity of All Saints (1 November).

It is truly right and just,
> our duty and our salvation,
always and everywhere to give you thanks,
Lord, holy Father,
> almighty and eternal God.

For today by your gift we celebrate
> the festival of your city,
the heavenly Jerusalem, our mother,
where the great array of
> our brothers and sisters
already gives you eternal praise.

Towards her, we eagerly hasten,
> as pilgrims advancing by faith,
rejoicing in the glory bestowed upon
> those exalted members of the Church
through whom you give us, in our frailty,
> both strength and good example.

And so, we glorify you with the multitude
> of Saints and Angels,
as with one voice of praise we acclaim:

Holy, Holy, Holy Lord God of hosts...

The following Prefaces are said in Masses for the Dead including the Commemoration of All the Faithful Departed (All Souls' Day) (2 November).

PREFACE I FOR THE DEAD

THE HOPE OF RESURRECTION IN CHRIST

It is truly right and just,
> our duty and our salvation,
always and everywhere to give you thanks,
Lord, holy Father,
> almighty and eternal God,
through Christ our Lord.

In him the hope of blessed resurrection
> has dawned,
that those saddened by the certainty
> of dying
might be consoled by the promise
> of immortality to come.

Indeed for your faithful, Lord,
life is changed not ended,
and, when this earthly dwelling
> turns to dust,
an eternal dwelling is made ready
> for them in heaven.

And so, with Angels and Archangels,
with Thrones and Dominions,
and with all the hosts and Powers of heaven,
we sing the hymn of your glory,
as without end we acclaim:

Holy, Holy, Holy Lord God of hosts...

PREFACE II FOR THE DEAD
CHRIST DIED SO THAT WE MIGHT LIVE

It is truly right and just,
    our duty and our salvation,
always and everywhere to give you thanks,
Lord, holy Father,
    almighty and eternal God,
through Christ our Lord.

For as one alone he accepted death,
so that we might all escape from dying;
as one man he chose to die,
so that in your sight
    we all might live for ever.

And so, in company
    with the choirs of Angels,
we praise you, and with joy we proclaim:

Holy, Holy, Holy Lord God of hosts...

PREFACE III FOR THE DEAD
CHRIST, THE SALVATION AND THE LIFE

It is truly right and just,
    our duty and our salvation,
always and everywhere to give you thanks,
Lord, holy Father,
    almighty and eternal God,
through Christ our Lord.

For he is the salvation of the world,
the life of the human race,
the resurrection of the dead.

Through him the host of Angels
    adores your majesty
and rejoices in your presence for ever.
May our voices, we pray, join with theirs
in one chorus of exultant praise,
    as we acclaim:

Holy, Holy, Holy Lord God of hosts...

PREFACE IV FOR THE DEAD
FROM EARTHLY LIFE TO HEAVENLY GLORY

It is truly right and just,
    our duty and our salvation,
always and everywhere to give you thanks,
Lord, holy Father,
    almighty and eternal God.

For it is at your summons
    that we come to birth,
by your will that we are governed,
and at your command that we return,
on account of sin,
to the earth from which we came.

And when you give the sign,
we who have been redeemed
    by the Death of your Son,
shall be raised up to the glory
    of his Resurrection.

And so, with the company
    of Angels and Saints,
we sing the hymn of your praise,
as without end we acclaim:

Holy, Holy, Holy Lord God of hosts...

PREFACE V FOR THE DEAD
OUR RESURRECTION THROUGH THE VICTORY
OF CHRIST

It is truly right and just,
    our duty and our salvation,
always and everywhere to give you thanks,
Lord, holy Father,
    almighty and eternal God.

For even though by our own fault
    we perish,
yet by your compassion and your grace,
when seized by death according to our sins,
we are redeemed
    through Christ's great victory,
and with him called back into life.

And so, with the Powers of heaven,
we worship you constantly on earth,
and before your majesty
without end we acclaim:

Holy, Holy, Holy Lord God of hosts...

THE MYSTERY OF THE CHURCH, THE BRIDE OF CHRIST AND THE TEMPLE OF THE SPIRIT

This Preface is said on the Feast of the Dedication of the Lateran Basilica (9 November).

It is truly right and just,
    our duty and our salvation,
always and everywhere to give you thanks,
Lord, holy Father,
    almighty and eternal God.

For in your benevolence you are pleased
to dwell in this house of prayer
in order to perfect us as the temple
    of the Holy Spirit,

supported by the perpetual help
    of your grace
and resplendent with the glory
    of a life acceptable to you.

Year by year you sanctify the Church,
    the Bride of Christ,
foreshadowed in visible buildings,
so that, rejoicing as the mother
    of countless children,
she may be given her place
    in your heavenly glory.

And so, with all the Angels and Saints,
we praise you, as without end
    we acclaim:

Holy, Holy, Holy Lord God of hosts...

LATIN TEXTS OF THE ORDER OF MASS

CONFITEOR

Confiteor Deo omnipotenti et vobis, fratres,
quia peccavi nimis
cogitatione, verbo, opere et omissione:
mea culpa, mea culpa, mea maxima culpa.
Ideo precor beatam Mariam semper Virginem,
omnes Angelos et Sanctos,
et vos, fratres, orare pro me
ad Dominum Deum nostrum. Amen

KYRIE

Kyrie, eleison
Kyrie, eleison.

Christe, eleison.
Christe, eleison.

Kyrie, eleison.
Kyrie, eleison.

GLORIA

Gloria in excelsis Deo
et in terra pax hominibus bonae voluntatis.
Laudamus te,
benedicimus te,
adoramus te,
glorificamus te,
gratias agimus tibi propter magnam
    gloriam tuam,
Domine Deus, Rex caelestis,
Deus Pater omnipotens.

Domine Fili unigenite, Jesu Christe,
Domine Deus, Agnus Dei, Filius Patris,
qui tollis peccata mundi, miserere nobis;
qui tollis peccata mundi,
    suscipe deprecationem nostram.
Qui sedes ad dexteram Patris,
    miserere nobis.
Quoniam tu solus Sanctus,
    tu solus Dominus,
    tu solus Altissimus,
Jesu Christe, cum Sancto Spiritu:
    in gloria Dei Patris. Amen.

CREDO

Credo in unum Deum,
Patrem Omnipotentem,
    factorem caeli et terrae,
visibilium omnium et invisibilium.
Et in unum Dominum Jesum Christum,
Filium Dei unigenitum,
    et ex Patre natum ante omnia saecula.
Deum de Deo, lumen de lumine,
    Deum verum de Deo vero,
genitum, non factum,
    consubstantialem Patri:
per quem omnia facta sunt.
Qui propter nos homines
    et propter nostram salutem
descendit de caelis.

Et incarnatus est de Spiritu Sancto
ex Maria Virgine; et homo factus est.

Crucifixus etiam pro nobis sub Pontio
  Pilato;
passus et sepultus est,
et resurrexit tertia die, secundum
  Scripturas,
et ascendit in caelum,
  sedet ad dexteram Patris.
Et iterum venturus est cum gloria,
  iudicare vivos et mortuos,
cuius regni non erit finis.
Et in Spiritum Sanctum,
  Dominum et vivificantem:
qui ex Patre Filioque procedit.
Qui cum Patre et Filio simul adoratur
  et conglorificatur:
qui locutus est per prophetas.
Et unam, sanctam, catholicam
  et apostolicam Ecclesiam.
Confiteor unum baptisma
  in remissionem peccatorum.
Et exspecto resurrectionem mortuorum,
et vitam venturi saeculi. Amen.

ORATE FRATRES

Orate fratres:
ut meum ac vestrum sacrificium
acceptabile fiat apud Deum
  Patrem omnipotentem.

Suscipiat Dominus sacrificium
  de manibus tuis
ad laudem et gloriam nominis sui,
ad utilitatem quoque nostram
totiusque Ecclesiae sanctae.

SURSUM CORDA

Dominus vobiscum.
Et cum spiritu tuo.

Sursum corda.
Habemus ad Dominum.

Gratias agamus Domine Deo nostro.
Dignum et iustum est.

SANCTUS

Sanctus, Sanctus, Sanctus Dominus
  Deus Sabaoth.
Pleni sunt caeli et terra gloria tua.
Hosanna in excelsis.
Benedictus qui venit in nomine Domini.
Hosanna in excelsis.

MYSTERIUM FIDEI

Mysterium Fidei.

1 Mortem tuam annuntiamus, Domine,
et tuam resurrectionem confitemur,
donec venias.

2 Quotiescumque manducamus panem
  hunc
et calicem bibimus
mortem tuam annuntiamus, Domine,
donec venias.

3 Salvator mundi, salva nos,
aui per crucem et resurrectionem tuam
liberasti nos.

PATER NOSTER

Praeceptis salutaribus moniti,
et divina insitutione formati,
audemus dicere:

Pater noster, qui es in caelis:
sanctificetur nomen tuum;
adveniat regnum tuum;
fiat voluntas tua, sicut in caelo,
  et in terra.
Panem nostrum cotidianum
  da nobis hodie;
et dimitte nobis debita nostra,
sicut et nos dimittimus debitoribus
  nostris
et ne nos inducas in tentationem;
sed libera nos a malo.

Libera nos, quaesumus, Domine,
  ab omnibus malis,...
...et adventum Salvatoris nostri Iesu Christi.

Quia tuum est regnum,
et potestas, et gloria
in saecula.

AGNUS DEI

Agnus Dei, qui tollis peccata mundi:
  miserere nobis.
Agnus Dei, qui tollis peccata mundi:
  miserere nobis.
Agnus Dei, qui tollis peccata mundi:
  dona nobis pacem.

CONTENTS OF THE PROPER OF TIME

COMMON RESPONSORIAL PSALMS

The Responsorial Psalm should correspond to each reading and should, as a rule, be taken from the Lectionary In order, however, that the people may be able to sing the Psalm response more readily, texts of some responses and psalms have been chosen for the various seasons of the year or for the various categories of Saints. These may be used in place of the text corresponding to the reading whenever the Psalm is sung.

General Instruction of the Roman Missal n 61

The Common Responsorial Psalms for Ordinary Time begin on the following page.

 # ORDINARY TIME

ABOUT THE SEASON

Besides the times of year that have their own distinctive character, there remain in the yearly cycle thirty-three or thirty-four weeks in which no particular aspect of the mystery of Christ is celebrated, but rather the mystery of Christ itself is honoured in its fullness, especially on Sundays. This period is known as Ordinary Time.

Universal Norms on the Liturgical Year and the Calendar n 43

ABOUT THE READINGS

On the Second Sunday of Ordinary Time the gospel continues to centre on the manifestation of the Lord, which Epiphany celebrates through the traditional passage about the wedding feast at Cana and two other passages from John.

Beginning with the Third Sunday, there is a semi-continuous reading of the Synoptic Gospels. This reading is arranged in such a way that as the Lord's life and preaching unfold the teaching proper to each of these Gospels is presented.

This distribution also provides a certain co-ordination between the meaning of each Gospel and the progress of the liturgical year. Thus after Epiphany the readings are on the beginning of the Lord's preaching and they fit in well with Christ's baptism and the first events in which he manifests himself. The liturgical year leads quite naturally to a termination in the eschatological theme proper to the last Sundays, since the chapters of the Synoptics that precede the account of the passion treat this eschatological theme rather extensively.

After the Sixteenth Sunday in Year B, five readings are incorporated from John 6 (the discourse on the bread of life). This is the proper place for these readings because the multiplication of the loaves from John takes the place of the same account in Mark.

Introduction to the Lectionary n 105

COMMON RESPONSORIAL PSALMS FOR ORDINARY TIME

COMMON RESPONSES

WITH A PSALM OF PRAISE

O give thanks to the Lord for he is good.

or

We thank you, Lord, for the wonders of all your creation.

or

O sing a new song to the Lord

WITH A PSALM OF PETITION

The Lord is close to all who call him.

or

Pay heed to us, Lord, and save us.

or

The Lord is compassion and love.

ORDINARY

COMMON PSALM 1   Psalm 18:8–11 response John 6:68; alternative response John 6:63

Lord, you have the message of eternal life.

or

Your words, Lord, are spirit and they are life.

1 The law of the Lord is perfect,
it revives the soul.
The rule of the Lord is to be trusted,
it gives wisdom to the simple.

3 The fear of the Lord is holy,
abiding for ever.
The decrees of the Lord are truth
and all of them just.

2 The precepts of the Lord are right,
they gladden the heart.
The command of the Lord is clear,
it gives light to the eyes.

4 They are more to be desired than gold,
than the purest of gold
and sweeter are they than honey,
than honey from the comb.

COMMON PSALM 2   Psalm 26:1, 4, 13–14 response v 1

The Lord is my light and my help.

1 The Lord is my light and my help;
whom shall I fear?
The Lord is the stronghold of my life;
before whom shall I shrink?

2 There is one thing I ask of the Lord,
for this I long,
to live in the house of the Lord,
all the days of my life,
to savour the sweetness of the Lord,
to behold his temple.

3 I am sure I shall see the Lord's goodness
in the land of the living.
Hope in him, hold firm and take heart.
Hope in the Lord!

COMMON PSALM 3   *Psalm 33:2–9 response v 2; alternative response v 9*

I will bless the Lord at all times.   *or*   **Taste and see that the Lord is good.**

1   I will bless the Lord at all times,
his praise always on my lips;
in the Lord my soul shall make its boast.
The humble shall hear and be glad.

2   Glorify the Lord with me.
Together let us praise his name
I sought the Lord and he answered me;
from all my terrors he set me free.

3   Look towards him and be radiant;
let your faces not be abashed.
This poor man called; the Lord heard him
and rescued him from all his distress.

4   The angel of the Lord is encamped
around those who revere him, to rescue them.
Taste and see that the Lord is good.
He is happy who seeks refuge in him.

COMMON PSALM 4   *Psalm 62:2–6, 8–9 response v 2*

For you my soul is thirsting, O Lord, my God.

1   O God, you are my God, for you I long;
for you my soul is thirsting.
My body pines for you
like a dry, weary land without water.

2   So I gaze on you in the sanctuary
to see your strength and your glory.
For your love is better than life,
my lips will speak your praise.

3   So I will bless you all my life,
in your name I will lift up my hands.
My soul shall be filled as with a banquet,
my mouth shall praise you with joy.

4   For you have been my help;
in the shadow of your wings I rejoice.
My soul clings to you;
your right hand holds me fast.

COMMON PSALM 5   *Psalm 94:1–2, 6–9 response v 8*

O that today you would listen to his voice!
Harden not your hearts.

1   Come, ring out our joy to the Lord;
hail the rock who saves us.
Let us come before him, giving thanks,
with songs let us hail the Lord.

2   Come in; let us bow and bend low,
let us kneel before the God who made us
for he is our God and we
the people who belong to his pasture,
the flock that is led by his hand.

3   O that today you would listen to his voice!
'Harden not your hearts as at Meribah,
as on that day at Massah in the desert
when your fathers put me to the test;
when they tried me, though they saw my work.'

COMMON PSALM 6   *Psalm 99:2, 3, 5 response v 3*

We are his people, the sheep of his flock.

1   Cry out with joy to the Lord, all the earth.
Serve the Lord with gladness.
Come before him, singing for joy.

2   Know that he, the Lord, is God.
He made us, we belong to him,
we are his people, the sheep of his flock.

3   Indeed, how good is the Lord,
eternal his merciful love.
He is faithful from age to age.

COMMON PSALM 7   *Psalm 102:1–4, 8, 10, 12–13 response v 8*

The Lord is compassion and love.

1   My soul, give thanks to the Lord,
all my being, bless his holy name.
My soul, give thanks to the Lord
and never forget all his blessings.

2   It is he who forgives all your guilt,
who heals every one of your ills,
who redeems your life from the grave,
who crowns you with love and compassion.

3   The Lord is compassion and love,
slow to anger and rich in mercy.
He does not treat us according to our sins
nor repay us according to our faults.

4   So far as the east is from the west
so far does he remove our sins.
As a father has compassion on his sons,
the Lord has pity on those who fear him.

ORDINARY

COMMON PSALM 8 *Psalm 144:1–2, 8–11, 13–14 response cf v 1*

I will bless your name for ever, O God my King.

1 I will give you glory, O God my King,
I will bless your name for ever.
I will bless you day after day
and praise your name for ever.

2 The Lord is kind and full of compassion,
slow to anger, abounding in love.
How good is the Lord to all,
compassionate to all his creatures.

3 All your creatures shall thank you, O Lord,
and your friends shall repeat their blessing.
They shall speak of the glory of your reign
and declare your might, O God.

4 The Lord is faithful in all his words
and loving in all his deeds.
The Lord supports all who fall
and raises all who are bowed down.

COMMON PSALM 9 For the Last Weeks of the Year *Psalm 121:1–9 response v 1*

Let us go to God's house, rejoicing.

1 I rejoiced when I heard them say:
'Let us go to God's house.'
And now our feet are standing
within your gates, O Jerusalem.

2 Jerusalem is built as a city
strongly compact.
It is there that the tribes go up,
the tribes of the Lord.

3 For Israel's law it is,
there to praise the Lord's name.
There were set the thrones of judgment
of the house of David.

4 For the peace of Jerusalem pray:
'Peace be to your homes!
May peace reign in your walls,
in your palaces, peace!'

5 For love of my brethren and friends
I say: 'Peace upon you!'
For love of the house of the Lord
I will ask for your good.

MOST HOLY TRINITY

ENTRANCE ANTIPHON
Blest be God the Father,
and the Only Begotten Son of God,
and also the Holy Spirit,
for he has shown us his merciful love.

▷ page 7

COLLECT
God our Father, who by sending into the world
the Word of truth and the Spirit of sanctification
made known to the human race your wondrous mystery,
grant us, we pray, that in professing the true faith,
we may acknowledge the Trinity of eternal glory
and adore your Unity, powerful in majesty.
Through our Lord Jesus Christ, your Son,
who lives and reigns with you in the unity of the Holy Spirit,
one God, for ever and ever.   **Amen.**

ORDINARY

FIRST READING   *Deuteronomy 4:32–34, 39–40*
*The Lord is God indeed, in heaven above as on earth
beneath, he and no other.*

Moses said to the people: 'Put this question to the ages that are past, that went before you, from the time God created man on earth: Was there ever a word so majestic, from one end of heaven to the other? Was anything ever heard? Did ever a people hear the voice of the living God speaking from the heart of the fire, as you heard it, and remain alive? Has any god ventured to take to himself one nation from the midst of another by ordeals, signs, wonders, war with mighty hand and outstretched arm, by fearsome terrors – all this that the Lord your God did for you before your eyes in Egypt?

'Understand this today, therefore, and take it to heart: The Lord is God indeed, in heaven above as on earth beneath, he and no other. Keep his laws and commandments as I give them to you today, so that you and your children may prosper and live long in the land that the Lord your God gives you for ever.'

The word of the Lord.
Thanks be to God.

RESPONSORIAL PSALM   *Psalm 32:4–6, 9, 18–20, 22 response v 12*

Happy the people the Lord has chosen as his own.

1   The word of the Lord is faithful
    and all his works to be trusted.
    The Lord loves justice and right
    and fills the earth with his love.

continued...

Happy the people the Lord has chosen as his own.

2 By his word the heavens were made,
   by the breath of his mouth all the stars.
   He spoke; and they came to be.
   He commanded; they sprang into being.

3 The Lord looks on those who revere him,
   on those who hope in his love,
   to rescue their souls from death,
   to keep them alive in famine.

4 Our soul is waiting for the Lord.
   The Lord is our help and our shield.
   May your love be upon us, O Lord,
   as we place all our hope in you.

SECOND READING   *Romans 8:14–17*

*You received the spirit of sons, and it makes us cry out,
'Abba, Father!'*

Everyone moved by the Spirit is a son of God. The spirit you received is not the spirit of slaves bringing fear into your lives again; it is the spirit of sons, and it makes us cry out, 'Abba, Father!' The Spirit himself and our spirit bear united witness that we are children of God. And if we are children we are heirs as well: heirs of God and coheirs with Christ, sharing his sufferings so as to share his glory.

The word of the Lord.
Thanks be to God.

GOSPEL ACCLAMATION   *cf Apocalypse 1:8*

Alleluia, alleluia!
**Glory be to the Father, and to the Son, and to the Holy Spirit,
the God who is, who was, and who is to come.
Alleluia!**

GOSPEL   *Matthew 28:16–20*

The Lord be with you.
And with your spirit.

A reading from the holy Gospel according to Matthew.
Glory to you, O Lord.

Baptise them in the name of the Father and of the Son and of the Holy Spirit.

The eleven disciples set out for Galilee, to the mountain where Jesus had arranged to meet them. When they saw him they fell down before him, though some hesitated. Jesus came up and spoke to them. He said, 'All authority in heaven and on earth has been given to me. Go, therefore, make disciples of all the nations; baptise them in the name of the Father and of the Son and of the Holy Spirit, and teach them to observe all the commands I gave you. And know that I am with you always; yes, to the end of time.'

The Gospel of the Lord.
Praise to you, Lord Jesus Christ.

▷ *page 11*

PRAYER OVER THE OFFERINGS
Sanctify by the invocation of your name,
we pray, O Lord our God,
this oblation of our service,
and by it make of us an eternal offering to you.
Through Christ our Lord.   **Amen.**

▷ *page 15*

Preface of The Mystery of the Most Holy Trinity, page 66.

COMMUNION ANTIPHON   *Galatians 4:6*
Since you are children of God,
God has sent into your hearts the Spirit of his Son,
the Spirit who cries out: Abba, Father.

▷ *page 59*

PRAYER AFTER COMMUNION
May receiving this Sacrament, O Lord our God,
bring us health of body and soul,
as we confess your eternal holy Trinity and undivided Unity.
Through Christ our Lord.   **Amen.**

▷ *page 59*

ORDINARY

MOST HOLY BODY AND BLOOD OF CHRIST

(CORPUS CHRISTI)
THURSDAY AFTER THE MOST HOLY TRINITY

*When the Solemnity of the Most Holy Body and Blood of Christ is not a Holyday of Obligation,
it is assigned to the Sunday after the Most Holy Trinity as its proper day.*

ENTRANCE ANTIPHON   *cf Psalm 80:17*
He fed them with the finest wheat
and satisfied them with honey from the rock.

▷ *page 7*

COLLECT
O God, who in this wonderful Sacrament
have left us a memorial of your Passion,
grant us, we pray,
so to revere the sacred mysteries of your Body and Blood
that we may always experience in ourselves
the fruits of your redemption.
Who live and reign with God the Father
in the unity of the Holy Spirit,
one God, for ever and ever.   **Amen.**

FIRST READING   *Exodus 24:3–8*
This is the blood of the Covenant that the Lord has made with you.

Moses went and told the people all the commands of the Lord and all the ordinances. In answer, all the people said with one voice, 'We will observe all the commands that the Lord has decreed.' Moses put all the commands of the Lord into writing, and early next morning he built an altar at the foot of the mountain, with twelve standing-stones for the twelve tribes of Israel. Then he directed certain young Israelites to offer holocausts and to immolate bullocks to the Lord as communion sacrifices. Half of the blood Moses took up and put into basins, the other half he cast on the altar. And taking the Book of the Covenant he read it to the listening people, and they said, 'We will observe all that the Lord has decreed; we will obey.' Then Moses took the blood and cast it towards the people. 'This' he said 'is the blood of the Covenant that the Lord has made with you, containing all these rules.'

The word of the Lord.
Thanks be to God.

RESPONSORIAL PSALM   *Psalm 115:12–13, 15–18 response v 13*

The cup of salvation I will raise;
I will call on the Lord's name

or

Alleluia! *(may be repeated two or three times)*

1   How can I repay the Lord
    for his goodness to me?
    The cup of salvation I will raise;
    I will call on the Lord's name.

2   O precious in the eyes of the Lord
    is the death of his faithful.
    Your servant, Lord, your servant am I;
    you have loosened my bonds.

3   A thanksgiving sacrifice I make;
    I will call on the Lord's name.
    My vows to the Lord I will fulfil
    before all his people.

SECOND READING   *Hebrews 9:11–15*

The blood of Christ can purify our inner self from dead actions.

Now Christ has come, as the high priest of all the blessings which were to come. He has passed through the greater, the more perfect tent, which is better than one made by men's hands because it is not of this created order; and he has entered the sanctuary once and for all, taking with him not the blood of goats and bull calves, but his own blood, having won an eternal redemption for us. The blood of goats and bulls and the ashes of a heifer are sprinkled on those who have incurred defilement and they restore the holiness of their outward lives; how much more effectively the blood of Christ, who offered himself as the perfect sacrifice to God through the eternal Spirit, can purify our inner self from dead actions so that we do our service to the living God.

He brings a new covenant, as the mediator, only so that the people who were called to an eternal inheritance may actually receive what was promised: his death took place to cancel the sins that infringed the earlier covenant.

The word of the Lord.
Thanks be to God.

SEQUENCE

The sequence may be said or sung in full, or using the shorter form indicated by the asterisked verses

Sing forth, O Zion, sweetly sing
The praises of thy Shepherd-King,
In hymns and canticles divine;
Dare all thou canst, thou hast no song
Worthy his praises to prolong,
So far surpassing powers like thine.

Today no theme of common praise
Forms the sweet burden of thy lays –
The living, life-dispensing food –
That food which at the sacred board
Unto the brethren twelve our Lord
His parting legacy bestowed.

Then be the anthem clear and strong,
Thy fullest-note, thy sweetest song,
The very music of the breast:
For now shines forth the day sublime
That brings remembrance of the time
When Jesus first his table blessed.

Within our new King's banquet-hall
They meet to keep the festival
That closed the ancient paschal rite:
The old is by the new replaced;
The substance hath the shadow chased;
And rising day dispels the night.

Christ willed what he himself had done
Should be renewed while time should run,
In memory of his parting hour:
Thus, tutored in his school divine,
We consecrate the bread and wine;
And lo – a Host of saving power.

This faith to Christian men is given –
Bread is made flesh by words from heaven:
Into his blood the wine is turned:
What though it baffles nature's powers
Of sense and sight? This faith of ours
Proves more than nature e'er discerned.

Concealed beneath the two-fold sign,
Meet symbols of the gifts divine,
There lie the mysteries adored:
The living body is our food;
Our drink the ever-precious blood;
In each, one undivided Lord.

Not he that eateth it divides
The sacred food, which whole abides
Unbroken still, nor knows decay;
Be one, or be a thousand fed,
They eat alike that living bread
Which, still received, ne'er wastes away.

The good, the guilty share therein,
With sure increase of grace or sin,
The ghostly life, or ghostly death:
Death to the guilty; to the good
Immortal life. See how one food
Man's joy or woe accomplisheth.

We break the Sacrament; but bold
And firm thy faith shall keep its hold;
Deem not the whole doth more enfold
Than in the fractured part resides:
Deem not that Christ doth broken lie;
'Tis but the sign that meets the eye;
The hidden deep reality
In all its fullness still abides.

* Behold the bread of angels, sent
For pilgrims in their banishment,
The bread for God's true children meant,
That may not unto dogs be given:
Oft in the olden types foreshowed;
In Isaac on the altar bowed,
And in the ancient paschal food,
And in the manna sent from heaven.

* Come then, good shepherd, bread divine,
Still show to us thy mercy sign;
Oh, feed us still, still keep us thine;
So may we see thy glories shine
In fields of immortality;

* O thou, the wisest, mightiest, best,
Our present food, our future rest,
Come, make us each thy chosen guest,
Co-heirs of thine, and comrades blest
With saints whose dwelling is with thee.

ORDINARY

GOSPEL ACCLAMATION *John 6:51–52*

Alleluia, alleluia!
I am the living bread which has come down from heaven,
says the Lord.
Anyone who eats this bread will live for ever.
Alleluia!

GOSPEL *Mark 14:12–16, 22–26*

The Lord be with you.
And with your spirit.

A reading from the holy Gospel according to Mark.
Glory to you, O Lord.

This is my body. This is my blood.

On the first day of Unleavened Bread, when the Passover lamb was sacrificed, his disciples said to Jesus, 'Where do you want us to go and make the preparations for you to eat the passover?' So he sent two of his disciples, saying to them, 'Go into the city and you will meet a man carrying a pitcher of water. Follow him, and say to the owner of the house which he enters, 'The Master says: Where is my dining room in which I can eat the passover with my disciples?' He will show you a large upper room furnished with couches, all prepared. Make the preparations for us there.' The disciples set out and went to the city and found everything as he had told them, and prepared the Passover.

And as they were eating he took some bread, and when he had said the blessing he broke it and gave it to them. 'Take it,' he said 'this is my body.' Then he took a cup, and when he had returned thanks he gave it to them, and all drank from it, and he said to them, 'This is my blood, the blood of the covenant, which is to be poured out for many. I tell you solemnly, I shall not drink any more wine until the day I drink the new wine in the Kingdom of God.'

After psalms had been sung they left for the Mount of Olives.

The Gospel of the Lord.
Praise to you, Lord Jesus Christ.

▷ *page 11*

PRAYER OVER THE OFFERINGS

Grant your Church, O Lord, we pray,
the gifts of unity and peace,
whose signs are to be seen in mystery
in the offerings we here present.
Through Christ our Lord.   **Amen.**

▷ *page 15*

Preface II or I of the Most Holy Eucharist, page 67.

COMMUNION ANTIPHON *John 6:57*

Whoever eats my flesh and drinks my blood
remains in me and I in him, says the Lord.

▷ *page 59*

PRAYER AFTER COMMUNION

Grant, O Lord, we pray,
that we may delight for all eternity
in that share in your divine life,
which is foreshadowed in the present age
by our reception of your precious Body and Blood.
Who live and reign for ever and ever.   **Amen.**

PROCESSION

It is desirable that a procession take place after the Mass in which the Host to be carried in the procession is consecrated. However, nothing prohibits a procession from taking place even after a public and lengthy period of adoration following the Mass. If a procession takes place after Mass, when the Communion of the faithful is over, the monstrance in which the consecrated host has been placed is set on the altar. When the Prayer after Communion has been said, the Concluding Rites are omitted and the procession forms.

If there is no procession   ▷ *page 59*

ORDINARY

NINTH SUNDAY IN ORDINARY TIME

ENTRANCE ANTIPHON   *cf Psalm 24:16, 18*

Turn to me and have mercy on me, O Lord,
for I am alone and poor.
See my lowliness and suffering
and take away all my sins, my God.

▷ *page 7*

COLLECT

O God, whose providence never fails in its design,
keep from us, we humbly beseech you,
all that might harm us
and grant all that works for our good.
Through our Lord Jesus Christ, your Son,
who lives and reigns with you in the unity of the Holy Spirit,
one God, for ever and ever.   **Amen.**

FIRST READING   *Deuteronomy 5:12–15*

Remember that you were a servant in the land of Egypt.

The Lord says this: 'Observe the sabbath day and keep it holy, as the Lord your God has commanded you. For six days you shall labour and do all your work but the seventh day is a sabbath for the Lord your God. You shall do no work that day, neither you nor your son nor your daughter nor your servants, men or women, nor your ox nor your donkey nor any of your animals, nor the stranger who lives with you. Thus your servant, man or woman, shall rest as you do. Remember that you were a servant in the land of Egypt, and that the Lord your God brought you out from there with mighty hand and outstretched arm; because of this, the Lord your God has commanded you to keep the sabbath day.'

The word of the Lord.
Thanks be to God.

RESPONSORIAL PSALM   *Psalm 80:3–8, 10–11 response v 2*

Ring out your joy to God our strength.

1   Raise a song and sound the timbrel,
    the sweet-sounding harp and the lute,
    blow the trumpet at the new moon,
    when the moon is full, on our feast.

2   For this is Israel's law,
    a command of the God of Jacob.
    He imposed it as a rule on Joseph,
    when he went out against the land of Egypt.

3   A voice I did not know said to me:
    'I freed your shoulder from the burden;
    your hands were freed from the load.
    You called in distress and I saved you.

4   'Let there be no foreign god among you,
    no worship of an alien god.
    I am the Lord your God,
    who brought you from the land of Egypt.'

SECOND READING   *2 Corinthians 4:6–11*

In our mortal flesh the life of Jesus is openly shown.

It is the same God that said, 'Let there be light shining out of darkness,' who has shone in our minds to radiate the light of the knowledge of God's glory, the glory on the face of Christ.

We are only earthenware jars that hold this treasure, to make it clear that such an overwhelming power comes from God and not from us. We are in difficulties on all sides, but never cornered; we see no answer to our problems, but never despair; we have been persecuted, but never deserted; knocked down, but never killed; always, wherever we may be, we carry with us in our body the death of Jesus, so that the life of Jesus, too, may always be seen in our body. Indeed, while we are still alive, we are consigned to our death every day, for the sake of Jesus, so that in our mortal flesh the life of Jesus, too, may be openly shown.

The word of the Lord.
Thanks be to God.

GOSPEL ACCLAMATION *cf John 6:63, 68*   **or**   *cf John 17:17*

Alleluia, alleluia!
Your words are spirit, Lord,
and they are life:
you have the message of eternal life.
Alleluia!

Alleluia, alleluia!
Your word is truth, O Lord,
consecrate us in the truth.
Alleluia!

GOSPEL   *Mark 2:23–3:6   Shorter form: Mark 2:23–28 (only read text with side line next to it).*

The Lord be with you.
And with your spirit.

A reading from the holy Gospel according to Mark.
Glory to you, O Lord.

The Son of Man is master even of the Sabbath.

One sabbath day Jesus happened to be taking a walk through the cornfields, and his disciples began to pick ears of corn as they went along. And the Pharisees said to him, 'Look, why are they doing something on the sabbath day that is forbidden?' And he replied, 'Did you ever read what David did in his time of need when he and his followers were hungry – how he went into the house of God when Abiathar was high priest, and ate the loaves of offering which only the priests are allowed to eat, and how he also gave some to the men with him?'

And he said to them, 'The sabbath was made for man, not man for the sabbath; so the Son of Man is master even of the sabbath.'

He went again into a synagogue, and there was a man there who had a withered hand. And they were watching him to see if he would cure him on the sabbath day, hoping for something to use against him. He said to the man with the withered hand, 'Stand up out in the middle!' Then he said to them, 'Is it against the law on the sabbath day to do good, or to do evil; to save life, or to kill?' But they said nothing. Then, grieved to find them so obstinate, he looked angrily round at them, and said to the man, 'Stretch out your hand.' He stretched it out and his hand was better. The Pharisees went out and at once began to plot with the Herodians against him, discussing how to destroy him.

The Gospel of the Lord.
Praise to you, Lord Jesus Christ.

▷ *page 11*

PRAYER OVER THE OFFERINGS

Trusting in your compassion, O Lord,
we come eagerly with our offerings to your sacred altar,
that, through the purifying action of your grace,
we may be cleansed by the very mysteries we serve.
Through Christ our Lord. **Amen.**

▷ *page 15*

ORDINARY

COMMUNION ANTIPHON   *cf Psalm 16:6*
To you I call, for you will surely heed me, O God;
turn your ear to me; hear my words.

or   *Mark 11:23, 24*

Amen, I say to you: Whatever you ask for in prayer,
believe you will receive it,
and it will be yours, says the Lord.

▷ *page 59*

PRAYER AFTER COMMUNION
Govern by your Spirit, we pray, O Lord,
those you feed with the Body and Blood of your Son,
that, professing you not just in word or in speech,
but also in works and in truth,
we may merit to enter the Kingdom of Heaven.   **Amen.**

▷ *page 59*

TENTH SUNDAY IN ORDINARY TIME

ENTRANCE ANTIPHON   *cf Psalm 26:1–2*
The Lord is my light and my salvation; whom shall I fear?
The Lord is the stronghold of my life; whom should I dread?
When those who do evil draw near, they stumble and fall.

▷ *page 7*

COLLECT
O God, from whom all good things come,
grant that we, who call on you in our need,
may at your prompting discern what is right,
and by your guidance do it.
Through our Lord Jesus Christ, your Son,
who lives and reigns with you in the unity of the Holy Spirit,
one God, for ever and ever.   **Amen.**

FIRST READING   *Genesis 3:9–15*

I will make you enemies of each other: you and the woman, your offspring and her offspring.

The Lord God called to the man after he had eaten of the tree. 'Where are you?' he asked. 'I heard the sound of you in the garden,' he replied 'I was afraid because I was naked, so I hid.' 'Who told you that you were naked?' he asked. 'Have you been eating of the tree I forbade you to eat?' The man replied, 'It was the woman you put with me; she gave me the fruit, and I ate it.' Then the Lord God asked the woman, 'What is this you have done?' The woman replied, 'The serpent tempted me and I ate.'

Then the Lord God said to the serpent, 'Because you have done this, be accursed beyond all cattle, all wild beasts. You shall crawl on your belly and eat dust every day of your life. I will make you enemies of each other: you and the woman, your offspring and her offspring. It will crush your head and you will strike its heel.'

The word of the Lord.
Thanks be to God.

RESPONSORIAL PSALM *Psalm 129 response v 7*

With the Lord there is mercy and fullness of redemption.

1 Out of the depths I cry to you, O Lord,
Lord, hear my voice!
O let your ears be attentive
to the voice of my pleading.

2 If you, O Lord, should mark our guilt,
Lord, who would survive?
But with you is found forgiveness:
for this we revere you.

3 My soul is waiting for the Lord,
I count on his word.
My soul is longing for the Lord
more than watchman for daybreak.

4 Because with the Lord there is mercy
and fullness of redemption,
Israel indeed he will redeem
from all its iniquity.

SECOND READING *2 Corinthians 4:13–5:1*
We believe, and therefore we speak.

As we have the same spirit of faith that is mentioned in scripture – I believed, and therefore I spoke – we too believe and therefore we too speak, knowing that he who raised the Lord Jesus to life will raise us with Jesus in our turn; and put us by his side and you with us. You see, all this is for your benefit, so that the more grace is multiplied among people, the more thanksgiving there will be, to the glory of God.

That is why there is no weakening on our part, and instead, though this outer man of ours may be falling into decay, the inner man is renewed day by day. Yes, the troubles which are soon over, though they weigh little, train us for the carrying of a weight of eternal glory which is out of all proportion to them. And so we have no eyes for things that are visible, but only for things that are invisible; for visible things last only for a time, and the invisible things are eternal.

For we know that when the tent that we live in on earth is folded up, there is a house built by God for us, an everlasting home not made by human hands, in the heavens.

The word of the Lord.
Thanks be to God.

ORDINARY

GOSPEL ACCLAMATION   *John 14:23*

Alleluia, alleluia!
If anyone loves me he will keep my word,
and my Father will love him,
and we shall come to him.
Alleluia!

or   John 12:31, 32

Alleluia, alleluia!
Now the prince of this world is to be overthrown,
says the Lord.
And when I am lifted up from the earth,
I shall draw all men to myself.
Alleluia!

GOSPEL   *Mark 3:20–35*

The Lord be with you.
And with your spirit.

A reading from the holy Gospel according to Mark.
Glory to you, O Lord.

It is the end of Satan.

Jesus went home with his disciples, and such a crowd collected that they could not even have a meal. When his relatives heard of this, they set out to take charge of him, convinced he was out of his mind.

The scribes who had come down from Jerusalem were saying, 'Beelzebul is in him,' and, 'It is through the prince of devils that he casts devils out.' So he called them to him and spoke to them in parables, 'How can Satan cast out Satan? If a kingdom is divided against itself, that kingdom cannot last. And if a household is divided against itself, that household can never stand. Now if Satan has rebelled against himself and is divided, he cannot stand either – it is the end of him. But no one can make his way into a strong man's house and burgle his property unless he has tied up the strong man first. Only then can he burgle his house.

'I tell you solemnly, all men's sins will be forgiven, and all their blasphemies; but let anyone blaspheme against the Holy Spirit and he will never have forgiveness: he is guilty of an eternal sin.' This was because they were saying, 'An unclean spirit is in him.'

His mother and brothers now arrived and, standing outside, sent in a message asking for him. A crowd was sitting round him at the time the message was passed to him, 'Your mother and brothers and sisters are outside asking for you.' He replied, 'Who are my mother and my brothers?' And looking round at those sitting in a circle about him, he said, 'Here are my mother and my brothers. Anyone who does the will of God, that person is my brother and sister and mother.'

The Gospel of the Lord.
Praise to you, Lord Jesus Christ.

▷ *page 11*

PRAYER OVER THE OFFERINGS
Look kindly upon our service, O Lord, we pray,
that what we offer
may be an acceptable oblation to you
and lead us to grow in charity.
Through Christ our Lord.   **Amen.**

▷ *page 15*

COMMUNION ANTIPHON   *Psalm 17:3*
The Lord is my rock, my fortress, and my deliverer;
my God is my saving strength.

or   *1 John 4:16*

God is love, and whoever abides in love
abides in God, and God in him.

▷ *page 59*

PRAYER AFTER COMMUNION
May your healing work, O Lord,
free us, we pray, from doing evil
and lead us to what is right.
Through Christ our Lord.   **Amen.**

▷ *page 59*

ORDINARY

ELEVENTH SUNDAY IN ORDINARY TIME

ENTRANCE ANTIPHON   *cf Psalm 26:7, 9*
O Lord, hear my voice, for I have called to you; be my help.
Do not abandon or forsake me, O God, my Saviour!

▷ *page 7*

COLLECT
O God, strength of those who hope in you,
graciously hear our pleas,
and, since without you mortal frailty can do nothing,
grant us always the help of your grace,
that in following your commands
we may please you by our resolve and our deeds.
Through our Lord Jesus Christ, your Son,
who lives and reigns with you in the unity of the Holy Spirit,
one God, for ever and ever.   **Amen.**

FIRST READING   *Ezekiel 17:22–24*
I make low trees grow.

The Lord says this:

'From the top of the cedar, from the highest branch I will take a shoot and plant it myself on a very high mountain. I will plant it on the high mountain of Israel. It will sprout branches and bear fruit, and become a noble cedar. Every kind of bird will live beneath it, every winged creature rest in the shade of its branches. And every tree of the field will learn that I, the Lord, am the one who stunts tall trees and makes the low ones grow, who withers green trees and makes the withered green. I, the Lord, have spoken, and I will do it.'

The word of the Lord.

Thanks be to God.

RESPONSORIAL PSALM   *Psalm 91:2–3, 13–16 response cf v 2*

It is good to give you thanks, O Lord.

1   It is good to give thanks to the Lord
to make music to your name, O Most High,
to proclaim your love in the morning
and your truth in the watches of the night.

2   The just will flourish like the palm-tree
and grow like a Lebanon cedar.

3   Planted in the house of the Lord
they will flourish in the courts of our God,
still bearing fruit when they are old,
still full of sap, still green,
to proclaim that the Lord is just.
In him, my rock, there is no wrong.

SECOND READING   *2 Corinthians 5:6–10*

Whether we are living in the body or exiled from it, we are intent on pleasing the Lord.

We are always full of confidence when we remember that to live in the body means to be exiled from the Lord, going as we do by faith and not by sight – we are full of confidence, I say, and actually want to be exiled from the body and make our home with the Lord. Whether we are living in the body or exiled from it, we are intent on pleasing him. For all the truth about us will be brought out in the law court of Christ, and each of us will get what he deserves for the things he did in the body, good or bad.

The word of the Lord.

Thanks be to God.

GOSPEL ACCLAMATION   *John 15:15*

> **Alleluia, alleluia!**
> **I call you friends, says the Lord,**
> **because I have made known to you**
> **everything I have learnt from my Father.**
> **Alleluia!**

or

> **Alleluia, alleluia!**
> **The seed is the word of God, Christ the sower;**
> **whoever finds the seed will remain for ever.**
> **Alleluia!**

GOSPEL   *Mark 4:26–34*

The Lord be with you.
And with your spirit.

A reading from the holy Gospel according to Mark.
Glory to you, O Lord.

It is the smallest of all the seeds; yet it grows into the biggest shrub of them all.

Jesus said to the crowds: 'This is what the Kingdom of God is like. A man throws seed on the land. Night and day, while he sleeps, when he is awake, the seed is sprouting and growing; how, he does not know. Of its own accord the land produces first the shoot, then the ear, then the full grain in the ear. And when the crop is ready, he loses no time: he starts to reap because the harvest has come.'

He also said, 'What can we say the kingdom of God is like? What parable can we find for it? It is like a mustard seed which at the time of its sowing in the soil is the smallest of all the seeds on earth; yet once it is sown it grows into the biggest shrub of them all and puts out big branches so that the birds of the air can shelter in its shade.'

Using many parables like these, he spoke the word to them, so far as they were capable of understanding it. He would not speak to them except in parables, but he explained everything to his disciples when they were alone.

The Gospel of the Lord.
Praise to you, Lord Jesus Christ.

▷ *page 11*

PRAYER OVER THE OFFERINGS

O God, who in the offerings presented here
provide for the twofold needs of human nature,
nourishing us with food
and renewing us with your Sacrament,
grant, we pray,
that the sustenance they provide
may not fail us in body or in spirit.
Through Christ our Lord. **Amen.**

▷ *page 15*

COMMUNION ANTIPHON   *Psalm 26:4*

There is one thing I ask of the Lord, only this do I seek:
to live in the house of the Lord all the days of my life.

or   *John 17:11*

Holy Father, keep in your name those you have given me,
that they may be one as we are one, says the Lord.

▷ *page 59*

PRAYER AFTER COMMUNION

As this reception of your Holy Communion, O Lord,
foreshadows the union of the faithful in you,
so may it bring about unity in your Church.
Through Christ our Lord. **Amen.**

▷ *page 59*

ORDINARY

✠ TWELFTH SUNDAY IN ORDINARY TIME

ENTRANCE ANTIPHON *cf Psalm 27:8–9*

The Lord is the strength of his people,
a saving refuge for the one he has anointed.
Save your people, Lord, and bless your heritage,
and govern them for ever.

▷ *page 7*

COLLECT

Grant, O Lord,
that we may always revere and love your holy name,
for you never deprive of your guidance
those you set firm on the foundation of your love.
Through our Lord Jesus Christ, your Son,
who lives and reigns with you in the unity of the Holy Spirit,
one God, for ever and ever. **Amen.**

FIRST READING *Job 38:1, 8–11*

Here your proud waves shall break.

From the heart of the tempest the Lord gave Job his answer. He said:

Who pent up the sea behind closed doors when it leapt tumultuous out of the womb, when I wrapped it in a robe of mist and made black clouds its swaddling bands; when I marked the bounds it was not to cross and made it fast with a bolted gate? Come thus far, I said, and no farther: here your proud waves shall break.

The word of the Lord.
Thanks be to God.

RESPONSORIAL PSALM *Psalm 106:23–26, 28–31 response v 1*

**O give thanks to the Lord,
for his love endures for ever.**   *or*   **Alleluia!** *(may be repeated two or three times)*

1 Some sailed to the sea in ships
   to trade on the mighty waters.
   These men have seen the Lord's deeds,
   the wonders he does in the deep.

2 For he spoke; he summoned the gale,
   tossing the waves of the sea
   up to heaven and back into the deep;
   their soul melted away in their distress.

3 Then they cried to the Lord in their need
   and he rescued them from their distress.
   He stilled the storm to a whisper:
   all the waves of the sea were hushed.

4 They rejoiced because of the calm
   and he led them to the haven they desired.
   Let them thank the Lord for his love,
   the wonders he does for men.

SECOND READING   *2 Corinthians 5:14–17*
Now the new creation is here.

The love of Christ overwhelms us when we reflect that if one man has died for all, then all men should be dead; and the reason he died for all was so that living men should live no longer for themselves, but for him who died and was raised to life for them. From now onwards, therefore, we do not judge anyone by the standards of the flesh. Even if we did once know Christ in the flesh, that is not how we know him now. And for anyone who is in Christ, there is a new creation; the old creation has gone, and now the new one is here.

The word of the Lord.
Thanks be to God.

GOSPEL ACCLAMATION   *cf Ephesians 1:17, 18*

Alleluia, alleluia!
**May the Father of our Lord Jesus Christ
enlighten the eyes of our mind,
so that we can see what hope his call holds for us.
Alleluia!**

or   *Luke 7:16*

Alleluia, alleluia!
**A great prophet has appeared among us;
God has visited his people.
Alleluia!**

GOSPEL   *Mark 4:35–41*

The Lord be with you.
And with your spirit.

A reading from the holy Gospel according to Mark.
Glory to you, O Lord.

Who can this be? Even the wind and the sea obey him.

With the coming of evening, Jesus said to his disciples, 'Let us cross over to the other side.' And leaving the crowd behind they took him, just as he was, in the boat; and there were other boats with him. Then it began to blow a gale and the waves were breaking into the boat so that it was almost swamped. But he was in the stern, his head on the cushion, asleep. They woke him and said to him, 'Master, do you not care? We are going down!' And he woke up and rebuked the wind and said to the sea, 'Quiet now! Be calm!' And the wind dropped, and all was calm again. Then he said to them, 'Why are you so frightened? How is it that you have no faith?' They were filled with awe and said to one another, 'Who can this be? Even the wind and the sea obey him.'

The Gospel of the Lord.
Praise to you, Lord Jesus Christ.

▷ *page 11*

ORDINARY

PRAYER OVER THE OFFERINGS

Receive, O Lord, the sacrifice of conciliation and praise
and grant that, cleansed by its action,
we may make offering of a heart pleasing to you.
Through Christ our Lord. **Amen.**

▷ *page 15*

COMMUNION ANTIPHON *Psalm 144:15*

The eyes of all look to you, Lord,
and you give them their food in due season.

or *John 10:11, 15*

I am the Good Shepherd,
and I lay down my life for my sheep, says the Lord.

▷ *page 59*

PRAYER AFTER COMMUNION

Renewed and nourished
by the Sacred Body and Precious Blood of your Son,
we ask of your mercy, O Lord,
that what we celebrate with constant devotion
may be our sure pledge of redemption.
Through Christ our Lord. **Amen.**

▷ *page 59*

THIRTEENTH SUNDAY IN ORDINARY TIME

ENTRANCE ANTIPHON *Psalm 46:2*

All peoples, clap your hands.
Cry to God with shouts of joy!

▷ *page 7*

COLLECT

O God, who through the grace of adoption
chose us to be children of light,
grant, we pray,
that we may not be wrapped in the darkness of error
but always be seen to stand in the bright light of truth.
Through our Lord Jesus Christ, your Son,
who lives and reigns with you in the unity of the Holy Spirit,
one God, for ever and ever. **Amen.**

FIRST READING   *Wisdom 1:13–15, 2:23–24*

It was the devil's envy that brought death into the world.

Death was not God's doing, he takes no pleasure in the extinction of the living. To be – for this he created all; the world's created things have health in them, in them no fatal poison can be found, and Hades holds no power on earth; for virtue is undying. Yet God did make man imperishable, he made him in the image of his own nature; it was the devil's envy that brought death into the world, as those who are his partners will discover.

The word of the Lord.

Thanks be to God.

RESPONSORIAL PSALM   *Psalm 29:2, 4–6, 11–13 response v 2*

I will praise you, Lord, you have rescued me.

1   I will praise you, Lord, you have rescued me
    and have not let my enemies rejoice over me.
    O Lord, you have raised my soul from the dead,
    restored me to life from those who sink into the grave.

2   Sing psalms to the Lord, you who love him,
    give thanks to his holy name.
    His anger lasts but a moment; his favour through life.
    At night there are tears, but joy comes with dawn.

3   The Lord listened and had pity.
    The Lord came to my help.
    For me you have changed my mourning into dancing,
    O Lord my God, I will thank you for ever.

SECOND READING   *2 Corinthians 8:7, 9, 13–15*

In giving relief to others, balance what happens to be your surplus now against their present need.

You always have the most of everything – of faith, of eloquence, of understanding, of keenness for any cause, and the biggest share of our affection – so we expect you to put the most into this work of mercy too. Remember how generous the Lord Jesus was: he was rich, but he became poor for your sake, to make you rich out of his poverty. This does not mean that to give relief to others you ought to make things difficult for yourselves: it is a question of balancing what happens to be your surplus now against their present need, and one day they may have something to spare that will supply your own need. That is how we strike a balance: as scripture says: The man who gathered much had none too much, the man who gathered little did not go short.

The word of the Lord.

Thanks be to God.

ORDINARY

GOSPEL ACCLAMATION   cf John 6:63, 68

Alleluia, alleluia!
Your words are spirit, Lord,
and they are life:
you have the message of eternal life.
Alleluia!

or   cf 2 Timothy 1:10

Alleluia, alleluia!
Our Saviour Christ Jesus abolished death,
and he has proclaimed life through the Good News.
Alleluia!

GOSPEL   Mark 5:21–43   Shorter form: 5:21–24, 35–43 (only read text with side line next to it).

The Lord be with you.
And with your spirit.

A reading from the holy Gospel according to Mark.
Glory to you, O Lord.

Little girl, I tell you to get up.

When Jesus had crossed in the boat to the other side, a large crowd gathered round him and he stayed by the lakeside. Then one of the synagogue officials came up, Jairus by name, and seeing him fell at his feet and pleaded with him earnestly, saying, 'My little daughter is desperately sick. Do come and lay your hands on her to make her better and save her life.' Jesus went with him and a large crowd followed him: they were pressing all round him.

Now there was a woman who had suffered from a haemorrhage for twelve years; after long and painful treatment under various doctors, she had spent all she had without being any the better for it, in fact, she was getting worse. She had heard about Jesus, and she came up behind him through the crowd and touched his cloak. 'If I can touch even his clothes,' she had told herself, 'I shall be well again.' And the source of the bleeding dried up instantly, and she felt in herself that she was cured of her complaint. Immediately aware that power had gone out from him, Jesus turned round in the crowd and said, 'Who touched my clothes?' His disciples said to him, 'You see how the crowd is pressing round you and yet you say, "Who touched me?"' But he continued to look all round to see who had done it. Then the woman came forward, frightened and trembling because she knew what had happened to her, and she fell at his feet and told him the whole truth. 'My daughter,' he said, 'your faith has restored you to health; go in peace and be free from your complaint.'

While he was still speaking some people arrived from the house of the synagogue official to say, 'Your daughter is dead: why put the Master to any further trouble?' But Jesus had overheard this remark of theirs and he said to the official, 'Do not be afraid; only have faith.' And he allowed no one to go with him except Peter and James and John the brother of James. So they came to the official's house and Jesus noticed all the commotion, with people weeping and wailing unrestrainedly. He went in and said to them, 'Why all this commotion and crying? The child is not dead, but asleep.' But they laughed at him. So he turned them all out and, taking with him the child's father and mother and his own companions, he went into the place where the child lay. And taking the child by the hand he said to her, 'Talitha, kum!' which means, 'Little girl, I tell you to get up.' The little girl got up at once and began to walk about, for she was twelve years old. At this they were overcome with astonishment, and he ordered them strictly not to let anyone know about it, and told them to give her something to eat.

The Gospel of the Lord.
Praise to you, Lord Jesus Christ.

▷ *page 11*

PRAYER OVER THE OFFERINGS

O God, who graciously accomplish
the effects of your mysteries,
grant, we pray,
that the deeds by which we serve you
may be worthy of these sacred gifts.
Through Christ our Lord.   **Amen.**

▷ *page 15*

COMMUNION ANTIPHON   *cf Psalm 102:1*

Bless the Lord, O my soul,
and all within me, his holy name.

or   *John 17:20–21*

O Father, I pray for them, that they may be one in us,
that the world may believe that you have sent me, says the Lord.

▷ *page 59*

PRAYER AFTER COMMUNION

May this divine sacrifice we have offered and received
fill us with life, O Lord, we pray,
so that, bound to you in lasting charity,
we may bear fruit that lasts for ever.
Through Christ our Lord.   **Amen.**

▷ *page 59*

FOURTEENTH SUNDAY IN ORDINARY TIME

ENTRANCE ANTIPHON   *cf Psalm 47:10–11*

Your merciful love, O God,
we have received in the midst of your temple.
Your praise, O God, like your name,
reaches the ends of the earth;
your right hand is filled with saving justice.

▷ *page 7*

COLLECT

O God, who in the abasement of your Son
have raised up a fallen world,
fill your faithful with holy joy,
for on those you have rescued from slavery to sin
you bestow eternal gladness.
Through our Lord Jesus Christ, your Son,
who lives and reigns with you in the unity of the Holy Spirit,
one God, for ever and ever. **Amen.**

FIRST READING   *Ezekiel 2:2–5*

*The sons are defiant and obstinate and they shall
know that there is a prophet among them.*

The spirit came into me and made me
stand up, and I heard the Lord speaking
to me. He said, 'Son of man, I am sending
you to the Israelites, to the rebels who
have turned against me. Till now they
and their ancestors have been in revolt
against me. The sons are defiant and
obstinate; I am sending you to them,
to say, "The Lord says this." Whether
they listen or not, this set of rebels shall
know there is a prophet among them.'

The word of the Lord.
Thanks be to God.

RESPONSORIAL PSALM   *Psalm 122 response v 2*

**Our eyes are on the Lord
till he show us his mercy.**

1 To you have I lifted up my eyes,
you who dwell in the heavens:
my eyes, like the eyes of slaves
on the hand of their lords.

2 Like the eyes of a servant
on the hand of his mistress,
so our eyes are on the Lord our God
till he show us his mercy.

3 Have mercy on us, Lord, have mercy.
We are filled with contempt.
Indeed all too full is our soul
with the scorn of the rich,
with the proud man's disdain.

SECOND READING   *2 Corinthians 12:7–10*

I shall be very happy to make my weaknesses my special boast so that the power of Christ may stay over me.

In view of the extraordinary nature
of these revelations, to stop me from
getting too proud I was given a thorn
in the flesh, an angel of Satan to beat
me and stop me from getting too proud!
About this thing, I have pleaded with
the Lord three times for it to leave me,
but he has said, 'My grace is enough for
you: my power is at its best in weakness.'
So I shall be very happy to make my
weaknesses my special boast so that the
power of Christ may stay over me, and
that is why I am quite content with my
weaknesses, and with insults, hardships,
persecutions, and the agonies I go
through for Christ's sake. For it is when
I am weak that I am strong.

The word of the Lord.
Thanks be to God.

GOSPEL ACCLAMATION   *John 1:14, 12*

Alleluia, alleluia!
The Word was made flesh and lived among us;
to all who did accept him
he gave power to become children of God.
Alleluia!

or   *cf Luke 4:18*

Alleluia, alleluia!
The Lord has sent me to bring the good news to the poor,
to proclaim liberty to captives.
Alleluia!

GOSPEL   *Mark 6:1–6*

The Lord be with you.
And with your spirit.

A reading from the holy Gospel according to Mark.
Glory to you, O Lord.

A prophet is only despised in his own country.

Jesus went to his home town and his disciples accompanied him. With the coming of the sabbath he began teaching in the synagogue and most of them were astonished when they heard him. They said, 'Where did the man get all this? What is this wisdom that has been granted him, and these miracles that are worked through him? This is the carpenter, surely, the son of Mary, the brother of James and Joset and Jude and Simon? His sisters, too, are they not here with us?' And they would not accept him. And Jesus said to them, 'A prophet is only despised in his own country, among his own relations and in his own house'; and he could work no miracle there, though he cured a few sick people by laying his hands on them. He was amazed at their lack of faith.

The Gospel of the Lord.
Praise to you, Lord Jesus Christ.

▷ *page 11*

PRAYER OVER THE OFFERINGS

May this oblation dedicated to your name
purify us, O Lord,
and day by day bring our conduct
closer to the life of heaven.
Through Christ our Lord.   **Amen.**

▷ *page 15*

COMMUNION ANTIPHON   *Psalm 33:9*

Taste and see that the Lord is good;
blessed the man who seeks refuge in him.

or   *Matthew 11:28*

Come to me, all who labour and are burdened,
and I will refresh you, says the Lord.

▷ *page 59*

ORDINARY

PRAYER AFTER COMMUNION

Grant, we pray, O Lord,
that, having been replenished by such great gifts,
we may gain the prize of salvation
and never cease to praise you.
Through Christ our Lord.   **Amen.**

▷ *page 59*

 # FIFTEENTH SUNDAY IN ORDINARY TIME

ENTRANCE ANTIPHON   *cf Psalm 16:15*

As for me, in justice I shall behold your face;
I shall be filled with the vision of your glory.

▷ *page 7*

COLLECT

O God, who show the light of your truth
to those who go astray,
so that they may return to the right path,
give all who for the faith they profess
are accounted Christians
the grace to reject whatever is contrary to the name of Christ
and to strive after all that does it honour.
Through our Lord Jesus Christ, your Son,
who lives and reigns with you in the unity of the Holy Spirit,
one God, for ever and ever.   **Amen.**

FIRST READING   *Amos 7:12–15*

Go, prophesy to my people.

Amaziah, the priest of Bethel, said to Amos, 'Go away, seer; get back to the land of Judah; earn your bread there, do your prophesying there. We want no more prophesying in Bethel; this is the royal sanctuary, the national temple.' 'I was no prophet, neither did I belong to any of the brotherhoods of prophets,' Amos replied to Amaziah, 'I was a shepherd, and looked after sycamores: but it was the Lord who took me from herding the flock, and the Lord who said, "Go, prophesy to my people Israel."'

The word of the Lord.
Thanks be to God.

RESPONSORIAL PSALM   *Psalm 84:9–14 response v 8*

**Let us see, O Lord, your mercy
and give us your saving help.**

1   I will hear what the Lord God has to say,
a voice that speaks of peace,
peace for his people.
His help is near for those who fear him
and his glory will dwell in our land.

2   Mercy and faithfulness have met;
    justice and peace have embraced.
    Faithfulness shall spring from the earth
    and justice look down from heaven.

3   The Lord will make us prosper
    and our earth shall yield its fruit.
    Justice shall march before him
    and peace shall follow his steps.

SECOND READING   *Ephesians 1:3–14   Shorter form: Ephesians 1:3–10 (only read text with side line next to it).*
Before the world was made, God chose us.

Blessed be God the Father of our Lord Jesus Christ, who has blessed us with all the spiritual blessings of heaven in Christ. Before the world was made he chose us, chose us in Christ, to be holy and spotless, and to live through love in his presence, determining that we should become his adopted sons, through Jesus Christ for his own kind purposes, to make us praise the glory of his grace, his free gift to us in the Beloved in whom, through his blood, we gain our freedom, the forgiveness of our sins. Such is the richness of the grace which he has showered on us in all wisdom and insight. He has let us know the mystery of his purpose, the hidden plan he so kindly made in Christ from the beginning to act upon when the times had run their course to the end:

that he would bring everything together under Christ, as head, everything in the heavens and everything on earth.

And it is in him that we were claimed as God's own, chosen from the beginning, under the predetermined plan of the one who guides all things as he decides by his own will; chosen to be, for his greater glory, the people who would put their hopes in Christ before he came. Now you too, in him, have heard the message of the truth and the good news of your salvation, and have believed it: and you too have been stamped with the seal of the Holy Spirit of the Promise, the pledge of our inheritance which brings freedom for those whom God has taken for his own, to make his glory praised.

The word of the Lord.
Thanks be to God.

GOSPEL ACCLAMATION   *cf John 6:63, 68*

Alleluia, alleluia!
**Your words are spirit, Lord,
and they are life:
you have the message of eternal life.
Alleluia!**

or   cf Ephesians 1:17, 18

Alleluia, alleluia!
**May the Father of our Lord Jesus Christ
enlighten the eyes of our mind,
so that we can see what hope his call holds for us.
Alleluia!**

GOSPEL   *Mark 6:7–13*

The Lord be with you.
And with your spirit.

A reading from the holy Gospel according to Mark.
Glory to you, O Lord.

He began to send them out.

Jesus summoned the Twelve and began to send them out in pairs giving them authority over the unclean spirits. And he instructed them to take nothing for the journey except a staff – no bread, no haversack, no coppers for their purses. They were to wear sandals but, he added, 'Do not take a spare tunic.' And he said to them, 'If you enter a house anywhere, stay there until you leave the district. And if any place does not welcome you and people refuse to listen to you, as you walk away shake off the dust from under your feet as a sign to them.' So they set off to preach repentance; and they cast out many devils, and anointed many sick people with oil and cured them.

The Gospel of the Lord.
Praise to you, Lord Jesus Christ.

▷ *page 11*

PRAYER OVER THE OFFERINGS

Look upon the offerings of the Church, O Lord,
as she makes her prayer to you,
and grant that, when consumed by those who believe,
they may bring ever greater holiness.
Through Christ our Lord.   **Amen.**

▷ *page 15*

COMMUNION ANTIPHON   *cf Psalm 83:4–5*

The sparrow finds a home,
and the swallow a nest for her young:
by your altars, O Lord of hosts, my King and my God.
Blessed are they who dwell in your house,
for ever singing your praise.

or   *John 6:57*

Whoever eats my flesh and drinks my blood
remains in me and I in him, says the Lord.

▷ *page 59*

PRAYER AFTER COMMUNION

Having consumed these gifts, we pray, O Lord,
that, by our participation in this mystery,
its saving effects upon us may grow.
Through Christ our Lord.   **Amen.**

▷ *page 59*

SIXTEENTH SUNDAY IN ORDINARY TIME

ENTRANCE ANTIPHON *Psalm 53:6, 8*
See, I have God for my help.
The Lord sustains my soul.
I will sacrifice to you with willing heart,
and praise your name, O Lord, for it is good.

▷ *page 7*

COLLECT
Show favour, O Lord, to your servants
and mercifully increase the gifts of your grace,
that, made fervent in hope, faith and charity,
they may be ever watchful in keeping your commands.
Through our Lord Jesus Christ, your Son,
who lives and reigns with you in the unity of the Holy Spirit,
one God, for ever and ever. **Amen.**

FIRST READING *Jeremiah 23:1–6*
The remnant of my flock I will gather and I will raise up shepherds to look after them.

'Doom for the shepherds who allow the flock of my pasture to be destroyed and scattered – it is the Lord who speaks! This, therefore, is what the Lord, the God of Israel, says about the shepherds in charge of my people: You have let my flock be scattered and go wandering and have not taken care of them. Right, I will take care of you for your misdeeds – it is the Lord who speaks! But the remnant of my flock I myself will gather from all the countries where I have dispersed them, and will bring them back to their pastures: they shall be fruitful and increase in numbers. I will raise up shepherds to look after them and pasture them; no fear, no terror for them any more; not one shall be lost – it is the Lord who speaks!

'See, the days are coming – it is the Lord who speaks – when I will raise a virtuous Branch for David, who will reign as true king and be wise, practising honesty and integrity in the land. In his days Judah will be saved and Israel dwell in confidence. And this is the name he will be called: The Lord-our-integrity.'

The word of the Lord.
Thanks be to God.

RESPONSORIAL PSALM *Psalm 22 response v 1*

> **The Lord is my shepherd;**
> **there is nothing I shall want.**

1 The Lord is my shepherd;
   there is nothing I shall want.
   Fresh and green are the pastures
   where he gives me repose.
   Near restful waters he leads me,
   to revive my drooping spirit.

continued…

**The Lord is my shepherd;
there is nothing I shall want.**

2   He guides me along the right path;
      he is true to his name.
      If I should walk in the valley of darkness
      no evil would I fear.
      You are there with your crook and your staff;
      with these you give me comfort.

3   You have prepared a banquet for me
      in the sight of my foes.
      My head you have anointed with oil;
      my cup is overflowing.

4   Surely goodness and kindness shall follow me
      all the days of my life.
      In the Lord's own house shall I dwell
      for ever and ever.

SECOND READING   *Ephesians 2:13–18*

Christ Jesus is the peace between us, and has made the two into one.

In Christ Jesus, you that used to be so far apart from us have been brought very close, by the blood of Christ. For he is the peace between us, and has made the two into one and broken down the barrier which used to keep them apart, actually destroying in his own person the hostility caused by the rules and decrees of the Law. This was to create one single New Man in himself out of the two of them and by restoring peace through the cross, to unite them both in a single Body and reconcile them with God. In his own person he killed the hostility. Later he came to bring the good news of peace, peace to you who were far away and peace to those who were near at hand. Through him, both of us have in the one Spirit our way to come to the Father.

The word of the Lord.
Thanks be to God.

GOSPEL ACCLAMATION   *John 10:27*

Alleluia, alleluia!
The sheep that belong to me listen to my voice,
says the Lord,
I know them and they follow me.
Alleluia!

GOSPEL   *Mark 6:30–34*

The Lord be with you.
And with your spirit.

A reading from the holy Gospel according to Mark.
Glory to you, O Lord.

They were like sheep without a shepherd.

The apostles rejoined Jesus and told him all they had done and taught. Then he said to them, 'You must come away to some lonely place all by yourselves and rest for a while'; for there were so many coming and going that the apostles had no time even to eat. So they went off in a boat to a lonely place where they could be by themselves. But people saw them going, and many could guess where; and from every town they all hurried to the place on foot and reached it before them. So as he stepped ashore he saw a large crowd; and he took pity on them because they were like sheep without a shepherd, and he set himself to teach them at some length.

The Gospel of the Lord.
Praise to you, Lord Jesus Christ.

▷ *page 11*

ORDINARY

PRAYER OVER THE OFFERINGS

O God, who in the one perfect sacrifice
brought to completion varied offerings of the law,
accept, we pray, this sacrifice from your faithful servants
and make it holy, as you blessed the gifts of Abel,
so that what each has offered to the honour of your majesty
may benefit the salvation of all.
Through Christ our Lord.   **Amen.**

▷ *page 15*

COMMUNION ANTIPHON   *Psalm 110:4–5*

The Lord, the gracious, the merciful,
has made a memorial of his wonders;
he gives food to those who fear him.

or   *Revelation 3:20*

Behold, I stand at the door and knock, says the Lord.
If anyone hears my voice and opens the door to me,
I will enter his house and dine with him, and he with me.

▷ *page 59*

PRAYER AFTER COMMUNION

Graciously be present to your people, we pray, O Lord,
and lead those you have imbued with heavenly mysteries
to pass from former ways to newness of life.
Through Christ our Lord.   **Amen.**

▷ *page 59*

SEVENTEENTH SUNDAY IN ORDINARY TIME

ENTRANCE ANTIPHON   *cf Psalm 67:6–7, 36*
God is in his holy place,
God who unites those who dwell in his house;
he himself gives might and strength to his people.

▷ *page 7*

COLLECT
O God, protector of those who hope in you,
without whom nothing has firm foundation, nothing is holy,
bestow in abundance your mercy upon us
and grant that, with you as our ruler and guide,
we may use the good things that pass
in such a way as to hold fast even now
to those that ever endure.
Through our Lord Jesus Christ, your Son,
who lives and reigns with you in the unity of the Holy Spirit,
one God, for ever and ever.   **Amen.**

FIRST READING   *2 Kings 4:42–44*

They will eat and have some left over.

A man came from Baal-shalishah, bringing Elisha, the man of God, bread from the first-fruits, twenty barley loaves and fresh grain in the ear. 'Give it to the people to eat,' Elisha said. But his servant replied, 'How can I serve this to a hundred men?' 'Give it to the people to eat,' he insisted, 'for the Lord says this, "They will eat and have some left over."' He served them; they ate and had some over, as the Lord had said.

The word of the Lord.
Thanks be to God.

RESPONSORIAL PSALM   *Psalm 144:10–11, 15–18 response v 16*

**You open wide your hand, O Lord,
and grant our desires.**

1   All your creatures shall thank you, O Lord,
    and your friends shall repeat their blessing.
    They shall speak of the glory of your reign
    and declare your might, O God.

2   The eyes of all creatures look to you
    and you give them their food in due time.
    You open wide your hand,
    grant the desires of all who live.

3   The Lord is just in all his ways
    and loving in all his deeds.
    He is close to all who call him,
    who call on him from their hearts.

SECOND READING   *Ephesians 4:1–6*
One Body, one Lord, one faith, one baptism.

I, the prisoner in the Lord, implore you to lead a life worthy of your vocation. Bear with one another charitably, in complete selflessness, gentleness and patience. Do all you can to preserve the unity of the Spirit by the peace that binds you together. There is one Body one Spirit, just as you were all called into one and the same hope when you were called. There is one Lord, one faith, one baptism, and one God who is Father of all, through all and within all.

The word of the Lord.
Thanks be to God.

GOSPEL ACCLAMATION   *cf John 6:63, 68*

Alleluia, alleluia!
Your words are spirit, Lord,
and they are life:
you have the message of eternal life.
Alleluia!

or   Luke 7:16

Alleluia, alleluia!
A great prophet has appeared among us;
God has visited his people.
Alleluia!

ORDINARY

GOSPEL   *John 6:1–15*

The Lord be with you.
And with your spirit.

A reading from the holy Gospel according to John.
Glory to you, O Lord.

Jesus gave out as much as was wanted to all who were sitting ready.

Jesus went off to the other side of the Sea of Galilee – or of Tiberias – and a large crowd followed him, impressed by the signs he gave by curing the sick. Jesus climbed the hillside, and sat down there with his disciples. It was shortly before the Jewish feast of Passover.

Looking up, Jesus saw the crowds approaching and said to Philip, 'Where can we buy some bread for these people to eat?' He only said this to test Philip; he himself knew exactly what he was going to do. Philip answered, 'Two hundred denarii would only buy enough to give them a small piece each.' One of his disciples, Andrew, Simon Peter's brother, said, 'There is a small boy here with five barley loaves and two fish; but what is that between so many?' Jesus said to them, 'Make the people sit down.' There was plenty of grass there, and as many as five thousand men sat down. Then Jesus took the loaves, gave thanks, and gave them out to all who were sitting ready; he then did the same with the fish, giving out as much as was wanted. When they had eaten enough he said to the disciples, 'Pick up the pieces left over, so that nothing gets wasted.' So they picked them up, and filled twelve hampers with scraps left over from the meal of five barley loaves. The people, seeing this sign that he had given, said, 'This really is the prophet who is to come into the world.' Jesus, who could see they were about to come and take him by force and make him king, escaped back to the hills by himself.

The Gospel of the Lord.
Praise to you, Lord Jesus Christ.

▷ *page 11*

PRAYER OVER THE OFFERINGS
Accept, O Lord, we pray, the offerings
which we bring from the abundance of your gifts,
that through the powerful working of your grace
these most sacred mysteries may sanctify our present way of life
and lead us to eternal gladness.
Through Christ our Lord.   **Amen.**

▷ *page 15*

COMMUNION ANTIPHON   *Psalm 102:2*
Bless the Lord, O my soul,
and never forget all his benefits.
or   *Matthew 5:7–8*

Blessed are the merciful, for they shall receive mercy.
Blessed are the clean of heart, for they shall see God.

▷ *page 59*

PRAYER AFTER COMMUNION

We have consumed, O Lord, this divine Sacrament,
the perpetual memorial of the Passion of your Son;
grant, we pray, that this gift,
which he himself gave us with love beyond all telling,
may profit us for salvation.
Through Christ our Lord.   **Amen.**

▷ *page 59*

EIGHTEENTH SUNDAY IN ORDINARY TIME

ENTRANCE ANTIPHON   *Psalm 69:2, 6*
O God, come to my assistance;
O Lord, make haste to help me!
You are my rescuer, my help;
O Lord, do not delay.

▷ *page 7*

COLLECT

Draw near to your servants, O Lord,
and answer their prayers with unceasing kindness,
that, for those who glory in you as their Creator and guide,
you may restore what you have created
and keep safe what you have restored.
Through our Lord Jesus Christ, your Son,
who lives and reigns with you in the unity of the Holy Spirit,
one God, for ever and ever. **Amen.**

FIRST READING   Exodus 16:2–4, 12–15

I will rain down bread for you from the heavens.

The whole community of the sons of Israel began to complain against Moses and Aaron in the wilderness and said to them, 'Why did we not die at the Lord's hand in the land of Egypt, when we were able to sit down to pans of meat and could eat bread to our heart's content! As it is, you have brought us to this wilderness to starve this whole company to death!'

Then the Lord said to Moses, 'Now I will rain down bread for you from the heavens. Each day the people are to go out and gather the day's portion; I propose to test them in this way to see whether they will follow my law or not.'

'I have heard the complaints of the sons of Israel. Say this to them, "Between the two evenings you shall eat meat, and in the morning you shall have bread to your heart's content. Then you will learn that I, the Lord, am your God."' And so it came about: quails flew up in the evening, and they covered the camp; in the morning there was a coating of dew all round the camp. When the coating of dew lifted, there on the surface of the desert was a thing delicate, powdery, as fine as hoarfrost on the ground. When they saw this, the sons of Israel said to one another, 'What is that?' not knowing what it was. 'That' said Moses to them 'is the bread the Lord gives you to eat.'

The word of the Lord.
Thanks be to God.

ORDINARY

RESPONSORIAL PSALM   Psalm 77:3–4, 23–25, 54 response v 24

The Lord gave them bread from heaven.

1 The things we have heard and understood,
   the things our fathers have told us,
   we will tell to the next generation:
   the glories of the Lord and his might.

2 He commanded the clouds above
   and opened the gates of heaven.
   He rained down manna for their food,
   and gave them bread from heaven.

3 Mere men ate the bread of angels.
   He sent them abundance of food.
   He brought them to his holy land,
   to the mountain which his right hand had won.

SECOND READING   *Ephesians 4:17, 20–24*

Put on the new self that has been created in God's way.

I want to urge you in the name of the Lord, not to go on living the aimless kind of life that pagans live. Now that is hardly the way you have learnt from Christ, unless you failed to hear him properly when you were taught what the truth is in Jesus. You must give up your old way of life; you must put aside your old self, which gets corrupted by following illusory desires. Your mind must be renewed by a spiritual revolution so that you can put on the new self that has been created in God's way, in the goodness and holiness of the truth.

The word of the Lord.
Thanks be to God.

GOSPEL ACCLAMATION   *John 14:5*

Alleluia, alleluia!
I am the Way, the Truth and the Life, says the Lord;
no one can come to the Father except through me.
Alleluia!

or   *Matthew 4:4*

Alleluia, alleluia!
Man does not live on bread alone,
but on every word that comes from the mouth of God.
Alleluia!

GOSPEL   *John 6:24–35*

The Lord be with you.
And with your spirit.

A reading from the holy Gospel according to John.
Glory to you, O Lord.

He who comes to me will never be hungry; he who believes in me will never thirst.

When the people saw that neither Jesus nor his disciples were there, they got into boats and crossed to Capernaum to look for Jesus. When they found him on the other side, they said to him, 'Rabbi, when did you come here?' Jesus answered:

'I tell you most solemnly, you are not looking for me because you have seen the signs but because you had all the bread you wanted to eat. Do not work for food that cannot last, but work for food that endures to eternal life, the kind of food the Son of Man is offering you, for on him the Father, God himself, has set his seal.'

Then they said to him, 'What must we do if we are to do the works that God wants?' Jesus gave them this answer, 'This is working for God: you must believe in the one he has sent.' So they said, 'What sign will you give to show us that we should believe in you? What work will you do? Our fathers had manna to eat in the desert; as scripture says: He gave them bread from heaven to eat.' Jesus answered: 'I tell you most solemnly, it was not Moses who gave you bread from heaven, it is my Father who gives you the bread from heaven, the true bread; for the bread of God is that which comes down from heaven and gives life to the world.'

'Sir,' they said 'give us that bread always.' Jesus answered: 'I am the bread of life. He who comes to me will never be hungry; he who believes in me will never thirst.'

The Gospel of the Lord.
Praise to you, Lord Jesus Christ.

▷ *page 11*

PRAYER OVER THE OFFERINGS

Graciously sanctify these gifts, O Lord, we pray,
and, accepting the oblation of this spiritual sacrifice,
make of us an eternal offering to you.
Through Christ our Lord. **Amen.**

▷ *page 15*

COMMUNION ANTIPHON   *Wisdom 16:20*

You have given us, O Lord, bread from heaven,
endowed with all delights and sweetness in every taste.

or   *John 6:35*

I am the bread of life, says the Lord;
whoever comes to me will not hunger
and whoever believes in me will not thirst.

▷ *page 59*

PRAYER AFTER COMMUNION

Accompany with constant protection, O Lord,
those you renew with these heavenly gifts
and, in your never-failing care for them,
make them worthy of eternal redemption.
Through Christ our Lord. **Amen.**

▷ *page 59*

NINETEENTH SUNDAY IN ORDINARY TIME

ENTRANCE ANTIPHON   *cf Psalm 73:20, 19, 22, 23*

Look to your covenant, O Lord,
and forget not the life of your poor ones for ever.
Arise, O God, and defend your cause,
and forget not the cries of those who seek you.

▷ *page 7*

COLLECT

Almighty ever-living God,
whom, taught by the Holy Spirit,
we dare to call our Father,
bring, we pray, to perfection in our hearts
the spirit of adoption as your sons and daughters,
that we may merit to enter into the inheritance
which you have promised.
Through our Lord Jesus Christ, your Son,
who lives and reigns with you in the unity of the Holy Spirit,
one God, for ever and ever. **Amen.**

FIRST READING   *1 Kings 19:4–8*

Strengthened by the food he walked until he reached the mountain of God.

Elijah went into the wilderness, a day's journey, and sitting under a furze bush wished he were dead. 'Lord,' he said 'I have had enough. Take my life; I am no better than my ancestors.' Then he lay down and went to sleep. But an angel touched him and said, 'Get up and eat.' He looked round, and there at his head was a scone baked on hot stones, and a jar of water. He ate and drank and then lay down again. But the angel of the Lord came back a second time and touched him and said, 'Get up and eat, or the journey will be too long for you.' So he got up and ate and drank, and strengthened by that food he walked for forty days and forty nights until he reached Horeb, the mountain of God.

The word of the Lord.
Thanks be to God.

RESPONSORIAL PSALM   *Psalm 33:2–9 response v 9*

Taste and see that the Lord is good.

1 I will bless the Lord at all times,
   his praise always on my lips;
   in the Lord my soul shall make its boast.
   The humble shall hear and be glad.

2 Glorify the Lord with me.
   Together let us praise his name
   I sought the Lord and he answered me;
   from all my terrors he set me free.

3 Look towards him and be radiant;
   let your faces not be abashed.
   This poor man called; the Lord heard him
   and rescued him from all his distress.

4 The angel of the Lord is encamped
   around those who revere him, to rescue them.
   Taste and see that the Lord is good.
   He is happy who seeks refuge in him.

SECOND READING   *Ephesians 4:30–5:2*

Follow Christ by loving as he loved you.

Do not grieve the Holy Spirit of God who has marked you with his seal for you to be set free when the day comes. Never have grudges against others, or lose your temper, or raise your voice to anybody, or call each other names, or allow any sort of spitefulness. Be friends with one another, and kind, forgiving each other as readily as God forgave you in Christ.

Try, then, to imitate God, as children of his that he loves, and follow Christ by loving as he loved you, giving himself up in our place as a fragrant offering and a sacrifice to God.

The word of the Lord.
Thanks be to God.

GOSPEL ACCLAMATION   *John 14:23*

> Alleluia, alleluia!
> If anyone loves me he will keep my word,
> and my Father will love him,
> and we shall come to him.
> Alleluia!

or   *John 6:51*

> Alleluia, alleluia!
> I am the living bread which has come down from heaven,
> says the Lord.
> Anyone who eats this bread will live for ever.
> Alleluia!

GOSPEL   *John 6:41–51*

The Lord be with you.
And with your spirit.

A reading from the holy Gospel according to John.
Glory to you, O Lord.

I am the living bread which has come down from heaven.

The Jews were complaining to each other about Jesus, because he had said, 'I am the bread that came down from heaven.' 'Surely this is Jesus son of Joseph' they said. 'We know his father and mother. How can he now say, "I have come down from heaven"?' Jesus said in reply, 'Stop complaining to each other.

'No one can come to me unless he is drawn by the Father who sent me, and I will raise him up at the last day. It is written in the prophets: They will all be taught by God, and to hear the teaching of the Father, and learn from it, is to come to me. Not that anybody has seen the Father, except the one who comes from God: he has seen the Father. I tell you most solemnly, everybody who believes has eternal life. I am the bread of life. Your fathers ate the manna in the desert and they are dead; but this is the bread that comes down from heaven, so that a man may eat it and not die. I am the living bread which has come down from heaven. Anyone who eats this bread will live for ever; and the bread that I shall give is my flesh, for the life of the world.'

The Gospel of the Lord.
Praise to you, Lord Jesus Christ.

▷ *page 11*

PRAYER OVER THE OFFERINGS
Be pleased, O Lord, to accept the offerings of your Church,
for in your mercy you have given them to be offered
and by your power you transform them
into the mystery of our salvation.
Through Christ our Lord.   **Amen.**

▷ *page 15*

COMMUNION ANTIPHON   *Psalm 147:12, 14*
O Jerusalem, glorify the Lord,
who gives you your fill of finest wheat.

or   *cf John 6:51*

The bread that I will give, says the Lord,
is my flesh for the life of the world.

▷ *page 59*

PRAYER AFTER COMMUNION
May the communion in your Sacrament
that we have consumed, save us, O Lord,
and confirm us in the light of your truth.
Through Christ our Lord.   **Amen.**

▷ *page 59*

TWENTIETH SUNDAY IN ORDINARY TIME

ENTRANCE ANTIPHON   *Psalm 83:10–11*
Turn your eyes, O God, our shield;
and look on the face of your anointed one;
one day within your courts
is better than a thousand elsewhere.

▷ *page 7*

COLLECT
O God, who have prepared for those who love you
good things which no eye can see,
fill our hearts, we pray, with the warmth of your love,
so that, loving you in all things and above all things,
we may attain your promises,
which surpass every human desire.
Through our Lord Jesus Christ, your Son,
who lives and reigns with you in the unity of the Holy Spirit,
one God, for ever and ever.   **Amen.**

FIRST READING   *Proverbs 9:1–6*

Eat my bread, drink the wine I have prepared for you.

Wisdom has built herself a house, she has erected her seven pillars, she has slaughtered her beasts, prepared her wine, she has laid her table. She has despatched her maidservants and proclaimed from the city's heights:

'Who is ignorant? Let him step this way.' To the fool she says, 'Come and eat my bread, drink the wine I have prepared! Leave your folly and you will live, walk in the ways of perception.'

The word of the Lord.

Thanks be to God.

RESPONSORIAL PSALM   *Psalm 33:2–3, 10–15 response v 9*

Taste and see that the Lord is good.

1 I will bless the Lord at all times,
   his praise always on my lips;
   in the Lord my soul shall make its boast.
   The humble shall hear and be glad.

2 Revere the Lord, you his saints.
   They lack nothing, those who revere him.
   Strong lions suffer want and go hungry
   but those who seek the Lord lack no blessing.

3 Come, children, and hear me
   that I may teach you the fear of the Lord.
   Who is he who longs for life
   and many days, to enjoy his prosperity?

4 Then keep your tongue from evil
   and your lips from speaking deceit.
   Turn aside from evil and do good;
   seek and strive after peace.

SECOND READING   *Ephesians 5:15–20*

Recognise what is the will of God.

Be very careful about the sort of lives you lead, like intelligent and not like senseless people. This may be a wicked age, but your lives should redeem it. And do not be thoughtless but recognise what is the will of the Lord. Do not drug yourselves with wine, this is simply dissipation; be filled with the Spirit. Sing the words and tunes of the psalms and hymns when you are together, and go on singing and chanting to the Lord in your hearts, so that always and everywhere you are giving thanks to God who is our Father in the name of our Lord Jesus Christ.

The word of the Lord.

Thanks be to God.

ORDINARY

GOSPEL ACCLAMATION   *John 1:14, 12*

Alleluia, alleluia!
The Word was made flesh and lived among us;
to all who did accept him
he gave power to become children of God.
Alleluia!

or   *John 6:56*

Alleluia, alleluia!
He who eats my flesh and drinks my blood
lives in me, and I live in him
says the Lord.
Alleluia!

GOSPEL   *John 6:51–58*

The Lord be with you.
And with your spirit.

A reading from the holy Gospel according to John.
Glory to you, O Lord.

My flesh is real food and my blood is real drink.

Jesus said to the crowd:

I am the living bread which has come down from heaven. Anyone who eats this bread will live for ever; and the bread that I shall give is my flesh, for the life of the world.'

Then the Jews started arguing with one another: 'How can this man give us his flesh to eat?' they said. Jesus replied:

'I tell you most solemnly, if you do not eat the flesh of the Son of Man and drink his blood, you will not have life in you. Anyone who does eat my flesh and drink my blood has eternal life, and I shall raise him up on the last day. For my flesh is real food and my blood is real drink. He who eats my flesh and drinks my blood lives in me and I live in him. As I, who am sent by the living Father, myself draw life from the Father, so whoever eats me will draw life from me. This is the bread come down from heaven; not like the bread our ancestors ate: they are dead, but anyone who eats this bread will live for ever.

The Gospel of the Lord.
Praise to you, Lord Jesus Christ.

▷ *page 11*

PRAYER OVER THE OFFERINGS

Receive our oblation, O Lord,
by which is brought about a glorious exchange,
that, by offering what you have given,
we may merit to receive your very self.
Through Christ our Lord.   **Amen.**

▷ *page 15*

COMMUNION ANTIPHON   *Psalm 129:7*

With the Lord there is mercy;
in him is plentiful redemption.

or John 6:51–52

I am the living bread that came down from heaven, says the Lord.
Whoever eats of this bread will live for ever.   ▷ *page 59*

PRAYER AFTER COMMUNION

Made partakers of Christ through these Sacraments,
we humbly implore your mercy, Lord,
that, conformed to his image on earth,
we may merit also to be his coheirs in heaven.
Who lives and reigns for ever and ever.   **Amen.**   ▷ *page 59*

TWENTY-FIRST SUNDAY IN ORDINARY TIME

ORDINARY

ENTRANCE ANTIPHON   *cf Psalm 85:1–3*

Turn your ear, O Lord, and answer me;
save the servant who trusts in you, my God.
Have mercy on me, O Lord, for I cry to you all the day long.

▷ *page 7*

COLLECT

O God, who cause the minds of the faithful
to unite in a single purpose,
grant your people to love what you command
and to desire what you promise,
that, amid the uncertainties of this world,
our hearts may be fixed on that place
where true gladness is found.
Through our Lord Jesus Christ, your Son,
who lives and reigns with you in the unity of the Holy Spirit,
one God, for ever and ever.   **Amen.**

FIRST READING   *Joshua 24:1–2, 15–18*
We will serve the Lord, for he is our God.

Joshua gathered all the tribes of Israel together at Shechem; then he called the elders, leaders, judges and scribes of Israel, and they presented themselves before God. Then Joshua said to all the people: 'If you will not serve the Lord, choose today whom you wish to serve, whether the gods that your ancestors served beyond the River, or the gods of the Amorites in whose land you are now living. As for me and my House, we will serve the Lord.'

The people answered, 'We have no intention of deserting the Lord our

God who brought us and our ancestors out of the land of Egypt, the house of slavery, who worked those great wonders before our eyes and preserved us all along the way we travelled and among all the peoples through whom we journeyed. We too will serve the Lord, for he is our God.'

The word of the Lord.

Thanks be to God.

RESPONSORIAL PSALM   *Psalm 33:2–3, 16–23 response v 9*

Taste and see that the Lord is good.

1   I will bless the Lord at all times,
his praise always on my lips;
in the Lord my soul shall make its boast
The humble shall hear and be glad.

2   The Lord turns his face against the wicked
to destroy their remembrance from the earth.
The Lord turns his eyes to the just
and his ears to their appeal.

3   They call and the Lord hears
and rescues them in all their distress.
The Lord is close to the broken-hearted;
those whose spirit is crushed he will save.

4   Many are the trials of the just man
but from them all the Lord will rescue him.
He will keep guard over all his bones,
not one of his bones shall be broken.

5   Evil brings death to the wicked;
those who hate the good are doomed.
The Lord ransoms the souls of his servants.
Those who hide in him shall not be condemned.

SECOND READING   *Ephesians 5:21–32*

This mystery has many implications for Christ and his Church.

Give way to one another in obedience to Christ. Wives should regard their husbands as they regard the Lord, since as Christ is head of the Church and saves the whole body, so is a husband the head of his wife; and as the Church submits to Christ, so should wives to their husbands, in everything. Husbands should love their wives just as Christ loved the Church and sacrificed himself for her to make her holy. He made her clean by washing her in water with a form of words, so that when he took her to himself she would be glorious, with no speck or wrinkle or anything like that, but holy and faultless. In the same way, husbands must love their wives as they love their own bodies; for a man to love his wife is for him to love himself. A man never hates his own body, but he feeds it and looks after it; and that is the way Christ treats the Church, because it is his body – and we are its living parts. For this reason, a man must leave his father and mother and be joined to his wife, and the two will become one body. This mystery has many implications; but I am saying it applies to Christ and the Church.

The word of the Lord.
Thanks be to God.

GOSPEL ACCLAMATION   *John 6:63, 68*

Alleluia, alleluia!
Your words are spirit, Lord,
and they are life:
you have the message of eternal life.
Alleluia!

GOSPEL   *John 6:60–69*

The Lord be with you.
And with your spirit.

A reading from the holy Gospel according to John.
Glory to you, O Lord.

Who shall we go to? You have the message of eternal life.

After hearing his doctrine many of the followers of Jesus said, 'This is intolerable language. How could anyone accept it?' Jesus was aware that his followers were complaining about it and said, 'Does this upset you? What if you should see the Son of Man ascend to where he was before?

'It is the spirit that gives life, the flesh has nothing to offer. The words I have spoken to you are spirit and they are life.

'But there are some of you who do not believe.' For Jesus knew from the outset those who did not believe, and who it was that would betray him. He went on, 'This is why I told you that no one could come to me unless the Father allows him.' After this, many of his disciples left him and stopped going with him.

Then Jesus said to the Twelve, 'What about you, do you want to go away too?' Simon Peter answered, 'Lord, who shall we go to? You have the message of eternal life, and we believe; we know that you are the Holy One of God.'

The Gospel of the Lord.
Praise to you, Lord Jesus Christ.

▷ *page 11*

PRAYER OVER THE OFFERINGS

O Lord, who gained for yourself a people by adoption
through the one sacrifice offered once for all,
bestow graciously on us, we pray,
the gifts of unity and peace in your Church.
Through Christ our Lord.   **Amen.**

▷ *page 15*

COMMUNION ANTIPHON   *cf Psalm 103:13–15*

The earth is replete with the fruits of your work, O Lord;
you bring forth bread from the earth
and wine to cheer the heart.

or   cf John 6:54

Whoever eats my flesh and drinks my blood
has eternal life, says the Lord,
and I will raise him up on the last day.

▷ *page 59*

PRAYER AFTER COMMUNION

Complete within us, O Lord, we pray,
the healing work of your mercy
and graciously perfect and sustain us,
so that in all things we may please you.
Through Christ our Lord.   **Amen.**

▷ *page 59*

 # TWENTY-SECOND SUNDAY IN ORDINARY TIME

ENTRANCE ANTIPHON   *cf Psalm 85:3, 5*

Have mercy on me, O Lord, for I cry to you all the day long.
O Lord, you are good and forgiving,
full of mercy to all who call to you.

▷ *page 7*

COLLECT

God of might, giver of every good gift,
put into our hearts the love of your name,
so that, by deepening our sense of reverence,
you may nurture in us what is good
and, by your watchful care,
keep safe what you have nurtured.
Through our Lord Jesus Christ, your Son,
who lives and reigns with you in the unity of the Holy Spirit,
one God, for ever and ever.   **Amen.**

FIRST READING   *Deuteronomy 4:1–2, 6–8*

Add nothing to what I command you, keep the commandments of the Lord.

Moses said to the people: 'Now, Israel, take notice of the laws and customs that I teach you today, and observe them, that you may have life and may enter and take possession of the land that the Lord the God of your fathers is giving you. You must add nothing to what I command you, and take nothing from it, but keep the commandments of the Lord your God just as I lay them down for you. Keep them, observe them, and they will demonstrate to the peoples your wisdom and understanding. When they come to know of all these laws they will exclaim, "No other people is as wise and prudent as this great nation." And indeed, what great nation is there that has its gods so near as the Lord our God is to us whenever we call to him?

And what great nation is there that has laws and customs to match this whole Law that I put before you today?'

The word of the Lord.

Thanks be to God.

RESPONSORIAL PSALM   *Psalm 14:2–5 response v 1*

The just will live in the presence of the Lord.

1   Lord, who shall dwell on your holy mountain?
    He who walks without fault;
    he who acts with justice
    and speaks the truth from his heart.

2   He who does no wrong to his brother,
    who casts no slur on his neighbour,
    who holds the godless in disdain,
    but honours those who fear the Lord.

3   He who keeps his pledge, come what may;
    who takes no interest on a loan
    and accepts no bribes against the innocent.
    Such a man will stand firm for ever.

SECOND READING   *James 1:17–18, 21–22, 27*

You must do what the word tells you.

It is all that is good, everything that is perfect, which is given us from above; it comes down from the Father of all light; with him there is no such thing as alteration, no shadow of a change. By his own choice he made us his children by the message of the truth so that we should be a sort of first-fruits of all that he had created.

Accept and submit to the word which has been planted in you and can save your souls. But you must do what the word tells you, and not just listen to it and deceive yourselves.

Pure, unspoilt religion, in the eyes of God our Father is this: coming to the help of orphans and widows when they need it, and keeping oneself uncontaminated by the world.

The word of the Lord.

Thanks be to God.

ORDINARY

GOSPEL ACCLAMATION   *cf John 6:63, 68*

Alleluia, alleluia!
Your words are spirit, Lord,
and they are life:
you have the message of eternal life.
Alleluia!

or   *James 1:18*

Alleluia, alleluia!
By his own choice the Father made us his children
by the message of the truth,
so that we should be a sort of first-fruits
of all that he created.
Alleluia!

GOSPEL   *Mark 7:1–8, 14–15, 21–23*

The Lord be with you.
And with your spirit.

A reading from the holy Gospel according to Mark.
Glory to you, O Lord.

You put aside the commandment of God to cling to human traditions.

The Pharisees and some of the scribes who had come from Jerusalem gathered round Jesus, and they noticed that some of his disciples were eating with unclean hands, that is, without washing them. For the Pharisees, and the Jews in general, follow the tradition of the elders and never eat without washing their arms as far as the elbow; and on returning from the market place they never eat without first sprinkling themselves. There are also many other observances which have been handed down to them concerning the washing of cups and pots and bronze dishes. So these Pharisees and scribes asked him, 'Why do your disciples not respect the tradition of the elders but eat their food with unclean hands?' He answered, 'It was of you hypocrites that Isaiah so rightly prophesied in this passage of scripture:

This people honours me only with lip-service, while their hearts are far from me. The worship they offer me is worthless, the doctrines they teach are only human regulations.

You put aside the commandment of God to cling to human traditions.'

He called the people to him again and said, 'Listen to me, all of you, and understand. Nothing that goes into a man from outside can make him unclean; it is the things that come out of a man that make him unclean. For it is from within, from men's hearts, that evil intentions emerge: fornication, theft, murder, adultery, avarice, malice, deceit, indecency, envy, slander, pride, folly. All these evil things come from within and make a man unclean.'

The Gospel of the Lord.
Praise to you, Lord Jesus Christ.

▷ *page 11*

PRAYER OVER THE OFFERINGS
May this sacred offering, O Lord,
confer on us always the blessing of salvation,
that what it celebrates in mystery
it may accomplish in power.
Through Christ our Lord. **Amen.**

▷ *page 15*

COMMUNION ANTIPHON   *Psalm 30:20*
How great is the goodness, Lord,
that you keep for those who fear you.
or   *Matthew 5:9–10*

Blessed are the peacemakers,
for they shall be called children of God.
Blessed are they who are persecuted for the sake of righteousness,
for theirs is the Kingdom of Heaven.

▷ *page 59*

ORDINARY

PRAYER AFTER COMMUNION
Renewed by this bread from the heavenly table,
we beseech you, Lord,
that, being the food of charity,
it may confirm our hearts
and stir us to serve you in our neighbour.
Through Christ our Lord. **Amen.**

▷ *page 59*

TWENTY-THIRD SUNDAY IN ORDINARY TIME

ENTRANCE ANTIPHON   *Psalm 118:137, 124*
You are just, O Lord, and your judgement is right;
treat your servant in accord with your merciful love.

▷ *page 7*

COLLECT
O God, by whom we are redeemed and receive adoption,
look graciously upon your beloved sons and daughters,
that those who believe in Christ
may receive true freedom
and an everlasting inheritance.
Through our Lord Jesus Christ, your Son,
who lives and reigns with you in the unity of the Holy Spirit,
one God, for ever and ever. **Amen.**

FIRST READING   *Isaiah 35:4–7*

The ears of the deaf shall be unsealed and the tongues of the dumb shall be loosed.

Say to all faint hearts, 'Courage! Do not be afraid.

Look, your God is coming, vengeance is coming, the retribution of God; he is coming to save you.'

Then the eyes of the blind shall be opened, the ears of the deaf unsealed,

then the lame shall leap like a deer and the tongues of the dumb sing for joy;

for water gushes in the desert, streams in the wasteland, the scorched earth becomes a lake, the parched land springs of water.

The word of the Lord.
Thanks be to God.

RESPONSORIAL PSALM   *Psalm 145:7–10 response v 1*

My soul, give praise to the Lord.

or

Alleluia! *(may be repeated two or three times)*

1 It is the Lord who keeps faith for ever,
   who is just to those who are oppressed.
   It is he who gives bread to the hungry,
   the Lord, who sets prisoners free.

2 It is the Lord who gives sight to the blind,
   who raises up those who are bowed down,
   the Lord who loves the just,
   the Lord, who protects the stranger.

3 The Lord upholds the widow and orphan,
   but thwarts the path of the wicked.
   The Lord will reign for ever,
   Zion's God, from age to age.

SECOND READING   *James 2:1–5*

God chose the poor to be the heirs to the kingdom.

My brothers, do not try to combine faith in Jesus Christ, our glorified Lord, with the making of distinctions between classes of people. Now suppose a man comes into your synagogue, beautifully dressed and with a gold ring on, and at the same time a poor man comes in, in shabby clothes, and you take notice of the well-dressed man, and say, 'Come this way to the best seats'; then you tell the poor man, 'Stand over there' or 'You can sit on the floor by my footrest.' Can't you see that you have used two different standards in your mind, and turned yourselves into judges, and corrupt judges at that?

Listen, my dear brothers: it was those who are poor according to the world that God chose, to be rich in faith and to be the heirs to the kingdom which he promised to those who love him.

The word of the Lord.
Thanks be to God.

GOSPEL ACCLAMATION   *1 Samuel 3:9; John 6:68*

Alleluia, alleluia!
Speak, Lord, your servant is listening:
you have the message of eternal life.
Alleluia!

or   *cf Matthew 4:23*

Alleluia, alleluia!
Jesus proclaimed the Good News of the kingdom,
and cured all kinds of sickness among the people.
Alleluia!

GOSPEL   *Mark 7:31–37*

The Lord be with you.
And with your spirit.

A reading from the holy Gospel according to Mark.
Glory to you, O Lord.

He makes the deaf hear and the dumb speak.

Returning from the district of Tyre, Jesus went by way of Sidon towards the Sea of Galilee, right through the Decapolis region. And they brought him a deaf man who had an impediment in his speech; and they asked him to lay his hand on him. He took him aside in private, away from the crowd, put his fingers into the man's ears and touched his tongue with spittle. Then looking up to heaven he sighed; and he said to him, 'Ephphatha', that is, 'Be opened.' And his ears were opened, and the ligament of his tongue was loosened and he spoke clearly. And Jesus ordered them to tell no one about it, but the more he insisted, the more widely they published it. Their admiration was unbounded. 'He has done all things well,' they said 'he makes the deaf hear and the dumb speak.'

The Gospel of the Lord.
Praise to you, Lord Jesus Christ.

▷ *page 11*

PRAYER OVER THE OFFERINGS

O God, who give us the gift of true prayer and of peace,
graciously grant that through this offering,
we may do fitting homage to your divine majesty
and, by partaking of the sacred mystery,
we may be faithfully united in mind and heart.
Through Christ our Lord.   **Amen.**

▷ *page 15*

ORDINARY

COMMUNION ANTIPHON   *cf Psalm 41:2–3*

Like the deer that yearns for running streams,
so my soul is yearning for you, my God;
my soul is thirsting for God, the living God.

or   *John 8:12*

I am the light of the world, says the Lord;
whoever follows me will not walk in darkness,
but will have the light of life.

▷ *page 59*

PRAYER AFTER COMMUNION

Grant that your faithful, O Lord,
whom you nourish and endow with life
through the food of your Word and heavenly Sacrament,
may so benefit from your beloved Son's great gifts
that we may merit an eternal share in his life.
Who lives and reigns for ever and ever.   **Amen.**

▷ *page 59*

 # TWENTY-FOURTH SUNDAY IN ORDINARY TIME

ENTRANCE ANTIPHON   *cf Sirach 36:18*

Give peace, O Lord, to those who wait for you,
that your prophets be found true.
Hear the prayers of your servant,
and of your people Israel.

▷ *page 7*

COLLECT

Look upon us, O God,
Creator and ruler of all things,
and, that we may feel the working of your mercy,
grant that we may serve you with all our heart.
Through our Lord Jesus Christ, your Son,
who lives and reigns with you in the unity of the Holy Spirit,
one God, for ever and ever.   **Amen.**

FIRST READING   *Isaiah 50:5–9*

I offered my back to those who struck me.

The Lord has opened my ear.

For my part, I made no resistance,
neither did I turn away. I offered my
back to those who struck me, my cheeks
to those who tore at my beard; I did not
cover my face against insult and spittle.

The Lord comes to my help, so that I
am untouched by the insults. So, too, I
set my face like flint; I know I shall not
be shamed.

My vindicator is here at hand. Does anyone start proceedings against me? Then let us go to court together. Who thinks he has a case against me? Let him approach me. The Lord is coming to my help, who dare condemn me?

The word of the Lord.
Thanks be to God.

RESPONSORIAL PSALM   *Psalm 114:1–6,8–9 response v 9*

> **I will walk in the presence of the Lord in the land of the living.**
>
> *or*
>
> **Alleluia!** *(may be repeated two or three times)*

1   I love the Lord for he has heard
the cry of my appeal;
for he turned his ear to me
in the day when I called him.

2   They surrounded me, the snares of death,
with the anguish of the tomb;
they caught me, sorrow and distress.
I called on the Lord's name.
O Lord my God, deliver me!

3   How gracious is the Lord, and just;
our God has compassion.
The Lord protects the simple hearts;
I was helpless so he saved me.

4   He has kept my soul from death,
my eyes from tears
and my feet from stumbling.
I will walk in the presence of the Lord
in the land of the living.

SECOND READING   *James 2:14–18*
If good words do not go with faith, it is quite dead.

Take the case, my brothers, of someone who has never done a single good act but claims that he has faith. Will that faith save him? If one of the brothers or one of the sisters is in need of clothes and has not enough food to live on, and one of you says to them, 'I wish you well; keep yourself warm and eat plenty', without giving them these bare necessities of life, then what good is that? Faith is like that: if good works do not go with it, it is quite dead.

This is the way to talk to people of that kind: 'You say you have faith and I have good deeds; I will prove to you that I have faith by showing you my good deeds – now you prove to me that you have faith without any good deeds to show.'

The word of the Lord.
Thanks be to God.

GOSPEL ACCLAMATION   *John 14:5*

Alleluia, alleluia!
I am the Way, the Truth and the Life, says the Lord;
no one can come to the Father except through me.
Alleluia!

or   Galatians 6:14

Alleluia, alleluia!
The only thing I can boast about is the cross of our Lord,
through whom the world is crucified to me, and I to the world.
Alleluia!

GOSPEL   *Mark 8:27–35*

The Lord be with you.
And with your spirit.

A reading from the holy Gospel according to Mark.
Glory to you, O Lord.

You are the Christ. The Son of Man is destined to suffer grievously.

Jesus and his disciples left for the villages round Caesarea Philippi. On the way he put this question to his disciples, 'Who do people say I am?' And they told him. 'John the Baptist,' they said, 'others Elijah; others again, one of the prophets.' 'But you,' he asked, 'who do you say I am?' Peter spoke up and said to him, 'You are the Christ.' And he gave them strict orders not to tell anyone about him.

And he began to teach them that the Son of Man was destined to suffer grievously, to be rejected by the elders and the chief priests and the scribes, and to be put to death, and after three days to rise again; and he said all this quite openly. Then, taking him aside, Peter started to remonstrate with him. But, turning and seeing his disciples, he rebuked Peter and said to him, 'Get behind me, Satan! Because the way you think is not God's way but man's.'

He called the people and his disciples to him and said, 'If anyone wants to be a follower of mine, let him renounce himself and take up his cross and follow me. For anyone who wants to save his life will lose it; but anyone who loses his life for my sake, and for the sake of the gospel, will save it.'

The Gospel of the Lord.
Praise to you, Lord Jesus Christ.

▷ *page 11*

PRAYER OVER THE OFFERINGS

Look with favour on our supplications, O Lord,
and in your kindness accept these, your servants' offerings,
that what each has offered to the honour of your name
may serve the salvation of all.
Through Christ our Lord.   **Amen.**

▷ *page 15*

COMMUNION ANTIPHON   *cf Psalm 35:8*
How precious is your mercy, O God!
The children of men seek shelter in the shadow of your wings.
or   *cf 1 Corinthians 10:16*

The chalice of blessing that we bless
is a communion in the Blood of Christ;
and the bread that we break
is a sharing in the Body of the Lord.

▷ *page 59*

PRAYER AFTER COMMUNION
May the working of this heavenly gift, O Lord, we pray,
take possession of our minds and bodies,
so that its effects, and not our own desires,
may always prevail in us.
Through Christ our Lord.   **Amen.**

▷ *page 59*

ORDINARY

TWENTY-FIFTH SUNDAY IN ORDINARY TIME

ENTRANCE ANTIPHON
I am the salvation of the people, says the Lord.
Should they cry to me in any distress,
I will hear them, and I will be their Lord for ever.

▷ *page 7*

COLLECT
O God, who founded all the commands of your sacred Law
upon love of you and of our neighbour,
grant that, by keeping your precepts,
we may merit to attain eternal life.
Through our Lord Jesus Christ, your Son,
who lives and reigns with you in the unity of the Holy Spirit,
one God, for ever and ever.   **Amen.**

FIRST READING   *Wisdom 2:12, 17–20*
Let us condemn him to a shameful death.

The godless say to themselves, 'Let us lie in wait for the virtuous man, since he annoys us and opposes our way of life, reproaches us for our breaches of the law and accuses us of playing false to our upbringing. Let us see if what he says is true, let us observe what kind of end he himself will have. If the virtuous man is God's son, God will take his part and rescue him from the clutches of his enemies. Let us test him with cruelty and with torture, and thus explore this gentleness of his and put his endurance to the proof. Let us condemn him to a shameful death since he will be looked after – we have his word for it.'

The word of the Lord.
Thanks be to God.

RESPONSORIAL PSALM *Psalm 53:3–6, 8 response v 6*

The Lord upholds my life.

1 O God, save me by your name;
by your power, uphold my cause.
O God, hear my prayer;
listen to the words of my mouth.

2 For proud men have risen against me,
ruthless men seek my life.
They have no regard for God.

3 But I have God for my help.
The Lord upholds my life.
I will sacrifice to you with willing heart
and praise your name for it is good.

SECOND READING *James 3:16–4:3*

Peacemakers when they work for peace, sow the seeds which will bear fruit in holiness.

Wherever you find jealousy and ambition, you find disharmony, and wicked things of every kind being done; whereas the wisdom that comes down from above is essentially something pure; it also makes for peace, and is kindly and considerate; it is full of compassion and shows itself by doing good; nor is there any trace of partiality or hypocrisy in it. Peacemakers, when they work for peace, sow the seeds which will bear fruit in holiness.

Where do these wars and battles between yourselves first start? Isn't it precisely in the desires fighting inside your own selves? You want something and you haven't got it; so you are prepared to kill. You have an ambition that you cannot satisfy; so you fight to get your way by force. Why you don't have what you want is because you don't pray for it; when you do pray and don't get it, it is because you have not prayed properly, you have prayed for something to indulge your own desires.

The word of the Lord.
Thanks be to God.

GOSPEL ACCLAMATION *John 8:12*

Alleluia, alleluia!
I am the light of the world, says the Lord,
anyone who follows me
will have the light of life.
Alleluia!

or *2 Thessalonians 2:14*

Alleluia, alleluia!
Through the Good News God called us
to share the glory of our Lord Jesus Christ.
Alleluia!

GOSPEL *Mark 9:30–37*

The Lord be with you.
And with your spirit.

A reading from the holy Gospel according to Mark.
Glory to you, O Lord.

The Son of Man will be delivered. If anyone wants to be first, he must make himself servant of all.

After leaving the mountain Jesus and his disciples made their way through Galilee; and he did not want anyone to know, because he was instructing his disciples; he was telling them, 'The Son of Man will be delivered into the hands of men; they will put him to death; and three days after he has been put to death he will rise again.' But they did not understand what he said and were afraid to ask him.

They came to Capernaum, and when he was in the house he asked them, 'What were you arguing about on the road?' They said nothing because they had been arguing which of them was the greatest. So he sat down, called the Twelve to him and said, 'If anyone wants to be first, he must make himself last of all and servant of all.' He then took a little child, set him in front of them, put his arms round him, and said to them, 'Anyone who welcomes one of these little children in my name, welcomes me; and anyone who welcomes me welcomes not me but the one who sent me.'

The Gospel of the Lord.
Praise to you, Lord Jesus Christ.

▷ *page 11*

PRAYER OVER THE OFFERINGS

Receive with favour, O Lord, we pray,
the offerings of your people,
that what they profess with devotion and faith
may be theirs through these heavenly mysteries.
Through Christ our Lord. **Amen.**

▷ *page 15*

COMMUNION ANTIPHON *Psalm 118:4–5*

You have laid down your precepts to be carefully kept;
may my ways be firm in keeping your statutes.

or *John 10:14*

I am the Good Shepherd, says the Lord;
I know my sheep, and mine know me.

▷ *page 59*

PRAYER AFTER COMMUNION

Graciously raise up, O Lord,
those you renew with this Sacrament,
that we may come to possess your redemption
both in mystery and in the manner of our life.
Through Christ our Lord. **Amen.**

▷ *page 59*

ORDINARY

✠ TWENTY-SIXTH SUNDAY IN ORDINARY TIME

ENTRANCE ANTIPHON   *Daniel 3:31, 29, 30, 43, 42*
All that you have done to us, O Lord,
you have done with true judgement,
for we have sinned against you
and not obeyed your commandments.
But give glory to your name
and deal with us according to the bounty of your mercy.   ▷ *page 7*

COLLECT
O God, who manifest your almighty power
above all by pardoning and showing mercy,
bestow, we pray, your grace abundantly upon us
and make those hastening to attain your promises
heirs to the treasures of heaven.
Through our Lord Jesus Christ, your Son,
who lives and reigns with you in the unity of the Holy Spirit,
one God, for ever and ever.   **Amen.**

FIRST READING   *Numbers 11:25–29*

Are you jealous on my account? If only the whole people of the Lord were prophets!

The Lord came down in the Cloud. He spoke with Moses, but took some of the spirit that was on him and put it on the seventy elders. When the spirit came on them they prophesied, but not again.

Two men had stayed back in the camp; one was called Eldad and the other Medad. The spirit came down on them; though they had not gone to the Tent, their names were enrolled among the rest. These began to prophesy in the camp. The young man ran to tell this to Moses, 'Look,' he said 'Eldad and Medad are prophesying in the camp.' Then said Joshua the son of Nun, who had served Moses from his youth, 'My Lord Moses, stop them!' Moses answered him, 'Are you jealous on my account? If only the whole people of the Lord were prophets, and the Lord gave his Spirit to them all!'

The word of the Lord.
Thanks be to God.

RESPONSORIAL PSALM   *Psalm 18:8, 10, 12–14 response v 9*

The precepts of the Lord gladden the heart.

1   The law of the Lord is perfect,
   it revives the soul.
   The rule of the Lord is to be trusted,
   it gives wisdom to the simple.

2   The fear of the Lord is holy,
   abiding for ever.
   The decrees of the Lord are truth
   and all of them just.

3 So in them your servant finds instruction;
   great reward is in their keeping.
   But who can detect all his errors?
   From hidden faults acquit me.

4 From presumption restrain your servant
   and let it not rule me.
   Then shall I be blameless,
   clean from grave sin.

SECOND READING   *James 5:1–6*

Your wealth is all rotting.

An answer for the rich. Start crying, weep for the miseries that are coming to you. Your wealth is all rotting, your clothes are all eaten up by moths. All your gold and your silver are corroding away, and the same corrosion will be your own sentence, and eat into your body. It was a burning fire that you stored up as your treasure for the last days. Labourers mowed your fields, and you cheated them – listen to the wages that you kept back, calling out; realise that the cries of the reapers have reached the ears of the Lord of hosts. On earth you have had a life of comfort and luxury; in the time of slaughter you went on eating to your heart's content. It was you who condemned the innocent and killed them; they offered you no resistance.

The word of the Lord.
Thanks be to God.

GOSPEL ACCLAMATION   *cf John 17:17*

Alleluia, alleluia!
Your word is truth, O Lord,
consecrate us in the truth.
Alleluia!

GOSPEL   *Mark 9:38–43, 45, 47–48*

The Lord be with you.
And with your spirit.

A reading from the holy Gospel according to Mark.
Glory to you, O Lord.

Anyone who is not against us is for us. If your hand should cause you to sin, cut it off.

John said to Jesus, 'Master, we saw a man who is not one of us casting out devils in your name; and because he was not one of us we tried to stop him.' But Jesus said, 'You must not stop him: no one who works a miracle in my name is likely to speak evil of me. Anyone who is not against us is for us.

'If anyone gives you a cup of water to drink just because you belong to Christ, then I tell you solemnly, he will most certainly not lose his reward.

'But anyone who is an obstacle to bring down one of these little ones who have faith, would be better thrown into the sea with a great millstone round his neck. And if your hand should cause you to sin, cut it off; it is better for you to enter into life crippled, than to have two hands and go to hell, into the fire that cannot be put out. And if your foot should cause you to sin, cut it off; it is better for you to enter into life lame, than to have two feet and be thrown into hell. And if your eye should cause you to sin, tear it out; it is better for you to enter into the kingdom of God with one eye, than to have two eyes and be thrown into hell where their worm does not die nor their fire go out.'

The Gospel of the Lord.

Praise to you, Lord Jesus Christ.

▷ *page 11*

PRAYER OVER THE OFFERINGS

Grant us, O merciful God,
that this our offering may find acceptance with you
and that through it the wellspring of all blessing
may be laid open before us.
Through Christ our Lord.   **Amen.**

▷ *page 15*

COMMUNION ANTIPHON   *cf Psalm 118:49–50*

Remember your word to your servant, O Lord,
by which you have given me hope.
This is my comfort when I am brought low.

or   *1 John 3:16*

By this we came to know the love of God:
that Christ laid down his life for us;
so we ought to lay down our lives for one another.

▷ *page 59*

PRAYER AFTER COMMUNION

May this heavenly mystery, O Lord,
restore us in mind and body,
that we may be coheirs in glory with Christ,
to whose suffering we are united
whenever we proclaim his Death.
Who lives and reigns for ever and ever.   **Amen.**

▷ *page 59*

✠ TWENTY-SEVENTH SUNDAY IN ORDINARY TIME

ENTRANCE ANTIPHON   *cf Esther 4:17*

Within your will, O Lord, all things are established,
and there is none that can resist your will.
For you have made all things, the heaven and the earth,
and all that is held within the circle of heaven;
you are the Lord of all.

▷ *page 7*

COLLECT

Almighty ever-living God,
who in the abundance of your kindness
surpass the merits and the desires of those who entreat you,
pour out your mercy upon us
to pardon what conscience dreads
and to give what prayer does not dare to ask.
Through our Lord Jesus Christ, your Son,
who lives and reigns with you in the unity of the Holy Spirit,
one God, for ever and ever.   **Amen.**

FIRST READING   *Genesis 2:18–24*

They become one body.

The Lord God said, 'It is not good that the man should be alone. I will make him a helpmate.' So from the soil the Lord God fashioned all the wild beasts and all the birds of heaven. These he brought to the man to see what he would call them; each one was to bear the name the man would give it. The man gave names to all the cattle, all the birds of heaven and all the wild beasts. But no helpmate suitable for man was found for him. So the Lord God made the man fall into a deep sleep. And while he slept, he took one of his ribs and enclosed it in flesh. The Lord God built the rib he had taken from the man into a woman, and brought her to the man. The man exclaimed:

'This at last is bone from my bones, and flesh from my flesh! This is to be called woman, for this was taken from man.'

This is why a man leaves his father and mother and joins himself to his wife, and they become one body.

The word of the Lord.
Thanks be to God.

RESPONSORIAL PSALM   *Psalm 127 response v 5*

May the Lord bless us all the days of our life.

1   O blessed are those who fear the Lord
    and walk in his ways!
    By the labour of your hands you shall eat.
    You will be happy and prosper.

2   Your wife like a fruitful vine
    in the heart of your house;
    your children like shoots of the olive,
    around your table.

3   Indeed thus shall be blessed
    the man who fears the Lord.
    May the Lord bless you from Zion
    all the days of your life!
    May you see your children's children.
    On Israel, peace!

SECOND READING   *Hebrews 2:9–11*

The one who sanctifies, and the ones who are sanctified, are of the same stock.

We see in Jesus one who was for a short while made lower than the angels and is now crowned with glory and splendour because he submitted to death; by God's grace he had to experience death for all mankind.

As it was his purpose to bring a great many of his sons into glory, it was appropriate that God, for whom everything exists and through whom everything exists, should make perfect, through suffering, the leader who would take them to their salvation. For the one who sanctifies, and the ones who are sanctified, are of the same stock; that is why he openly calls them brothers.

The word of the Lord.
Thanks be to God.

GOSPEL ACCLAMATION   *cf John 17:17*

Alleluia, alleluia!
Your word is truth, O Lord,
consecrate us in the truth.
Alleluia!

or   *1 John 4:12*

Alleluia, alleluia!
As long as we love one another
God will live in us
and his love will be complete in us.
Alleluia!

GOSPEL   *Mark 10:2–16*   *Shorter form: Mark 10:2–12 (only read text with side line next to it).*

The Lord be with you.
And with your spirit.

A reading from the holy Gospel according to Mark.
Glory to you, O Lord.

What God has united, man must not divide.

Some Pharisees approached Jesus and asked, 'Is it against the law for a man to divorce his wife?' They were testing him. He answered them, 'What did Moses command you?' 'Moses allowed us' they said 'to draw up a writ of dismissal and so to divorce.' Then Jesus said to them, 'It was because you were so unteachable that he wrote his commandment for you. But from the beginning of creation God made them male and female. This is why a man must leave father and mother, and the two become one body. They are no longer two, therefore, but one body. So then, what God has united, man must not divide.' Back in the house the disciples questioned him again about this, and he said to them, 'The man who divorces his wife and marries another is guilty of adultery against her. And if a woman divorces her husband and marries another she is guilty of adultery too.'

People were bringing little children to him, for him to touch them. The disciples turned them away, but when Jesus saw this he was indignant and said to them, 'Let the little children come to me; do not stop them; for it is to such as these that the kingdom of God belongs. I tell you solemnly, anyone who does not welcome the kingdom of God like a little child will never enter it.' Then he put his arms round them, laid his hands on them and gave them his blessing.

The Gospel of the Lord.
Praise to you, Lord Jesus Christ.

▷ *page 11*

PRAYER OVER THE OFFERINGS
Accept, O Lord, we pray,
the sacrifices instituted by your commands
and, through the sacred mysteries,
which we celebrate with dutiful service,
graciously complete the sanctifying work
by which you are pleased to redeem us.
Through Christ our Lord.   **Amen.**

▷ page 15

COMMUNION ANTIPHON   *Lamentations 3:25*
The Lord is good to those who hope in him,
to the soul that seeks him.

or   *cf 1 Corinthians 10:17*

Though many, we are one bread, one body,
for we all partake of the one Bread and one Chalice.

▷ page 59

PRAYER AFTER COMMUNION
Grant us, almighty God,
that we may be refreshed and nourished
by the Sacrament which we have received,
so as to be transformed into what we consume.
Through Christ our Lord.   **Amen.**

▷ page 59

TWENTY-EIGHTH SUNDAY IN ORDINARY TIME

ENTRANCE ANTIPHON   *Psalm 129:3–4*
If you, O Lord, should mark iniquities,
Lord, who could stand?
But with you is found forgiveness,
O God of Israel.

▷ page 7

COLLECT
May your grace, O Lord, we pray,
at all times go before us and follow after
and make us always determined
to carry out good works.
Through our Lord Jesus Christ, your Son,
who lives and reigns with you in the unity of the Holy Spirit,
one God, for ever and ever.   **Amen.**

FIRST READING *Wisdom 7:7–11*

Compared with wisdom, I held riches as nothing.

I prayed, and understanding was given me; I entreated, and the spirit of Wisdom came to me. I esteemed her more than sceptres and thrones; compared with her, I held riches as nothing. I reckoned no priceless stone to be her peer, for compared with her, all gold is a pinch of sand, and beside her silver ranks as mud. I loved her more than health or beauty, preferred her to the light, since her radiance never sleeps. In her company all good things came to me, at her hands riches not to be numbered.

The word of the Lord.

Thanks be to God.

RESPONSORIAL PSALM *Psalm 89:12–17 response v 14*

Fill us with your love that we may rejoice.

1 Make us know the shortness of our life
that we may gain wisdom of heart.
Lord, relent! Is your anger for ever?
Show pity to your servants.

2 In the morning, fill us with your love;
we shall exult and rejoice all our days.
Give us joy to balance our affliction
for the years when we knew misfortune.

3 Show forth your work to your servants;
let your glory shine on their children.
Let the favour of the Lord be upon us:
give success to the work of our hands.

SECOND READING *Hebrews 4:12–13*

The word of God can judge secret emotions and thoughts.

The word of God is something alive and active: it cuts like any double-edged sword but more finely: it can slip through the place where the soul is divided from the spirit, or joints from the marrow; it can judge the secret emotions and thoughts. No created thing can hide from him; everything is uncovered and open to the eyes of the one to whom we must give account of ourselves.

The word of the Lord.

Thanks be to God.

GOSPEL ACCLAMATION *cf Matthew 11:25*

Alleluia, alleluia!
Blessed are you, Father,
Lord of heaven and earth,
for revealing the mysteries of the kingdom
to mere children.
alleluia!

or   *Matthew 5:3*

Alleluia, alleluia!
How happy are the poor in spirit;
theirs is the kingdom of heaven.
Alleluia!

GOSPEL   *Mark 10:17–30   Shorter form: Mark 10:17–27 (only read text with side line next to it).*

The Lord be with you.
And with your spirit.

A reading from the holy Gospel according to Mark.
Glory to you, O Lord.

Go and sell everything you own and follow me.

Jesus was setting out on a journey when a man ran up, knelt before him and put this question to him, 'Good master, what must I do to inherit eternal life?' Jesus said to him, 'Why do you call me good? No one is good but God alone. You know the commandments: You must not kill; You must not commit adultery; You must not steal; You must not bring false witness; You must not defraud; Honour your father and mother.' And he said to him, 'Master, I have kept all these from my earliest days.' Jesus looked steadily at him and loved him, and he said, 'There is one thing you lack. Go and sell everything you own and give the money to the poor, and you will have treasure in heaven; then come, follow me.' But his face fell at these words and he went away sad, for he was a man of great wealth.

Jesus looked round and said to his disciples, 'How hard it is for those who have riches to enter the kingdom of God!' The disciples were astounded by these words, but Jesus insisted, 'My children,' he said to them 'how hard it is to enter the kingdom of God! It is easier for a camel to pass through the eye of a needle than for a rich man to enter the kingdom of God.' They were more astonished than ever. 'In that case' they said to one another 'who can be saved?' Jesus gazed at them. 'For men' he said 'it is impossible, but not for God: because everything is possible for God.'

Peter took this up. 'What about us?' he asked him. 'We have left everything and followed you.' Jesus said, 'I tell you solemnly, there is no one who has left house, brothers, sisters, father, children or land for my sake and for the sake of the gospel who will not be repaid a hundred times over, houses, brothers, sisters, mothers, children and land – not without persecutions – now in this present time and, in the world to come, eternal life.'

The Gospel of the Lord.
Praise to you, Lord Jesus Christ.

▷ *page 11*

PRAYER OVER THE OFFERINGS
Accept, O Lord, the prayers of your faithful
with the sacrificial offerings,
that, through these acts of devotedness,
we may pass over to the glory of heaven.
Through Christ our Lord.   **Amen.**

▷ *page 15*

ORDINARY

COMMUNION ANTIPHON   *cf Psalm 33:11*

The rich suffer want and go hungry,
but those who seek the Lord lack no blessing.

or   *1 John 3:2*

When the Lord appears, we shall be like him,
for we shall see him as he is.

▷ *page 59*

PRAYER AFTER COMMUNION

We entreat your majesty most humbly, O Lord,
that, as you feed us with the nourishment
which comes from the most holy Body and Blood of your Son,
so you may make us sharers of his divine nature.
Who lives and reigns for ever and ever.   **Amen.**

▷ *page 59*

 # TWENTY-NINTH SUNDAY IN ORDINARY TIME

ENTRANCE ANTIPHON   *cf Psalm 16:6, 8*

To you I call; for you will surely heed me, O God;
turn your ear to me; hear my words.
Guard me as the apple of your eye;
in the shadow of your wings protect me.

▷ *page 7*

COLLECT

Almighty ever-living God,
grant that we may always conform our will to yours
and serve your majesty in sincerity of heart.
Through our Lord Jesus Christ, your Son,
who lives and reigns with you in the unity of the Holy Spirit,
one God, for ever and ever.   **Amen.**

FIRST READING   *Isaiah 53:10–11*

If he offers his life in atonement, he shall see his heirs,
he shall have a long life.

The Lord has been pleased to crush his
servant with suffering. If he offers his
life in atonement, he shall see his heirs,
he shall have a long life and through
him what the Lord wishes will be done.

His soul's anguish over he shall see the
light and be content. By his sufferings
shall my servant justify many, taking
their faults on himself.

The word of the Lord.
Thanks be to God.

RESPONSORIAL PSALM   *Psalm 32:4–5, 18–20, 22 response v 22*

May your love be upon us, O Lord,
as we place all our hope in you.

1   The word of the Lord is faithful
and all his works to be trusted.
The Lord loves justice and right
and fills the earth with his love.

2   The Lord looks on those who revere him,
on those who hope in his love,
to rescue their souls from death,
to keep them alive in famine.

3   Our soul is waiting for the Lord.
The Lord is our help and our shield.
May your love be upon us, O Lord,
as we place all our hope in you.

SECOND READING   *Hebrews 4:14–16*

Let us be confident in approaching the throne of grace.

Since in Jesus, the Son of God, we have the supreme high priest who has gone through to the highest heaven, we must never let go of the faith that we have professed. For it is not as if we had a high priest who was incapable of feeling our weaknesses with us; but we have one who has been tempted in every way that we are, though he is without sin. Let us be confident, then, in approaching the throne of grace, that we shall have mercy from him and find grace when we are in need of help.

The word of the Lord.
Thanks be to God.

GOSPEL ACCLAMATION   *John 14:5*

Alleluia, alleluia!
I am the Way, the Truth and the Life, says the Lord;
no one can come to the Father except through me.
Alleluia!

or   *Mark 10:45*

Alleluia, alleluia!
The Son of Man came to serve,
and to give his life as a ransom for many.
Alleluia!

ORDINARY

GOSPEL   *Mark 10:35–45   Shorter form: Mark 10:42–45 (only read text with side line next to it).*

The Lord be with you.
And with your spirit.

A reading from the holy Gospel according to Mark.
Glory to you, O Lord.

The Son of Man came to give his life as a ransom for many.

James and John, the sons of Zebedee, approached Jesus. 'Master,' they said to him 'we want you to do us a favour.' He said to them, 'What is it you want me to do for you?' They said to him, 'Allow us to sit one at your right hand and the other at your left in your glory.' 'You do not know what you are asking' Jesus said to them. 'Can you drink the cup that I must drink, or be baptised with the baptism with which I must be baptised?' They replied, 'We can.' Jesus said to them, 'The cup that I must drink you shall drink, and with the baptism with which I must be baptised you shall be baptised, but as for seats at my right hand or my left, these are not mine to grant: they belong to those to whom they have been allotted.'

When the other ten heard this they began to feel indignant with James and John, so *Jesus called them to him and said to them, 'You know that among the pagans their so-called rulers lord it over them, and their great men make their authority felt. This is not to happen among you. No; anyone who wants to become great among you must be your servant, and anyone who wants to be first among you must be slave to all. For the Son of Man himself did not come to be served but to serve, and to give his life as a ransom for many.'

The Gospel of the Lord.
Praise to you, Lord Jesus Christ.

▷ *page 11*

* The shorter version of this reading begins:

Jesus called his disciples to him and said to them: 'You know...

PRAYER OVER THE OFFERINGS
Grant us, Lord, we pray,
a sincere respect for your gifts,
that, through the purifying action of your grace,
we may be cleansed by the very mysteries we serve.
Through Christ our Lord.   **Amen.**

▷ *page 15*

COMMUNION ANTIPHON   *cf Psalm 32:18–19*
Behold, the eyes of the Lord
are on those who fear him,
who hope in his merciful love,
to rescue their souls from death,
to keep them alive in famine.

or   *Mark 10:45*

The Son of Man has come
to give his life as a ransom for many.

▷ *page 59*

PRAYER AFTER COMMUNION
Grant, O Lord, we pray,
that, benefiting from participation in heavenly things,
we may be helped by what you give in this present age
and prepared for the gifts that are eternal.
Through Christ our Lord. **Amen.**

▷ *page 59*

THIRTIETH SUNDAY IN ORDINARY TIME

ENTRANCE ANTIPHON   *cf Psalm 104:3–4*
Let the hearts that seek the Lord rejoice;
turn to the Lord and his strength;
constantly seek his face.

▷ *page 7*

ORDINARY

COLLECT
Almighty ever-living God,
increase our faith, hope and charity,
and make us love what you command,
so that we may merit what you promise.
Through our Lord Jesus Christ, your Son,
who lives and reigns with you in the unity of the Holy Spirit,
one God, for ever and ever. **Amen.**

FIRST READING   *Jeremiah 31:7–9*
I will comfort the blind and the lame as I lead them back.

The Lord says this:

Shout with joy for Jacob! Hail the chief of nations! Proclaim! Praise! Shout: 'The Lord has saved his people, the remnant of Israel!' See, I will bring them back from the land of the North and gather them from the far ends of earth; all of them: the blind and the lame, women with child, women in labour: a great company returning here. They had left in tears, I will comfort them as I lead them back; I will guide them to streams of water, by a smooth path where they will not stumble. For I am a father to Israel, and Ephraim is my first-born son.

The word of the Lord.
Thanks be to God.

RESPONSORIAL PSALM   *Psalm 125 response v 3*

**What marvels the Lord worked for us!
Indeed we were glad.**

1 When the Lord delivered Zion from bondage,
    it seemed like a dream.
    Then was our mouth filled with laughter,
    on our lips there were songs.

continued...

What marvels the Lord worked for us!
Indeed we were glad.

2 The heathens themselves said: 'What marvels
the Lord worked for them!'
What marvels the Lord worked for us!
Indeed we were glad.

3 Deliver us, O Lord, from our bondage
as streams in dry land.
Those who are sowing in tears
will sing when they reap.

4 They go out, they go out, full of tears
carrying seed for the sowing:
they come back, they come back, full of song,
carrying their sheaves.

SECOND READING   *Hebrews 5:1–6*

You are a priest of the order of Melchizedek, and for ever.

Every high priest has been taken out of mankind and is appointed to act for men in their relations with God, to offer gifts and sacrifices for sins; and so he can sympathise with those who are ignorant or uncertain because he too lives in the limitations of weakness. That is why he has to make sin offerings for himself as well as for the people. No one takes this honour on himself, but each one is called by God, as Aaron was. Nor did Christ give himself the glory of becoming high priest, but he had it from the one who said to him; You are my son today I have become your father, and in another text: You are a priest of the order of Melchizedek, and for ever.

The word of the Lord.
Thanks be to God.

GOSPEL ACCLAMATION   *John 8:12*

Alleluia, alleluia!
I am the light of the world, says the Lord,
anyone who follows me
will have the light of life.
Alleluia!

or   cf 2 Timothy 1:10

Alleluia, alleluia!
Our Saviour Christ Jesus abolished death,
and he has proclaimed life through the Good News.
Alleluia!

GOSPEL   Mark 10:46–52

The Lord be with you.
And with your spirit.

A reading from the holy Gospel according to Mark.
Glory to you, O Lord.

Master, let me see again.

As Jesus left Jericho with his disciples and a large crowd, Bartimaeus (that is, the son of Timaeus), a blind beggar, was sitting at the side of the road. When he heard that it was Jesus of Nazareth, he began to shout and to say, 'Son of David, Jesus, have pity on me.' And many of them scolded him and told him to keep quiet, but he only shouted all the louder, 'Son of David, have pity on me.' Jesus stopped and said, 'Call him here.' So they called the blind man. 'Courage,' they said 'get up; he is calling you.' So throwing off his cloak, he jumped up and went to Jesus. Then Jesus spoke, 'What do you want me to do for you?' 'Rabbuni,' the blind man said to him 'Master, let me see again.' Jesus said to him, 'Go; your faith has saved you.' And immediately his sight returned and he followed him along the road.

The Gospel of the Lord.
Praise to you, Lord Jesus Christ.

▷ page 11

PRAYER OVER THE OFFERINGS

Look, we pray, O Lord,
on the offerings we make to your majesty,
that whatever is done by us in your service
may be directed above all to your glory.
Through Christ our Lord. **Amen.**

▷ page 15

COMMUNION ANTIPHON   cf Psalm 19:6

We will ring out our joy at your saving help
and exult in the name of our God.

or   Ephesians 5:2

Christ loved us and gave himself up for us,
as a fragrant offering to God.

▷ page 59

PRAYER AFTER COMMUNION

May your Sacraments, O Lord, we pray,
perfect in us what lies within them,
that what we now celebrate in signs
we may one day possess in truth.
Through Christ our Lord. **Amen.**

▷ page 59

ORDINARY

✠ THIRTY-FIRST SUNDAY IN ORDINARY TIME

ENTRANCE ANTIPHON   *cf Psalm 37:22–23*
Forsake me not, O Lord, my God;
be not far from me!
Make haste and come to my help,
O Lord, my strong salvation!

▷ *page 7*

COLLECT
Almighty and merciful God,
by whose gift your faithful offer you
right and praiseworthy service,
grant, we pray,
that we may hasten without stumbling
to receive the things you have promised.
Through our Lord Jesus Christ, your Son,
who lives and reigns with you in the unity of the Holy Spirit,
one God, for ever and ever.   **Amen.**

FIRST READING   *Deuteronomy 6:2–6*
Listen, Israel: You shall love the Lord your God with all your heart.

Moses said to the people: 'If you fear the Lord your God all the days of your life and if you keep all his laws and commandments which I lay on you, you will have a long life, you and your son and your grandson. Listen then, Israel, keep and observe what will make you prosper and give you great increase, as the Lord God of your fathers has promised you, giving you a land where milk and honey flow.

'Listen, Israel: The Lord our God is the one Lord. You shall love the Lord your God with all your heart, with all your soul, with all your strength. Let these words I urge on you today be written on your heart.'

The word of the Lord.
Thanks be to God.

RESPONSORIAL PSALM   *Psalm 17:2–4, 47, 51 response v 2*

I love you, Lord, my strength.

1   I love you, Lord, my strength,
    my rock, my fortress, my saviour.
    My God is the rock where I take refuge;
    my shield, my mighty help, my stronghold.
    The Lord is worthy of all praise:
    when I call I am saved from my foes.

2   Long life to the Lord, my rock!
    Praised be the God who saves me.
    He has given great victories to his king
    and shown his love for his anointed.

SECOND READING   *Hebrews 7:23–28*

Because he remains for ever, Christ can never lose his priesthood.

There used to be a great number of priests under the former covenant, because death put an end to each one of them; but this one, Christ, because he remains for ever, can never lose his priesthood. It follows then, that his power to save is utterly certain, since he is living for ever to intercede for all who come to God through him.

To suit us, the ideal high priest would have to be holy, innocent and uncontaminated, beyond the influence of sinners, and raised up above the heavens; one who would not need to offer sacrifices every day, as the other high priests do for their own sins and then for those of the people, because he has done this once and for all by offering himself. The Law appoints high priests who are men subject to weakness; but the promise on oath, which came after the Law, appointed the Son who is made perfect for ever.

The word of the Lord.
Thanks be to God.

GOSPEL ACCLAMATION   *cf John 6:63, 68*

**Alleluia, alleluia!
Your words are spirit, Lord,
and they are life:
you have the message of eternal life.
Alleluia!**

or   *John 14:23*

**Alleluia, alleluia!
If anyone loves me he will keep my word,
and my Father will love him,
and we shall come to him.
Alleluia!**

GOSPEL   *Mark 12:28–34*

The Lord be with you.
And with your spirit.

A reading from the holy Gospel according to Mark.
Glory to you, O Lord.

This is the first commandment. The second is like it.

One of the scribes came up to Jesus and put a question to him, 'Which is the first of all the commandments?' Jesus replied, 'This is the first: Listen, Israel, the Lord our God is the one Lord, and you must love the Lord your God with all your heart, with all your soul, with all your mind and with all your strength. The second is this: You must love your neighbour as yourself. There is no commandment greater than these.' The scribe said to him, 'Well spoken, Master; what you have said is true: that he is one and there is no other. To love with all your heart, with all your understanding and strength and to love your neighbour as yourself, this is far more important than any holocaust or sacrifice.' Jesus, seeing how wisely he had spoken, said, 'You are not far from the kingdom of God.' And after that no one dared to question him any more.

The Gospel of the Lord.
Praise to you, Lord Jesus Christ.

▷ *page 11*

PRAYER OVER THE OFFERINGS
May these sacrificial offerings, O Lord,
become for you a pure oblation,
and for us a holy outpouring of your mercy.
Through Christ our Lord.   **Amen.**

▷ *page 15*

COMMUNION ANTIPHON   *cf Psalm 15:11*
You will show me the path of life,
the fullness of joy in your presence, O Lord.

or *John 6:58*

Just as the living Father sent me
and I have life because of the Father,
so whoever feeds on me
shall have life because of me, says the Lord.

▷ *page 59*

PRAYER AFTER COMMUNION

May the working of your power, O Lord,
increase in us, we pray,
so that, renewed by these heavenly Sacraments,
we may be prepared by your gift
for receiving what they promise.
Through Christ our Lord.   **Amen.**

▷ *page 59*

THIRTY-SECOND SUNDAY IN ORDINARY TIME

ENTRANCE ANTIPHON   *cf Psalm 87:3*
Let my prayer come into your presence.
Incline your ear to my cry for help, O Lord.

▷ *page 7*

COLLECT

Almighty and merciful God,
graciously keep from us all adversity,
so that, unhindered in mind and body alike,
we may pursue in freedom of heart
the things that are yours.
Through our Lord Jesus Christ, your Son,
who lives and reigns with you in the unity of the Holy Spirit,
one God, for ever and ever. **Amen.**

FIRST READING   1 Kings 17:10–16

The widow made a little scone from her meal and brought it to Elijah.

Elijah the Prophet went off to Sidon. And when he reached the city gate, there was a widow gathering sticks; addressing her he said, 'Please bring a little water in a vessel for me to drink.' She was setting off to bring it when he called after her. 'Please' he said 'bring me a scrap of bread in your hand.' 'As the Lord your God lives,' she replied 'I have no baked bread, but only a handful of meal in a jar and a little oil in a jug; I am just gathering a stick or two to go and prepare this for myself and my son to eat, and then we shall die.' But Elijah said to her, 'Do not be afraid, go and do as you have said; but first make a little scone of it for me and bring it to me, and then make some for yourself and for your son. For thus the Lord speaks, the God of Israel:

"Jar of meal shall not be spent, jug of oil shall not be emptied, before the day when the Lord sends rain on the face of the earth."'

The woman went and did as Elijah told her and they ate the food, she, himself and her son. The jar of meal was not spent nor the jug of oil emptied, just as the Lord had foretold through Elijah.

The word of the Lord.
Thanks be to God.

RESPONSORIAL PSALM   Psalm 145:7–10 response v 2

My soul, give praise to the Lord.

or

Alleluia! *(may be repeated two or three times)*

1   It is the Lord who keeps faith for ever,
who is just to those who are oppressed.
It is he who gives bread to the hungry,
the Lord, who sets prisoners free.

2   It is the Lord who gives sight to the blind,
who raises up those who are bowed down.
It is the Lord who loves the just,
the Lord, who protects the stranger.

3   The Lord upholds the widow and orphan
but thwarts the path of the wicked.
The Lord will reign for ever,
Zion's God, from age to age.

SECOND READING   *Hebrews 9:24–28*

Christ offers himself only once to take the faults of many on himself.

It is not as though Christ had entered a man-made sanctuary which was only modelled on the real one; but it was heaven itself, so that he could appear in the actual presence of God on our behalf. And he does not have to offer himself again and again, like the high priest going into the sanctuary year after year with the blood that is not his own, or else he would have had to suffer over and over again since the world began. Instead of that, he has made his appearance once and for all, now at the end of the last age, to do away with sin by sacrificing himself. Since men only die once, and after that comes judgement, so Christ, too, offers himself only once to take the faults of many on himself, and when he appears a second time, it will not be to deal with sin but to reward with salvation those who are waiting for him.

The word of the Lord.
Thanks be to God.

GOSPEL ACCLAMATION   *Apocalypse 2:10*   or   *Matthew 5:3*

Alleluia, alleluia!
Even if you have to die, says the Lord,
keep faithful, and I will give you
the crown of life.
Alleluia!

Alleluia, alleluia!
How happy are the poor in spirit;
theirs is the kingdom of heaven.
Alleluia!

GOSPEL   *Mark 12:38–44   Shorter form: Mark 12:41–44 (only read text with side line next to it).*

The Lord be with you.
And with your spirit.

A reading from the holy Gospel according to Mark.
Glory to you, O Lord.

This poor widow has put in more than all.

In his teaching Jesus said, 'Beware of the scribes who like to walk about in long robes, to be greeted obsequiously in the market squares, to take the front seats in the synagogues and the places of honour at banquets; these are the men who swallow the property of widows, while making a show of lengthy prayers. The more severe will be the sentence they receive.'

*He sat down opposite the treasury and watched the people putting money into the treasury, and many of the rich put in a great deal. A poor widow came and put in two small coins, the equivalent of a penny. Then he called his disciples and said to them, 'I tell you solemnly, this poor widow has put more in than all who have contributed to the treasury; for they have all put in money they had over, but she from the little she had has put in everything she possessed, all she had to live on.'

The Gospel of the Lord.
Praise to you, Lord Jesus Christ.

▷ *page 11*

---

* The shorter version of this reading begins:
Jesus sat down opposite the treasury...

PRAYER OVER THE OFFERINGS

Look with favour, we pray, O Lord,
upon the sacrificial gifts offered here,
that, celebrating in mystery the Passion of your Son,
we may honour it with loving devotion.
Through Christ our Lord.   **Amen.**

▷ *page 15*

COMMUNION ANTIPHON   *cf Psalm 22:1–2*

The Lord is my shepherd; there is nothing I shall want.
Fresh and green are the pastures where he gives me repose,
near restful waters he leads me.

or   *cf Luke 24:35*

The disciples recognized the Lord Jesus in the breaking of bread.

▷ *page 59*

ORDINARY

PRAYER AFTER COMMUNION

Nourished by this sacred gift, O Lord,
we give you thanks and beseech your mercy,
that, by the pouring forth of your Spirit,
the grace of integrity may endure
in those your heavenly power has entered.
Through Christ our Lord.   **Amen.**

▷ *page 59*

THIRTY-THIRD SUNDAY IN ORDINARY TIME

ENTRANCE ANTIPHON   *Jeremiah 29:11, 12, 14*

The Lord said: I think thoughts of peace and not of affliction.
You will call upon me, and I will answer you,
and I will lead back your captives from every place.

▷ *page 7*

COLLECT

Grant us, we pray, O Lord our God,
the constant gladness of being devoted to you,
for it is full and lasting happiness
to serve with constancy
the author of all that is good.
Through our Lord Jesus Christ, your Son,
who lives and reigns with you in the unity of the Holy Spirit,
one God, for ever and ever.   **Amen.**

FIRST READING   *Daniel 12:1–13*

When that time comes, your own people will be spared.

'At that time Michael will stand up, the great prince who mounts guard over your people. There is going to be a time of great distress, unparalleled since nations first came into existence. When that time comes, your own people will be spared, all those whose names are found written in the Book. Of those who lie sleeping in the dust of the earth many will awake, some to everlasting life, some to shame and everlasting disgrace. The learned will shine as brightly as the vault of heaven, and those who have instructed many in virtue, as bright as stars for all eternity.'

The word of the Lord.

Thanks be to God.

RESPONSORIAL PSALM   *Psalm 15:5, 8–11 response v1*

Preserve me, God, I take refuge in you.

1   O Lord, it is you who are my portion and cup;
it is you yourself who are my prize
I keep the Lord ever in my sight:
since he is at my right hand, I shall stand firm.

2   And so my heart rejoices, my soul is glad;
even my body shall rest in safety.
For you will not leave my soul among the dead,
nor let your beloved know decay.

3   You will show me the path of life,
the fullness of joy in your presence,
at your right hand happiness for ever.

SECOND READING   *Hebrews 10:11–14, 18*

By virtue of one single offering, he has achieved the eternal perfection of all whom he is sanctifying.

All the priests stand at their duties every day, offering over and over again the same sacrifices which are quite incapable of taking sins away. Christ, on the other hand, has offered one single sacrifice for sins, and then taken his place for ever, at the right hand of God, where he is now waiting until his enemies are made into a footstool for him. By virtue of that one single offering, he has achieved the eternal perfection of all whom he is sanctifying. When all sins have been forgiven, there can be no more sin offerings.

The word of the Lord.

Thanks be to God.

GOSPEL ACCLAMATION   *Matthew 24:42, 44*

Alleluia, alleluia!
Stay awake and stand ready,
because you do not know the hour
when the Son of Man is coming.
Alleluia!

or   *Luke 21:36*

Alleluia, alleluia!
Stay awake, praying at all times
for the strength to stand with confidence
before the Son of Man.
Alleluia!

GOSPEL   *Mark 13:24–32*

The Lord be with you.
And with your spirit.

A reading from the holy Gospel according to Mark.
Glory to you, O Lord.

He will gather his chosen from the four winds.

Jesus said to his disciples: 'In those days, after the time of distress, the sun will be darkened, the moon will lose its brightness, the stars will come falling from heaven and the powers in the heavens will be shaken. And then they will see the Son of Man coming in the clouds with great power and glory; then too he will send the angels to gather his chosen from the four winds, from the ends of the world to the ends of heaven. Take the fig tree as a parable: as soon as its twigs grow supple and its leaves come out, you know that summer is near. So with you, when you see these things happening: know that he is near, at the very gates. I tell you solemnly, before this generation has passed away all these things will have taken place. Heaven and earth will pass away, but my words will not pass away.

'But as for that day or hour, nobody knows it, neither the angels of heaven, nor the Son; no one but the Father.'

The Gospel of the Lord.
Praise to you, Lord Jesus Christ.

▷ *page 11*

PRAYER OVER THE OFFERINGS

Grant, O Lord, we pray,
that what we offer in the sight of your majesty
may obtain for us the grace of being devoted to you
and gain us the prize of everlasting happiness.
Through Christ our Lord. **Amen.**

▷ *page 15*

COMMUNION ANTIPHON   *Psalm 72:28*

To be near God is my happiness,
to place my hope in God the Lord.

or   *Mark 11:23–24*

Amen, I say to you: Whatever you ask in prayer,
believe that you will receive,
and it shall be given to you, says the Lord.

▷ *page 59*

PRAYER AFTER COMMUNION

We have partaken of the gifts of this sacred mystery,
humbly imploring, O Lord,
that what your Son commanded us to do
in memory of him
may bring us growth in charity.
Through Christ our Lord.   **Amen.**

▷ *page 59*

 # OUR LORD JESUS CHRIST, KING OF THE UNIVERSE

ENTRANCE ANTIPHON   *Revelation 5:12; 1:6*

How worthy is the Lamb who was slain,
to receive power and divinity,
and wisdom and strength and honour.
To him belong glory and power for ever and ever.

▷ *page 7*

COLLECT

Almighty ever-living God,
whose will is to restore all things
in your beloved Son, the King of the universe,
grant, we pray,
that the whole creation, set free from slavery,
may render your majesty service
and ceaselessly proclaim your praise.
Through our Lord Jesus Christ, your Son,
who lives and reigns with you in the unity of the Holy Spirit,
one God, for ever and ever.   **Amen.**

FIRST READING   *Daniel 7:13–14*

His sovereignty is an eternal sovereignty.

I gazed into the visions of the night. And I saw, coming on the clouds of heaven, one like a son of man. He came to the one of great age and was led into his presence. On him was conferred sovereignty, glory and kingship, and men of all peoples, nations and languages became his servants. His sovereignty is an eternal sovereignty which shall never pass away, nor will his empire be destroyed.

The word of the Lord.
Thanks be to God.

RESPONSORIAL PSALM   *Psalm 92:1–2, 5 response v 1*

The Lord is king, with majesty enrobed.

1   The Lord is king, with majesty enrobed;
the Lord has robed himself with might,
he has girded himself with power.

2   The world you made firm, not to be moved;
your throne has stood firm from of old.
From all eternity, O Lord, you are.

3   Truly your decrees are to be trusted.
Holiness is fitting to your house,
O Lord, until the end of time.

SECOND READING   *Apocalypse 1:5–8*

Rulers of the kings of the earth... he made us a line of kings, priests to serve his God.

Jesus Christ is the faithful witness, the First-born from the dead, the Ruler of the kings of the earth. He loves us and has washed away our sins with his blood, and made us a line of kings, priests to serve his God and Father; to him, then, be glory and power for ever and ever. Amen. It is he who is coming on the clouds; everyone will see him, even those who pierced him, and all the races of the earth will mourn over him. This is the truth. Amen. 'I am the Alpha and the Omega' says the Lord God, who is, who was, and who is to come, the Almighty.

The word of the Lord.
Thanks be to God.

GOSPEL ACCLAMATION   *Mark 11:9, 10*

**Alleluia, alleluia!
Blessings on him who comes in the name of the Lord!
Blessings on the coming kingdom of our father David!
Alleluia!**

GOSPEL   *John 18:33–37*

The Lord be with you.
And with your spirit.

A reading from the holy Gospel according to John.
Glory to you, O Lord.

It is you who say that I am a king.

'Are you the king of the Jews?' Pilate asked. Jesus replied, 'Do you ask this of your own accord, or have others spoken to you about me?' Pilate answered, 'Am I a Jew? It is your own people and the chief priests who have handed you over to me: what have you done?' Jesus replied, 'Mine is not a kingdom of this world; if my kingdom were of this world, my men would have fought to prevent my being surrendered to the Jews. But my kingdom is not of this kind.' 'So you are a king then?' said Pilate. 'It is you who say it' answered Jesus. 'Yes, I am a king. I was born for this I came into the world for this: to bear witness to the truth; and all who are on the side of truth listen to my voice.'

The Gospel of the Lord.
Praise to you, Lord Jesus Christ.

▷ page 11

PRAYER OVER THE OFFERINGS

As we offer you, O Lord, the sacrifice
by which the human race is reconciled to you,
we humbly pray,
that your Son himself may bestow on all nations
the gifts of unity and peace.
Through Christ our Lord.   **Amen.**

▷ page 15

Preface: Christ, King of the Universe, page 70.

COMMUNION ANTIPHON   *Psalm 28:10–11*

The Lord sits as King for ever.
The Lord will bless his people with peace.

▷ page 59

PRAYER AFTER COMMUNION

Having received the food of immortality,
we ask, O Lord,
that, glorying in obedience
to the commands of Christ, the King of the universe,
we may live with him eternally in his heavenly Kingdom.
Who lives and reigns for ever and ever.   **Amen.**

▷ page 59

PROPER OF SAINTS

NATIVITY OF ST JOHN THE BAPTIST — VIGIL MASS

24 JUNE

If this Solemnity falls on a Sunday, it replaces the Sunday in Ordinary Time.
This Mass is used on the evening of 23 June.

ENTRANCE ANTIPHON   *Luke 1:15, 14*

He will be great in the sight of the Lord
and will be filled with the Holy Spirit,
even from his mother's womb;
and many will rejoice at his birth.

▷ *page 7*

The Gloria is sung (said)

COLLECT

Grant, we pray, almighty God,
that your family may walk in the way of salvation
and, attentive to what Saint John the Precursor urged,
may come safely to the One he foretold,
our Lord Jesus Christ.
Who lives and reigns with you in the unity of the Holy Spirit,
one God, for ever and ever.   **Amen.**

FIRST READING   *Jeremiah 1:4–10*

Before I formed you in the womb, I knew you.

The word of the Lord was addressed to me, saying,

'Before I formed you in the womb I knew you; before you came to birth I consecrated you; I have appointed you as prophet to the nations.'

I said, 'Ah, Lord; look, I do not know how to speak: I am a child!' But the Lord replied,

'Do not say, "I am a child." Go now to those to whom I send you and say whatever I command you. Do not be afraid of them, for I am with you to protect you – it is the Lord who speaks!'

Then the Lord put out his hand and touched my mouth and said to me:

'There! I am putting my words into your mouth. Look, today I am setting you over nations and over kingdoms, to tear up and to knock down, to destroy and to overthrow, to build and to plant.'

The word of the Lord.
Thanks be to God.

RESPONSORIAL PSALM   *Psalm 70:1–6, 15, 17 response v 6*

From my mother's womb you have been my help.

1   In you, O Lord, I take refuge:
    let me never be put to shame.
    In your justice rescue me, free me:
    pay heed to me and save me.

2   Be a rock where I can take refuge,
    a mighty stronghold to save me;
    for you are my rock, my stronghold.
    Free me from the hand of the wicked.

3   It is you, O Lord, who are my hope,
     my trust, O Lord, since my youth.
     On you I have leaned from my birth,
     from my mother's womb you have been my help.

4   My lips will tell of your justice
     and day by day of your help.
     O God, you have taught me from my youth
     and I proclaim your wonders still.

SECOND READING   *1 Peter 1:8–12*

It was this salvation that the prophets were looking and searching so hard for.

You not see Jesus Christ, yet you love him; and still without seeing him, you are already filled with a joy so glorious that it cannot he described, because you believe; and you are sure of the end to which your faith looks forward, that is, the salvation of your souls.

It was this salvation that the prophets were looking and searching so hard for; their prophecies were about the grace which was to come to you. The Spirit of Christ which was in them foretold the sufferings of Christ and the glories that would come after them, and they tried to find out at what time and in what circumstances all this was to be expected. It was revealed to them that the news they brought of all the things which have now been announced to you, by those who preached to you the Good News through the Holy Spirit sent from heaven, was for you and not for themselves. Even the angels long to catch a glimpse of these things.

The word of the Lord.
Thanks be to God.

GOSPEL ACCLAMATION   *John 1:7; Luke 1:17*

Alleluia, alleluia!
He came as a witness,
to speak for the light,
preparing for the Lord a people fit for him
Alleluia!

GOSPEL   *Luke 1:5–17*

The Lord be with you.
And with your spirit.

A reading from the holy Gospel according to Luke.
Glory to you, O Lord.

She is to bear you a son and you must name him John.

In the days of King Herod of Judaea there lived a priest called Zechariah who belonged to the Abijah section of the priesthood, and he had a wife, Elizabeth by name, who was a descendant of Aaron. Both were worthy in the sight of God, and scrupulously observed all the commandments and observances of the Lord. But they were childless: Elizabeth was barren and they were both getting on in years.

Now it was the turn of Zechariah's section to serve, and he was exercising his priestly office before God when it fell to him by lot, as the ritual custom was, to enter the Lord's sanctuary and burn incense there. And at the hour of incense the whole congregation was outside, praying.

Then there appeared to him the angel of the Lord, standing on the right of the altar of incense. The sight disturbed Zechariah and he was overcome with fear. But the angel said to him, 'Zechariah, do not be afraid, your prayer has been heard. Your wife Elizabeth is to bear you a son and you must name him John. He will be your joy and delight and many will rejoice at his birth, for he will be great in the sight of the Lord; he must drink no wine, no strong drink. Even from his mother's womb he will be filled with the Holy Spirit, and he will bring back many of the sons of Israel to the Lord their God. With the spirit and power of Elijah, he will go before him to turn the hearts of fathers towards their children and the disobedient back to the wisdom that the virtuous have, preparing for the Lord a people fit for him.'

The Gospel of the Lord.
Praise to you, Lord Jesus Christ.

▷ page 11

PROFESSION OF FAITH
The Profession of Faith is said.

PRAYER OVER THE OFFERINGS
Look with favour, O Lord,
upon the offerings made by your people
on the Solemnity of Saint John the Baptist,
and grant that what we celebrate in mystery
we may follow with deeds of devoted service.
Through Christ our Lord.   **Amen.**

▷ page 15

Preface: The mission of the Precursor, page 71.

COMMUNION ANTIPHON   *Luke 1:68*
Blessed be the Lord, the God of Israel!
He has visited his people and redeemed them.

▷ page 59

PRAYER AFTER COMMUNION
May the marvellous prayer of Saint John the Baptist
accompany us who have eaten our fill
at this sacrificial feast, O Lord,
and, since Saint John proclaimed your Son
to be the Lamb who would take away our sins,
may he implore now for us your favour.
Through Christ our Lord.   **Amen.**

▷ page 59

NATIVITY OF ST JOHN THE BAPTIST – MASS DURING THE DAY

24 JUNE

If this Solemnity falls on a Sunday, it replaces the Sunday in Ordinary Time.

ENTRANCE ANTIPHON   *John 1: 6–7; Luke 1:17*
A man was sent from God, whose name was John.
He came to testify to the light,
to prepare a people fit for the Lord.

▷ *page 7*

The Gloria is sung (said)

COLLECT
O God, who raised up Saint John the Baptist
to make ready a nation fit for Christ the Lord,
give your people, we pray,
the grace of spiritual joys
and direct the hearts of all the faithful
into the way of salvation and peace.
Through our Lord Jesus Christ, your Son,
who lives and reigns with you in the unity of the Holy Spirit,
one God, for ever and ever.   **Amen.**

SAINTS

FIRST READING   *Isaiah 49:1–6*
I will make you the light of the nations.

Islands, listen to me, pay attention remotest peoples. The Lord called me before I was born, from my mother's womb he pronounced my name.

He made my mouth a sharp sword, and hid me in the shadow of his hand. He made me into a sharpened arrow. and concealed me in his quiver.

He said to me, 'You are my servant (Israel) in whom I shall be glorified': while I was thinking, 'I have toiled in vain, I have exhausted myself for nothing':

and all the while my cause was with the Lord, my reward with my God. I was honoured in the eyes of the Lord, my God was my strength.

And now the Lord has spoken, he who formed me in the womb to be his servant, to bring Jacob back to him, to gather Israel to him:

'It is not enough for you to be my servant, to restore the tribes of Jacob and bring back the survivors of Israel; I will make you the light of the nations so that my salvation may reach to the ends of the earth.'

The word of the Lord.
Thanks be to God.

RESPONSORIAL PSALM   *Psalm 138:1–3, 13–15 response v 14*

I thank you for the wonder of my being.

1   O Lord, you search me and you know me,
you know my resting and my rising,
you discern my purpose from afar.
You mark when I walk or lie down,
all my ways lie open to you.

continued...

I thank you for the wonder of my being.

2 For it was you who created my being,
   knit me together in my mother's womb.
   I thank you for the wonder of my being,
   for the wonders of all your creation.

3 Already you knew my soul,
   my body held no secret from you
   when I was being fashioned in secret
   and moulded in the depths of the earth.

SECOND READING   *Acts 13:22–26*

Jesus, whose coming was heralded by John.

Paul said: 'God made David the king of our ancestors, of whom he approved in these words. "I have selected David son of Jesse, a man after my own heart, who will carry out my whole purpose." To keep his promise, God has raised up for Israel one of David's descendants, Jesus, as Saviour, whose coming was heralded by John when he proclaimed a baptism of repentance for the whole people of Israel. Before John ended his career he said, "I am not the one you imagine me to be; that one is coming after me and I am not fit to undo his sandal."

'My brothers, sons of Abraham's race, and all you who fear God, this message of salvation is meant for you.'

The word of the Lord.
Thanks be to God.

GOSPEL ACCLAMATION   *cf Luke 1:76*

Alleluia, alleluia!
As for you, little child, you shall be called
a prophet of God, the Most High.
You shall go ahead of the Lord
to prepare his ways before him.
Alleluia!

GOSPEL   *Luke 1:57–66, 80*

The Lord be with you.
And with your spirit.

A reading from the holy Gospel according to Luke.
Glory to you, O Lord.

His name is John.

The time came for Elizabeth to have her child, and she gave birth to a son; and when her neighbours and relations heard that the Lord had shown her so great a kindness, they shared her joy.

Now on the eighth day they came to circumcise the child; they were going to call him Zechariah after his father, but his mother spoke up. 'No,' she said 'he is to be called John.' They said to her, 'But no one in your family has that name', and made signs to his father to find out what he wanted him called. The father asked for a writing tablet and wrote, 'His name is John.' And they were all astonished. At that instant his power of speech returned and he spoke and praised God. All their neighbours were filled with awe and the whole affair was talked about throughout the hill country of Judaea. All those who heard of it treasured it in their hearts. 'What will this child turn out to be?' they wondered. And indeed the hand of the Lord was with him. The child grew up and his spirit matured. And he lived out in the wilderness until the day he appeared openly to Israel.

The Gospel of the Lord.
Praise to you, Lord Jesus Christ.

▷ *page 11*

PROFESSION OF FAITH
The Profession of Faith is said.

PRAYER OVER THE OFFERINGS
We place these offerings on your altar, O Lord,
to celebrate with fitting honour the nativity of him
who both foretold the coming of the world's Saviour
and pointed him out when he came.
Who lives and reigns for ever and ever.   **Amen.**

▷ *page 15*

Preface: The mission of the Precursor, page 71.

COMMUNION ANTIPHON   *cf Luke 1:78*
Through the tender mercy of our God,
the Dawn from on high will visit us.

▷ *page 59*

PRAYER AFTER COMMUNION
Having feasted at the banquet of the heavenly Lamb,
we pray, O Lord,
that, finding joy in the nativity of Saint John the Baptist,
your Church may know as the author of her rebirth
the Christ whose coming John foretold.
Who lives and reigns for ever and ever.   **Amen.**

▷ *page 59*

SS PETER AND PAUL, APOSTLES — VIGIL MASS

29 JUNE

This Mass is used on the evening before the Solemnity.

If this Solemnity falls on a Sunday, it replaces the Sunday in Ordinary Time.
In certain territories, this Solemnity may be transferred to the nearest Sunday,
replacing the Sunday in Ordinary Time.

ENTRANCE ANTIPHON
Peter the Apostle, and Paul the teacher of the Gentiles,
these have taught us your law, O Lord.

The Gloria is sung (said)

▷ *page 7*

COLLECT

Grant, we pray, O Lord our God,
that we may be sustained
by the intercession of the blessed Apostles Peter and Paul,
that, as through them you gave your Church
the foundations of her heavenly office,
so through them you may help her to eternal salvation.
Through our Lord Jesus Christ, your Son,
who lives and reigns with you in the unity of the Holy Spirit,
one God, for ever and ever. **Amen.**

FIRST READING   Acts 3:1–10

I will give you what I have: in the name of Jesus stand up and walk!

Once, when Peter and John were going up to the Temple for the prayers at the ninth hour, it happened that there was a man being carried past. He was a cripple from birth; and they used to put him down every day near the Temple entrance called the Beautiful Gate so that he could beg from the people going in. When this man saw Peter and John on their way into the Temple he begged from them. Both Peter and John looked straight at him and said, 'Look at us.' He turned to them expectantly, hoping to get something from them, but Peter said, 'I have neither silver nor gold, but I will give you what I have: in the name of Jesus Christ the Nazarene, walk!' Peter then took him by the hand and helped him to stand up. Instantly his feet and ankles became firm, he jumped up, stood, and began to walk, and he went with them into the Temple, walking and jumping and praising God. Everyone could see him walking and praising God, and they recognised him as the man who used to sit begging at the Beautiful Gate of the Temple. They were all astonished and unable to explain what had happened to him.

The word of the Lord.
Thanks be to God.

RESPONSORIAL PSALM   Psalm 18:2–5 response v 5

Their word goes forth through all the earth.

1 The heavens proclaim the glory of God
and the firmament shows forth the work of his hands.
Day unto day takes up the story
and night unto night makes known the message.

2 No speech, no word, no voice is heard
yet their span extends through all the earth,
their words to the utmost bounds of the world.

SECOND READING   Galatians 1:11–20

God specially chose me while I was still in my mother's womb.

The Good News I preached is not a human message that I was given by men, it is something I learnt only through a revelation of Jesus Christ. You must have heard of my career as a practising Jew, how merciless I was in persecuting the Church of God, how much damage I did to it, how I stood out among other Jews of my generation, and how enthusiastic I was for the traditions of my ancestors.

Then God, who had specially chosen me while I was still in my mother's womb, called me through his grace and chose to reveal his Son to me, so that I might preach the Good News about him to the pagans. I did not stop to discuss this with any human being, nor did I go up to Jerusalem to see those who were already apostles before me, but I went off to Arabia at once and later went straight back from there to Damascus. Even when after three years I went up to Jerusalem to visit Cephas and stayed with him for fifteen days, I did not see any of the other apostles; I only saw James, the brother of the Lord, and I swear before God that what I have just written is the literal truth.

The word of the Lord.
Thanks be to God.

GOSPEL ACCLAMATION   *John 21:17*

Alleluia, alleluia!
Lord, you know everything;
you know I love you.
Alleluia!

GOSPEL   *John 21:15–19*

The Lord be with you.
And with your spirit.

A reading from the holy Gospel according to John.
Glory to you, O Lord.

Feed my lambs, feed my sheep.

After Jesus had shown himself to his disciples and eaten with them, he said to Simon Peter, 'Simon son of John, do you love me more than these others do?' He answered, 'Yes, Lord, you know I love you.' Jesus said to him, 'Feed my lambs.' A second time he said to him, 'Simon son of John, do you love me?' He replied, 'Yes, Lord, you know I love you.' Jesus said to him, 'Look after my sheep.' Then he said to him a third time, 'Simon son of John, do you love me?' Peter was upset that he asked him the third time, 'Do you love me?' and said, 'Lord, you know everything; you know I love you.' Jesus said to him, 'Feed my sheep.

'I tell you most solemnly, when you were young you put on your own belt and walked where you liked; but when you grow old you will stretch out your hands, and somebody else will put a belt round you and take you where you would rather not go.'

In these words he indicated the kind of death by which Peter would give glory to God. After this he said, 'Follow me.'

The Gospel of the Lord.
Praise to you, Lord Jesus Christ.

▷ *page 11*

PROFESSION OF FAITH
The Profession of Faith is said.

SAINTS

PRAYER OVER THE OFFERINGS

We bring offerings to your altar, O Lord,
as we glory in the solemn feast
of the blessed Apostles Peter and Paul,
so that the more we doubt our own merits,
the more we may rejoice that we are to be saved
by your loving kindness.
Through Christ our Lord.   **Amen.**

▷ *page 15*

Preface: The twofold mission of Peter and Paul in the Church, page 71.

COMMUNION ANTIPHON   *cf John 21:15, 17*

Simon, Son of John, do you love me more than these?
Lord, you know everything; you know that I love you.

▷ *page 59*

PRAYER AFTER COMMUNION

By this heavenly Sacrament, O Lord, we pray,
strengthen your faithful,
whom you have enlightened with the teaching of the Apostles.
Through Christ our Lord.   **Amen.**

▷ *page 59*

A solemn blessing may be used.

 # SS PETER AND PAUL, APOSTLES — MASS DURING THE DAY

If this Solemnity falls on a Sunday, it replaces the Sunday in Ordinary Time.
In certain territories, this Solemnity may be transferred to the nearest Sunday,
replacing the Sunday in Ordinary Time.

ENTRANCE ANTIPHON

These are the ones who, living in the flesh,
planted the Church with their blood;
they drank the chalice of the Lord
and became the friends of God.

▷ *page 7*

The Gloria is sung (said).

COLLECT

O God, who on the Solemnity of the Apostles Peter and Paul
give us the noble and holy joy of this day,
grant, we pray, that your Church
may in all things follow the teaching
of those through whom she received
the beginnings of right religion.
Through our Lord Jesus Christ, your Son,
who lives and reigns with you in the unity of the Holy Spirit,
one God, for ever and ever.   **Amen.**

FIRST READING   *Acts 12:1–11*

Now I know the Lord really did save me from Herod.

King Herod started persecuting certain members of the Church. He beheaded James the brother of John, and when he saw that this pleased the Jews he decided to arrest Peter as well. This was during the days of Unleavened Bread, and he put Peter in prison, assigning four squads of four soldiers each to guard him in turns. Herod meant to try Peter in public after the end of the Passover week. All the time Peter was under guard the Church prayed to God for him unremittingly.

On the night before Herod was to try him, Peter was sleeping between two soldiers, fastened with double chains, while guards kept watch at the main entrance to the prison. Then suddenly the angel of the Lord stood there, and the cell was filled with light. He tapped Peter on the side and woke him. 'Get up!' he said 'Hurry!' – and the chains fell from his hands. The angel then said, 'Put on your belt and sandals.' After he had done this, the angel next said, 'Wrap your cloak round you and follow me.' Peter followed him, but had no idea that what the angel did was all happening in reality; he thought he was seeing a vision. They passed through two guard posts one after the other, and reached the iron gate leading to the city. This opened of its own accord; they went through it and had walked the whole length of one street when suddenly the angel left him. It was only then that Peter came to himself. 'Now I know it is all true,' he said. 'The Lord really did send his angel and has saved me from Herod and from all that the Jewish people were so certain would happen to me.'

The word of the Lord.
Thanks be to God.

RESPONSORIAL PSALM   *Psalm 33:2–9 response v 5; alternative response v 8*

From all my terrors the Lord set me free.

or

The angel of the Lord rescues those who revere him.

1   I will bless the Lord at all times,
    his praise always on my lips;
    in the Lord my soul shall make its boast.
    The humble shall hear and be glad.

2   Glorify the Lord with me.
    Together let us praise his name
    I sought the Lord and he answered me;
    from all my terrors he set me free.

3   Look towards him and be radiant;
    let your faces not be abashed.
    This poor man called; the Lord heard him
    and rescued him from all his distress.

4   The angel of the Lord is encamped
    around those who revere him, to rescue them.
    Taste and see that the Lord is good.
    He is happy who seeks refuge in him.

SECOND READING   *2 Timothy 4:6–8, 17–18*

All there is to come now is the crown of righteousness reserved for me.

My life is already being poured away as a libation, and the time has come for me to be gone. I have fought the good fight to the end; I have run the race to the finish; I have kept the faith; all there is to come now is the crown of righteousness reserved for me, which the Lord, the righteous judge, will give to me on that Day; and not only to me but to all those who have longed for his Appearing.

The Lord stood by me and gave me power, so that through me the whole message might be proclaimed for all the pagans to hear; and so I was rescued from the lion's mouth. The Lord will rescue me from all evil attempts on me, and bring me safely to his heavenly kingdom. To him be glory for ever and ever. Amen.

The word of the Lord.
Thanks be to God.

GOSPEL ACCLAMATION   *Matthew 16:18*

Alleluia, alleluia!
You are Peter and on this rock I will build my Church.
And the gates of the underworld can never hold out against it.
Alleluia!

GOSPEL   *Matthew 16:13–19*

The Lord be with you.
And with your spirit.

A reading from the holy Gospel according to Matthew.
Glory to you, O Lord.

You are Peter, and I will give you the keys of the kingdom of heaven.

When Jesus came to the region of Caesarea Philippi he put this question to his disciples, 'Who do people say the Son of Man is?' And they said, 'Some say he is John the Baptist, some Elijah, and others Jeremiah or one of the prophets.' 'But you,' he said, 'who do you say I am?' Then Simon Peter spoke up. 'You are the Christ,' he said 'the Son of the living God.' Jesus replied, 'Simon son of Jonah, you are a happy man! Because it was not flesh and blood that revealed this to you but my Father in heaven. So I now say to you: You are Peter and on this rock I will build my Church. And the gates of the underworld can never hold out against it. I will give you the keys of the kingdom of heaven: whatever you bind on earth shall be considered bound in heaven; whatever you loose on earth shall be considered loosed in heaven.'

The Gospel of the Lord.
Praise to you, Lord Jesus Christ.

▷ *page 11*

PROFESSION OF FAITH
The Profession of Faith is said.

PRAYER OVER THE OFFERINGS
May the prayer of the Apostles, O Lord,
accompany the sacrificial gift
that we present to your name for consecration,
and may their intercession make us devoted to you
in celebration of the sacrifice.
Through Christ our Lord.   **Amen.**

▷ *page 15*

Preface: The twofold mission of Peter and Paul in the Church, page 71.

COMMUNION ANTIPHON   *cf Matthew 16:16, 18*
Peter said to Jesus: You are the Christ, the Son of the living God.
And Jesus replied: You are Peter,
and upon this rock I will build my Church.

▷ *page 59*

PRAYER AFTER COMMUNION
Grant us, O Lord,
who have been renewed by this Sacrament,
so to live in the Church,
that, persevering in the breaking of the Bread
and in the teaching of the Apostles,
we may be one heart and one soul,
made steadfast in your love.
Through Christ our Lord.   **Amen.**

▷ *page 59*

A solemn blessing may be used.

SAINTS

TRANSFIGURATION OF THE LORD

6 AUGUST
If this feast falls on a Sunday, it replaces the Sunday in Ordinary Time.
When the Feast is celebrated on a weekday there is only one reading before the Gospel.

ENTRANCE ANTIPHON   *cf Matthew 17:5*
In a resplendent cloud the Holy Spirit appeared.
The Father's voice was heard: This is my beloved Son,
with whom I am well pleased. Listen to him.

▷ *page 7*

The Gloria is sung (said)

COLLECT
O God, who in the glorious Transfiguration
of your Only Begotten Son
confirmed the mysteries of faith by the witness of the Fathers
and wonderfully prefigured our full adoption to sonship,
grant, we pray, to your servants,
that, listening to the voice of your beloved Son,
we may merit to become coheirs with him.
Who lives and reigns with you in the unity of the Holy Spirit,
one God, for ever and ever.   **Amen.**

FIRST READING   *Daniel 7:9–10, 13–14*

His robe was white as snow.

As I watched: Thrones were set in place and one of great age took his seat. His robe was white as snow, the hair of his head as pure as wool. His throne was a blaze of flames, its wheels were a burning fire. A stream of fire poured out, issuing from his presence. A thousand thousand waited on him, ten thousand times ten thousand stood before him. A court was held and the books were opened. I gazed into the visions of the night. And I saw, coming on the clouds of heaven, one like a son of man. He came to the one of great age and was led into his presence. On him was conferred sovereignty, glory and kingship, and men of all peoples, nations and languages became his servants. His sovereignty is an eternal sovereignty which shall never pass away, nor will his empire ever be destroyed.

The word of the Lord.
Thanks be to God.

RESPONSORIAL PSALM   *Psalm 96:1–2, 5–6, 9 response vv 1, 9*

The Lord is king,
most high above all the earth.

1   The Lord is king, let earth rejoice,
let all the coastlands be glad.
Cloud and darkness are his raiment;
his throne, justice and right.

2   The mountains melt like wax
before the Lord of all the earth.
The skies proclaim his justice;
all peoples see his glory.

3   For you indeed are the Lord
most high above all the earth
exalted far above all spirits.

SECOND READING   *2 Peter 1:16–19*

We heard this ourselves, spoken from heaven.

It was not any cleverly invented myths that we were repeating when we brought you the knowledge of the power and the coming of our Lord Jesus Christ; we had seen his majesty for ourselves. He was honoured and glorified by God the Father, when the Sublime Glory itself spoke to him and said, 'This is my Son, the Beloved; he enjoys my favour.' We heard this ourselves, spoken from heaven, when we were with him on the holy mountain.

So we have confirmation of what was said in prophecies; and you will be right to depend on prophecy and take it as a lamp for lighting a way through the dark until the dawn comes and the morning star rises in your minds.

The word of the Lord.
Thanks be to God.

GOSPEL ACCLAMATION   *Matthew 17:5*

Alleluia, alleluia!
This is my Son, the Beloved,
he enjoys my favour;
listen to him.
Alleluia!

GOSPEL   *Mark 9:2–10*

The Lord be with you.
And with your spirit.

A reading from the holy Gospel according to Mark.
Glory to you, O Lord.

This is my Son, the Beloved.

Jesus took with him Peter and James and John and led them up a high mountain where they could be alone by themselves. There in their presence he was transfigured: his clothes became dazzlingly white, whiter than any earthly bleacher could make them. Elijah appeared to them with Moses; and they were talking with Jesus. Then Peter spoke to Jesus: 'Rabbi,' he said 'it is wonderful for us to be here; so let us make three tents, one for you, one for Moses and one for Elijah.' He did not know what to say; they were so frightened. And a cloud came, covering them in shadow; and there came a voice from the cloud, 'This is my Son, the Beloved. Listen to him.' Then suddenly, when they looked round, they saw no one with them any more but only Jesus.

As they came down from the mountain he warned them to tell no one what they had seen, until after the Son of Man had risen from the dead. They observed the warning faithfully, though among themselves they discussed what 'rising from the dead' could mean.

The Gospel of the Lord.
Praise to you, Lord Jesus Christ.

▷ *page 11*

SAINTS

PROFESSION OF FAITH
The Profession of Faith is said when this feast is celebrated on Sunday.

PRAYER OVER THE OFFERINGS
Sanctify, O Lord, we pray,
these offerings here made to celebrate
the glorious Transfiguration of your Only Begotten Son,
and by his radiant splendour
cleanse us from the stains of sin.
Through Christ our Lord.   **Amen.**

▷ *page 15*

Preface: The Mystery of the Transfiguration, page 72.

COMMUNION ANTIPHON   *cf 1 John 3:2*
When Christ appears, we shall be like him,
for we shall see him as he is.

▷ *page 59*

PRAYER AFTER COMMUNION
May the heavenly nourishment we have received,
O Lord, we pray,
transform us into the likeness of your Son,
whose radiant splendour you willed to make manifest
in his glorious Transfiguration.
Who lives and reigns for ever and ever.   **Amen.**

▷ *page 59*

ASSUMPTION OF THE BLESSED VIRGIN — VIGIL MASS

ASSUMPTION OF THE BLESSED VIRGIN MARY
15 AUGUST

This Mass is used on the evening before the Solemnity.

If this Solemnity falls on a Sunday, it replaces the Sunday in Ordinary Time.
In certain territories, this Solemnity may be transferred to the nearest Sunday,
replacing the Sunday in Ordinary Time.

ENTRANCE ANTIPHON

Glorious things are spoken of you, O Mary,
who today were exalted above the choirs of Angels
into eternal triumph with Christ.

▷ *page 7*

The Gloria is sung (said)

COLLECT

O God, who, looking on the lowliness of the Blessed Virgin Mary,
raised her to this grace,
that your Only Begotten Son was born of her according to the flesh
and that she was crowned this day with surpassing glory,
grant through her prayers,
that, saved by the mystery of your redemption,
we may merit to be exalted by you on high.
Through our Lord Jesus Christ, your Son,
who lives and reigns with you in the unity of the Holy Spirit,
one God, for ever and ever. **Amen.**

FIRST READING   *1 Chronicles 15:3–4, 15–16; 16:1–2*

They brought in the ark of God and set it inside the tent which David had pitched for it.

David gathered all Israel together in Jerusalem to bring the ark of God up to the place he had prepared for it. David called together the sons of Aaron and the sons of Levi. And the Levites carried the ark of God with the shafts on their shoulders, as Moses had ordered in accordance with the word of the Lord.

David then told the heads of the Levites to assign duties for their kinsmen as cantors, with their various instruments of music, harps and lyres and cymbals, to play joyful tunes. They brought the ark of God in and put it inside the tent that David had pitched for it: and they offered holocausts before God, and communion sacrifices. And when David had finished offering holocausts and communion sacrifices, he blessed the people in the name of the Lord.

The word of the Lord.
Thanks be to God.

RESPONSORIAL PSALM *Psalm 131:6–7, 9–10, 13–14 response v 8*

**Go up, Lord, to the place of your rest,
you and the ark of your strength.**

1 At Ephrata we heard of the ark;
we found it in the plains of Yearim.
'Let us go to the place of his dwelling;
let us go to kneel at his footstool.'

2 Your priests shall be clothed with holiness:
your faithful shall ring out their joy.
For the sake of David your servant
do not reject your anointed.

3 For the Lord has chosen Zion;
he has desired it for his dwelling:
'This is my resting-place for ever,
here have I chosen to live.'

SECOND READING *1 Corinthians 15:54–57*

He gave us victory through our Lord Jesus Christ.

When this perishable nature has put on imperishability, and when this mortal nature has put on immortality, then the words of scripture will come true: Death is swallowed up in victory. Death, where is your victory? Death, where is your sting? Now the sting of death is sin and sin gets its power from the Law. So let us thank God for giving us the victory through our Lord Jesus Christ.

The word of the Lord.
Thanks be to God.

GOSPEL ACCLAMATION *Luke 11:28*

**Alleluia, alleluia!
Happy are those
who hear the word of God,
and keep it.
Alleluia!**

GOSPEL *Luke 11:27–28*

The Lord be with you.
And with your spirit.

A reading from the holy Gospel according to Luke.
Glory to you, O Lord.

Happy the womb that bore you

As Jesus was speaking, a woman in the crowd raised her voice and said, 'Happy the womb that bore you and the breasts you sucked!' But he replied, 'Still happier those who hear the word of God and keep it!'

The Gospel of the Lord.
Praise to you, Lord Jesus Christ.

▷ page 11

SAINTS

PROFESSION OF FAITH
The Profession of Faith is said.

PRAYER OVER THE OFFERINGS
Receive, we pray, O Lord,
the sacrifice of conciliation and praise,
which we celebrate on the Assumption of the holy Mother of God,
that it may lead us to your pardon
and confirm us in perpetual thanksgiving.
Through Christ our Lord.   **Amen.**

▷ *page 15*

Preface: The Glory of Mary assumed into heaven, page 72.

COMMUNION ANTIPHON   *cf Luke 11:27*
Blessed is the womb of the Virgin Mary,
which bore the Son of the eternal Father.

▷ *page 59*

PRAYER AFTER COMMUNION
Having partaken of this heavenly table,
we beseech your mercy, Lord our God,
that we, who honour the Assumption of the Mother of God,
may be freed from every threat of harm.
Through Christ our Lord.   **Amen.**

▷ *page 59*

A solemn blessing may be used.

ASSUMPTION OF THE BLESSED VIRGIN — DURING THE DAY

ASSUMPTION OF THE BLESSED VIRGIN MARY
15 AUGUST

If this Solemnity falls on a Sunday, it replaces the Sunday in Ordinary Time.
In certain territories, this Solemnity may be transferred to the nearest Sunday,
replacing the Sunday in Ordinary Time.

ENTRANCE ANTIPHON   *cf Revelation 12:1*
A great sign appeared in heaven:
a woman clothed with the sun, and the moon beneath her feet,
and on her head a crown of twelve stars.
or

Let us all rejoice in the Lord,
as we celebrate the feast day in honour of the Virgin Mary,
at whose Assumption the Angels rejoice
and praise the Son of God.

The Gloria is sung (said)

▷ *page 7*

COLLECT

Almighty ever-living God,
who assumed the Immaculate Virgin Mary, the Mother of your Son,
body and soul into heavenly glory,
grant, we pray,
that, always attentive to the things that are above,
we may merit to be sharers of her glory.
Through our Lord Jesus Christ, your Son,
who lives and reigns with you in the unity of the Holy Spirit,
one God, for ever and ever.   **Amen.**

FIRST READING   *Apocalypse 11:19; 12:1–6, 10*

A woman adorned with the sun, standing on the moon.

The sanctuary of God in heaven opened, and the ark of the covenant could be seen inside it.

Now a great sign appeared in heaven: a woman, adorned with the sun, standing on the moon, and with the twelve stars on her head for a crown. She was pregnant, and in labour, crying aloud in the pangs of childbirth. Then a second sign appeared in the sky, a huge red dragon which had seven heads and ten horns, and each of the seven heads crowned with a coronet. Its tail dragged a third of the stars from the sky and dropped them to the earth, and the dragon stopped in front of the woman as she was having the child, so that he could eat it as soon as it was born from its mother. The woman brought a male child into the world, the son who was to rule all the nations with an iron sceptre, and the child was taken straight up to God and to his throne, while the woman escaped into the desert, where God had made a place of safety ready. Then I heard a voice shout from heaven. 'Victory and power and empire for ever have been won by our God, and all authority for his Christ.'

The word of the Lord.

Thanks be to God.

RESPONSORIAL PSALM   *Psalm 44:10–12, 16 response v 10*

**On your right stands the queen,
in garments of gold.**

1   The daughters of kings are among your loved ones.
    On your right stands the queen in gold of Ophir.
    Listen, O daughter, give ear to my words:
    forget your own people and your father's house.

2   So will the king desire your beauty:
    he is your lord, pay homage to him.
    They are escorted amid gladness and joy;
    they pass within the palace of the king.

SECOND READING   *1 Corinthians 15:20–26*

Christ as the first-fruits and then, those who belong to him.

Christ has been raised from the dead, the first-fruits of all who have fallen asleep. Death came through one man and in the same way the resurrection of the dead has come through one man. Just as all men die in Adam, so all men will be brought to life in Christ; but all of them in their proper order: Christ as the first-fruits and then, after the coming of Christ, those who belong to him. After that will come the end, when he hands over the kingdom to God the Father, having done away with every sovereignty, authority and power. For he must be king until he has put all his enemies under his feet and the last of the enemies to be destroyed is death, for everything is to be put under his feet.

The word of the Lord.
Thanks be to God.

GOSPEL ACCLAMATION

Alleluia, alleluia!
Mary has been taken up into heaven;
all the choirs of angels are rejoicing.
Alleluia!

GOSPEL   *Luke 1:39–56*

The Lord be with you.
And with your spirit.

A reading from the holy Gospel according to Luke.
Glory to you, O Lord.

The Almighty has done great things for me, he has exalted the lowly.

Mary set out and went as quickly as she could to a town in the hill country of Judah. She went into Zechariah's house and greeted Elizabeth. Now as soon as Elizabeth heard Mary's greeting, the child leapt in her womb and Elizabeth was filled with the Holy Spirit. She gave a loud cry and said, 'Of all women you are the most blessed, and blessed is the fruit of your womb. Why should I be honoured with a visit from the mother of my Lord? For the moment your greeting reached my ears, the child in my womb leapt for joy. Yes, blessed is she who believed that the promise made her by the Lord would be fulfilled.'

And Mary said:

'My soul proclaims the greatness of the Lord and my spirit exults in God my saviour; because he has looked upon his lowly handmaid. Yes, from this day forward all generations will call me blessed, for the Almighty has done great things for me. Holy is his name, and his mercy reaches from age to age for those who fear him. He has shown the power of his arm, he has routed the proud of heart. He has pulled down princes from their thrones and exalted the lowly. The hungry he has filled with good things, the rich sent empty away. He has come to the help of Israel his servant, mindful of his mercy – according to the promise he made to our ancestors – of his mercy to Abraham and to his descendants for ever.'

Mary stayed with Elizabeth about three months and then went back home.

The Gospel of the Lord.
Praise to you, Lord Jesus Christ.

▷ page 11

PROFESSION OF FAITH
The Profession of Faith is said.

PRAYER OVER THE OFFERINGS
May this oblation, our tribute of homage,
rise up to you, O Lord,
and, through the intercession of the most Blessed Virgin Mary,
whom you assumed into heaven,
may our hearts, aflame with the fire of love,
constantly long for you.
Through Christ our Lord. **Amen.**

▷ *page 15*

Preface: The Glory of Mary assumed into heaven, page 72.

COMMUNION ANTIPHON   *Luke 1:48–49*
All generations will call me blessed,
for he who is mighty has done great things for me.

▷ *page 59*

PRAYER AFTER COMMUNION
Having received the Sacrament of salvation,
we ask you to grant, O Lord,
that, through the intercession of the Blessed Virgin Mary,
whom you assumed into heaven,
we may be brought to the glory of the resurrection.
Through Christ our Lord. **Amen.**

▷ *page 59*

A solemn blessing may be used.

SAINTS

EXALTATION OF THE HOLY CROSS

14 SEPTEMBER
If this feast falls on a Sunday, it replaces the Sunday in Ordinary Time.
When the Feast is celebrated on a weekday there is only one reading before the Gospel.

ENTRANCE ANTIPHON   *cf Galatians 6:14*
We should glory in the Cross of our Lord Jesus Christ,
in whom is our salvation, life and resurrection,
through whom we are saved and delivered.

▷ *page 7*

The Gloria is sung (said)

COLLECT
O God, who willed that your Only Begotten Son
should undergo the Cross to save the human race,
grant, we pray,
that we, who have known his mystery on earth,
may merit the grace of his redemption in heaven.
Through our Lord Jesus Christ, your Son,
who lives and reigns with you in the unity of the Holy Spirit,
one God, for ever and ever. **Amen.**

FIRST READING　*Numbers 21:4-9*

If anyone was bitten by a serpent, he looked at the bronze serpent and lived.

On the way through the wilderness, the Israelites lost patience. They spoke against God and against Moses. 'Why did you bring us out of Egypt to die in this wilderness? For there is neither bread nor water here: we are sick of this unsatisfying food.'

At this God sent fiery serpents among the people; their bite brought death to many in Israel. The people came and said to Moses, 'We have sinned by speaking against the Lord and against you. Intercede for us with the Lord to save us from these serpents.' Moses interceded for the people, and the Lord answered him, 'Make a fiery serpent and put it on a standard. If anyone is bitten and looks at it he shall live.' So Moses fashioned a bronze serpent which he put on a standard, and if anyone was bitten by a serpent, he looked at the bronze serpent and lived.

The word of the Lord.
Thanks be to God.

RESPONSORIAL PSALM　*Psalm 77:1-2, 34-38 response v 7*

Never forget the deeds of the Lord.

1　Give heed, my people, to my teaching;
　　turn your ear to the words of my mouth.
　　I will open my mouth in a parable
　　and reveal hidden lessons of the past.

2　When he slew them then they would seek him,
　　return and seek him in earnest.
　　They would remember that God was their rock,
　　God the Most High their redeemer.

3　But the words they spoke were mere flattery;
　　they lied to him with their lips.
　　For their hearts were not truly with him;
　　they were not faithful to his covenant.

4　Yet he who is full of compassion
　　forgave their sin and spared them.
　　So often he held back his anger
　　when he might have stirred up his rage.

SECOND READING　*Philippians 2:6-11*

He humbled himself, therefore God raised him high.

The state of Jesus Christ was divine, yet he did not cling to his equality with God but emptied himself to assume the condition of a slave, and became as men are; and being as all men are, he was humbler yet, even to accepting death, death on a cross. But God raised him high and gave him the name which is above all other names so that all beings in the heavens, on earth and in the underworld, should bend the knee at the name of Jesus and that every tongue should acclaim Jesus Christ as Lord, to the glory of God the Father.

The word of the Lord.
Thanks be to God.

GOSPEL ACCLAMATION

Alleluia, alleluia!
We adore you, O Christ,
and we bless you;
because by your cross
you have redeemed the world.
Alleluia!

GOSPEL *John 3:13–17*

The Lord be with you.
And with your spirit.

A reading from the holy Gospel according to John.
Glory to you, O Lord.

The Son of Man must be lifted up.

Jesus said to Nicodemus:

'No one has gone up to heaven except the one who came down from heaven, the Son of Man who is in heaven; and the Son of Man must be lifted up as Moses lifted up the serpent in the desert, so that everyone who believes may have eternal life in him. Yes, God loved the world so much that he gave his only Son, so that everyone who believes in him may not be lost but may have eternal life. For God sent his Son into the world not to condemn the world, but so that through him the world might be saved.'

The Gospel of the Lord.
Praise to you, Lord Jesus Christ.

▷ page 11

PROFESSION OF FAITH

The Profession of Faith is said when this feast is celebrated on Sunday.

PRAYER OVER THE OFFERINGS

May this oblation, O Lord,
which on the altar of the Cross
cancelled the offence of the whole world,
cleanse us, we pray, of all our sins.
Through Christ our Lord.   **Amen.**

▷ page 15

Preface: The victory of the glorious Cross, page 72 or Preface I of the Passion of the Lord, page 73.

COMMUNION ANTIPHON *John 12:32*

When I am lifted up from the earth,
I will draw everyone to myself, says the Lord.

▷ page 59

PRAYER AFTER COMMUNION

Having been nourished by your holy banquet,
we beseech you, Lord Jesus Christ,
to bring those you have redeemed
by the wood of your life-giving Cross
to the glory of the resurrection.
Who live and reign for ever and ever.   **Amen.**

▷ page 59

SAINTS

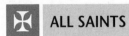 ALL SAINTS

1 NOVEMBER

If this Solemnity falls on a Sunday, it replaces the Sunday in Ordinary Time.
In certain territories, this Solemnity may be transferred to the nearest Sunday,
replacing the Sunday in Ordinary Time.

ENTRANCE ANTIPHON

Let us all rejoice in the Lord,
as we celebrate the feast day in honour of all the Saints,
at whose festival the Angels rejoice
and praise the Son of God.

▷ *page 7*

The Gloria is sung (said)

COLLECT

Almighty ever-living God,
by whose gift we venerate in one celebration
the merits of all the Saints,
bestow on us, we pray,
through the prayers of so many intercessors,
an abundance of the reconciliation with you
for which we earnestly long.
Through our Lord Jesus Christ, your Son,
who lives and reigns with you in the unity of the Holy Spirit,
one God, for ever and ever. **Amen.**

FIRST READING   *Apocalypse 7:2–4, 9–14*

I saw a huge number, impossible to count, of people
from every nation, race, tribe and language.

I, John, saw another angel rising where the sun rises, carrying the seal of the living God; he called in a powerful voice to the four angels whose duty was to devastate land and sea, 'Wait before you do any damage on land or at sea or to the trees, until we have put the seal on the foreheads of the servants of our God.' Then I heard how many were sealed: a hundred and forty-four thousand, out of all the tribes of Israel.

After that I saw a huge number, impossible to count, of people from every nation, race, tribe and language; they were standing in front of the throne and in front of the Lamb, dressed in white robes and holding palms in their hands. They shouted aloud, 'Victory to our God, who sits on the throne, and to the Lamb!' And all the angels who were standing in a circle round the throne, surrounding the elders and the four animals, prostrated themselves before the throne, and touched the ground with their foreheads, worshipping God with these words, 'Amen. Praise and glory and wisdom and thanksgiving and honour and power and strength to our God for ever and ever. Amen.'

One of the elders then spoke, and asked me, 'Do you know who these people are, dressed in white robes, and where they have come from?' I answered him, 'You can tell me, my Lord.' Then he said, 'These are the people who have been through the great persecution, and they have washed their robes white again in the blood of the Lamb.'

The word of the Lord.
Thanks be to God.

RESPONSORIAL PSALM   *Psalm 23:1–6 response cf v 6*

> ### Such are the men who seek your face, O Lord.

1   The Lord's is the earth and its fullness,
the world and all its peoples.
It is he who set it on the seas;
on the waters he made it firm.

2   Who shall climb the mountain of the Lord?
Who shall stand in his holy place?
The man with clean hands and pure heart,
who desires not worthless things.

3   He shall receive blessings from the Lord
and reward from the God who saves him.
Such are the men who seek him,
seek the face of the God of Jacob.

SECOND READING   *1 John 3:1–3*

We shall see God as he really is.

Think of the love that the Father has lavished on us, by letting us be called God's children; and that is what we are. Because the world refused to acknowledge him, therefore it does not acknowledge us. My dear people, we are already the children of God but what we are to be in the future has not yet been revealed; all we know is, that when it is revealed we shall be like him because we shall see him as he really is. Surely everyone who entertains this hope must purify himself, must try to be as pure as Christ.

The word of the Lord.
Thanks be to God.

GOSPEL ACCLAMATION   *Matthew 11:28*

> **Alleluia, alleluia!**
> **Come to me, all you who labour and are overburdened,**
> **and I will give you rest, says the Lord.**
> **Alleluia!**

GOSPEL   *Matthew 5:1–12*

The Lord be with you.
And with your spirit.

A reading from the holy Gospel according to Matthew.
Glory to you, O Lord.

Rejoice and be glad, for your reward will be great in heaven.

Seeing the crowds, Jesus went up the hill. There he sat down and was joined by his disciples. Then he began to speak. This is what he taught them:

'How happy are the poor in spirit; theirs is the kingdom of heaven. Happy the gentle: they shall have the earth for their heritage. Happy those who mourn: they shall be comforted. Happy those who hunger and thirst for what is right: they shall be satisfied. Happy the merciful: they shall have mercy shown them. Happy the pure in heart: they shall see God. Happy the peacemakers: they shall be called sons of God. Happy those who are persecuted in the cause of right: theirs is the kingdom of heaven.

'Happy are you when people abuse you and persecute you and speak all kinds of calumny against you on my account. Rejoice and be glad, for your reward will be great in heaven.'

The Gospel of the Lord.
Praise to you, Lord Jesus Christ.

▷ *page 11*

PROFESSION OF FAITH
The Profession of Faith is said.

PRAYER OVER THE OFFERINGS
May these offerings we bring in honour of all the Saints
be pleasing to you, O Lord,
and grant that, just as we believe the Saints
to be already assured of immortality,
so we may experience their concern for our salvation.
Through Christ our Lord.   **Amen.**

▷ *page 15*

Preface: The glory of Jerusalem, our mother, page 73.

COMMUNION ANTIPHON   *Matthew 5:8–10*
Blessed are the clean of heart, for they shall see God.
Blessed are the peacemakers,
for they shall be called children of God.
Blessed are they who are persecuted for the sake of righteousness,
for theirs is the Kingdom of Heaven.

▷ *page 59*

PRAYER AFTER COMMUNION
As we adore you, O God, who alone are holy
and wonderful in all your Saints,
we implore your grace,
so that, coming to perfect holiness in the fullness of your love,
we may pass from this pilgrim table
to the banquet of our heavenly homeland.
Through Christ our Lord.   **Amen.**

▷ *page 59*

A solemn blessing may be used.

ALL SOULS' DAY

COMMEMORATION OF ALL THE FAITHFUL DEPARTED (ALL SOULS' DAY)
2 NOVEMBER

*If All Souls' Day falls on a Sunday, it replaces the Sunday in Ordinary Time
unless the Solemnity of All Saints is transferred to Sunday 2 November.
In this case All Souls' Day is transferred to 3 November.*

The celebrant may choose any of the three Masses which follow.

ENTRANCE ANTIPHON

First Mass   *cf 1 Thessalonians 4:14; 1 Corinthians 15:22*

Just as Jesus died and has risen again,
so through Jesus God will bring with him
those who have fallen asleep;
and as in Adam all die,
so also in Christ will all be brought to life.

Second Mass *cf 4 Esdras 2:34–35*

Eternal rest grant unto them, O Lord,
and let perpetual light shine upon them.

Third Mass   *cf Romans 8:11*

God, who raised Jesus from the dead,
will give life also to your mortal bodies,
through his Spirit that dwells in you.

▷ *page 7*

The Gloria is sung (said) when this commemoration is celebrated on Sunday.

COLLECT

First Mass

Listen kindly to our prayers, O Lord,
and, as our faith in your Son,
raised from the dead, is deepened,
so may our hope of resurrection for your departed servants
also find new strength.
Through our Lord Jesus Christ, your Son,
who lives and reigns with you in the unity of the Holy Spirit,
one God, for ever and ever. **Amen.**

Second Mass

O God, glory of the faithful and life of the just,
by the Death and Resurrection of whose Son
we have been redeemed,
look mercifully on your departed servants,
that, just as they professed the mystery of our resurrection,
so they may merit to receive the joys of eternal happiness.
Through our Lord Jesus Christ, your Son,
who lives and reigns with you in the unity of the Holy Spirit,
one God, for ever and ever. **Amen.**

COLLECT
Third Mass

O God, who willed that your Only Begotten Son,
having conquered death,
should pass over into the realm of heaven,
grant, we pray, to your departed servants
that, with the mortality of this life overcome,
they may gaze eternally on you,
their Creator and Redeemer.
Through our Lord Jesus Christ, your Son,
who lives and reigns with you in the unity of the Holy Spirit,
one God, for ever and ever. **Amen.**

The following readings are provided in the Lectionary Volume I.
Alternative readings from the Masses for the Dead (Lectionary Volume III) may be chosen.

FIRST READING   *Isaiah 25:6–9*

The Lord will destroy Death for ever.

On this mountain, the Lord of hosts
will prepare for all peoples a banquet
of rich food. On this mountain, he will
remove the mourning veil covering all
peoples, and the shroud enwrapping
all nations; he will destroy Death for
ever. The Lord will wipe away the tears
from every cheek; he will take away his
people's shame everywhere on earth, for
the Lord has said so. That day, it will be
said: See, this is our God in whom we
hoped for salvation; the Lord is the one
in whom we hoped. We exult and we
rejoice that he has saved us.

The word of the Lord.
Thanks be to God.

RESPONSORIAL PSALM   *Psalm 26:1, 4, 7–9 13–14 response v 1; alternative response v 13*

The Lord is my light and my help

or

I am sure I shall see the Lord's goodness
in the land of the living.

1 The Lord is my light and my help;
   whom shall I hear?
   The Lord is the stronghold of my life;
   before whom shall I shrink?

2 There is one thing I ask of the Lord,
   for this I long,
   to live in the house of the Lord,
   all the days of my life,
   to savour the sweetness of the Lord,
   to behold his temple.

3 O Lord, hear my voice when I call;
   have mercy and answer.
   It is your face, O Lord, that I seek;
   hide not your face.

4   I am sure I shall see the Lord's goodness
     in the land of the living.
     Hope in him, hold firm and take heart.
     Hope in the Lord!

SECOND READING   *Romans 5:5–11*

Having died to make us righteous, is it likely that he would now fail to save us from God's anger?

Hope is not deceptive, because the love of God has been poured into our hearts by the Holy Spirit which has been given us. We were still helpless when at his appointed moment Christ died for sinful men. It is not easy to die even for a good man – though of course for someone really worthy, a man might be prepared to die – but what proves that God loves us is that Christ died for us while we were still sinners. Having died to make us righteous, is it likely that he would now fail to save us from God's anger? When we were reconciled to God by the death of his Son, we were still enemies; now that we have been reconciled, surely we may count on being saved by the life of his Son? Not merely because we have been reconciled but because we are filled with joyful trust in God, through our Lord Jesus Christ, through whom we have already gained our reconciliation.

The word of the Lord.
Thanks be to God.

GOSPEL ACCLAMATION   *John 6:39*

Alleluia, alleluia!
It is my Father's will, says the Lord,
that I should lose nothing of all that he has given me,
and that I should raise it up on the last day.
Alleluia!

GOSPEL   *Mark 15:33–39; 16:1–6   Shorter form: Mark 15:33–39 (only read text with side line next to it).*

The Lord be with you.
And with your spirit.

A reading from the holy Gospel according to Mark.
Glory to you, O Lord.

Jesus gave a loud cry and breathed his last.

When the sixth hour came there was darkness over the whole land until the ninth hour. And at the ninth hour Jesus cried out in a loud voice, 'Eloi, Eloi, lama sabachthani?' which means, 'My God, my God, why have you deserted me?' When some of those who stood by heard this, they said, 'Listen, he is calling on Elijah.' Someone ran and soaked a sponge in vinegar and, putting it on a reed, gave it him to drink saying, 'Wait and see if Elijah will come to take him down'. But Jesus gave a loud cry and breathed his last. And the veil of the Temple was torn in two from top to bottom. The centurion, who was standing in front of him, had seen how he had died and he said, 'In truth this man was a son of God'.

When the sabbath was over, Mary of Magdala, Mary the mother of James, and Salome, bought spices with which to go and anoint him. And very early in the morning on the first day of the week they went to the tomb, just as the sun was rising.

They had been saying to one another, 'Who will roll away the stone for us from the entrance to the tomb?' But when they looked they could see that the stone – which was very big – had already been rolled back. On entering the tomb they saw a young man in a white robe seated on the right-hand side, and they were struck with amazement. But he said to them, 'There is no need for alarm. You are looking for Jesus of Nazareth, who was crucified: he has risen, he is not here. See, here is the place where they laid him.'

The Gospel of the Lord.

Praise to you, Lord Jesus Christ.

▷ page 11

PROFESSION OF FAITH
The Profession of Faith is said when this commemoration is celebrated on Sunday.

PRAYER OVER THE OFFERINGS
First Mass
Look favourably on our offerings, O Lord,
so that your departed servants
may be taken up into glory with your Son,
in whose great mystery of love we are all united.
Who lives and reigns for ever and ever.   **Amen.**

Second Mass
Almighty and merciful God,
by means of these sacrificial offerings
wash away, we pray, in the Blood of Christ,
the sins of your departed servants,
for you purify unceasingly by your merciful forgiveness
those you once cleansed in the waters of Baptism.
Through Christ our Lord.   **Amen.**

Third Mass
Receive, Lord, in your kindness,
the sacrificial offering we make
for all your servants who sleep in Christ,
that, set free from the bonds of death
by this singular sacrifice,
they may merit eternal life.
Through Christ our Lord.   **Amen.**

▷ page 15

Preface for the Dead I–V, pages 73–74.

COMMUNION ANTIPHON
First Mass   *cf John 11:25–26*
I am the Resurrection and the Life, says the Lord.
Whoever believes in me, even though he dies, will live,
and everyone who lives and believes in me will not die for ever.

Second Mass   *cf 4 Esdras 2:35, 34*
Let perpetual light shine upon them, O Lord,
with your Saints for ever, for you are merciful.

Third Mass   *cf Philippians 3:20–21*

We await a saviour, the Lord Jesus Christ,
who will change our mortal bodies,
to conform with his glorified body.

▷ *page 59*

PRAYER AFTER COMMUNION
First Mass

Grant we pray, O Lord, that your departed servants,
for whom we have celebrated this paschal Sacrament,
may pass over to a dwelling place of light and peace.
Through Christ our Lord.   **Amen.**

Second Mass

Having received the Sacrament of your Only Begotten Son,
who was sacrificed for us and rose in glory,
we humbly implore you, O Lord,
for your departed servants,
that, cleansed by the paschal mysteries,
they may glory in the gift of the resurrection to come.
Through Christ our Lord.   **Amen.**

Third Mass

Through these sacrificial gifts
which we have received, O Lord,
bestow on your departed servants your great mercy
and, to those you have endowed with the grace of Baptism,
grant also the fullness of eternal joy.
Through Christ our Lord.   **Amen.**

▷ *page 59*

A solemn blessing may be used.

DEDICATION OF THE LATERAN BASILICA

9 NOVEMBER
If this feast falls on a Sunday, it replaces the Sunday in Ordinary Time.
When the Feast is celebrated on a weekday there is only one reading before the Gospel.

ENTRANCE ANTIPHON   *cf Revelation 21:2*

I saw the holy city, a new Jerusalem,
coming down out of heaven from God,
prepared like a bride adorned for her husband.

or   *cf Revelation 21:3*

Behold God's dwelling with the human race.
He will dwell with them and they will be his people,
and God himself with them will be their God.

▷ *page 7*

The Gloria is sung (said).

COLLECT

O God, who from living and chosen stones
prepare an eternal dwelling for your majesty,
increase in your Church the spirit of grace you have bestowed,
so that by new growth your faithful people
may build up the heavenly Jerusalem.
Through our Lord Jesus Christ, your Son,
who lives and reigns with you in the unity of the Holy Spirit,
one God, for ever and ever. **Amen.**

or

O God, who were pleased to call your Church the Bride,
grant that the people that serves your name
may revere you, love you and follow you,
and may be led by you
to attain your promises in heaven.
Through our Lord Jesus Christ, your Son,
who lives and reigns with you in the unity of the Holy Spirit,
one God, for ever and ever. **Amen.**

FIRST READING   *Ezekiel 47:1–2, 8–9, 12*
I saw a stream of water coming from the Temple, bringing life to all wherever it flowed.

The angel brought me to the entrance of the Temple, where a stream came out from under the Temple threshold and flowed eastwards, since the Temple faced east. The water flowed from under the right side of the Temple, south of the altar. He took me out by the north gate and led me right round outside as far as the outer east gate where the water flowed out on the right-hand side. The man went to the east holding his measuring line and measured off a thousand cubits; he then made me wade across the stream; the water reached my ankles. He measured off another thousand and made me wade across the stream again; the water reached my knees. He measured off another thousand and made me wade across again; the water reached my waist. He measured off another thousand; it was now a river which I could not cross; the stream had swollen and was now deep water, a river impossible to cross. He then said: 'Do you see, son of man?' He took me further, then brought me back to the bank of the river. When I got back, there were many trees on each bank of the river. He said, 'This water flows east down to the Arabah and to the sea; and flowing into the sea it makes its waters wholesome. Wherever the river flows, all living creatures teeming in it will live. Fish will be very plentiful, for wherever the water goes it brings health, and life teems wherever the river flows. Along the river, on either bank, will grow every kind of fruit tree with leaves that never wither and fruit that never fails; they will bear new fruit every month, because this water comes from the sanctuary. And their fruit will be good to eat and the leaves medicinal.'

The word of the Lord.
Thanks be to God.

RESPONSORIAL PSALM   *Psalm 45:2–3, 5–6 8–9 response v 5*

The waters of a river give joy to God's city,
the holy place where the Most High dwells.

1   God is for us a refuge and strength,
    a helper close at hand, in time of distress;
    so we shall not fear though the earth should rock,
    though the mountains fall into the depths of the sea.

2   The waters of a river give joy to God's city,
    the holy place where the Most High dwells.
    God is within, it cannot be shaken;
    God will help it at the dawning of the day.

3   The Lord of hosts is with us:
    the God of Jacob is our stronghold.
    Come, consider the works of the Lord,
    the redoubtable deeds he has done on the earth.

SECOND READING   *1 Corinthians 3:9–11, 16–17*
You are the temple of God.

You are God's building. By the grace God gave me, I succeeded as an architect and laid the foundations, on which someone else is doing the building. Everyone doing the building must work carefully. For the foundation, nobody can lay any other than the one which has already been laid, that is Jesus Christ.

Didn't you realise that you were God's temple and that the Spirit of God was living among you? If anybody should destroy the temple of God, God will destroy him, because the temple of God is sacred; and you are that temple.

The word of the Lord.
Thanks be to God.

GOSPEL ACCLAMATION   *2 Chronicles 7:16*

Alleluia, alleluia!
I have chosen and consecrated this house, says the Lord,
for my name to be there for ever.
Alleluia!

GOSPEL   *John 2:13–22*

The Lord be with you.
And with your spirit.

A reading from the holy Gospel according to John.
Glory to you, O Lord.

He was speaking of the sanctuary that was his body.

Just before the Jewish Passover Jesus went up to Jerusalem, and in the Temple he found people selling cattle and sheep and pigeons, and the money changers sitting at their counters there. Making a whip out of some cord, he drove them all out of the Temple, cattle and sheep as well, scattered the money changers'

SAINTS

coins, knocked their tables over and said to the pigeon-sellers, 'Take all this out of here and stop turning my Father's house into a market.' Then his disciples remembered the words of scripture: Zeal for your house will devour me. The Jews intervened and said, 'What sign can you show us to justify what you have done?' Jesus answered, 'Destroy this sanctuary, and in three days I will raise it up.'

The Jews replied, 'It has taken forty-six years to build this sanctuary: are you going to raise it up in three days?' But he was speaking of the sanctuary that was his body, and when Jesus rose from the dead, his disciples remembered that he had said this, and they believed the scripture and the words he had said.

The Gospel of the Lord.
Praise to you, Lord Jesus Christ.

▷ page 11

PROFESSION OF FAITH
The Profession of Faith is said when this feast is celebrated on Sunday.

PRAYER OVER THE OFFERINGS
Accept, we pray, O Lord, the offering made here
and grant that by it those who seek your favour
may receive in this place
the power of the Sacraments
and the answer to their prayers.
Through Christ our Lord.   **Amen.**

▷ page 15

Preface: The Mystery of the Church, the Bride of Christ and the Temple of the Spirit, page 75.

COMMUNION ANTIPHON   *cf 1 Peter 2:5*
Be built up like living stones,
into a spiritual house, a holy priesthood.

▷ page 59

PRAYER AFTER COMMUNION
O God, who chose to foreshadow for us
the heavenly Jerusalem
through the sign of your Church on earth,
grant, we pray,
that, by our partaking of this Sacrament,
we may be made the temple of your grace
and may enter the dwelling place of your glory.
Through Christ our Lord.   **Amen.**

▷ page 59

A solemn blessing may be used.

OTHER CELEBRATIONS

COMMON OF THE DEDICATION OF A CHURCH

COMMON OF THE DEDICATION OF A CHURCH
ON THE ANNIVERSARY OF THE DEDICATION
I   IN THE CHURCH THAT WAS DEDICATED

ENTRANCE ANTIPHON   *Psalm 67:36*

Wonderful are you, O God in your holy place.
The God of Israel himself gives his people strength and courage.
Blessed be God!

▷ *page 7*

The Gloria is sung (or said).

COLLECT

O God, who year by year renew for us the day
when this your holy temple was consecrated,
hear the prayers of your people
and grant that in this place
for you there may always be pure worship
and for us, fullness of redemption.
Through our Lord Jesus Christ, your Son,
who lives and reigns with you in the unity of the Holy Spirit,
one God, for ever and ever.   **Amen.**

FIRST READING

*The Lectionary notes that the pairings of Readings with Responsorial Psalms are suggestions only.
Any other suitable pairing may be used, having regard to the pastoral needs of the occasion.*

One of the following readings is chosen:

1   1 Kings 8:22–23, 27–30
     Let your eyes watch over this house.

2   2 Chronicles 5:6–11, 13–6:2
     *I have built you a dwelling, a place
     for you to live in for ever.*

3   Isaiah 56:1, 6–7
     My house will be called a house of prayer for all the peoples.

4   Ezekiel 43:1–2, 4–7
     I saw the glory of the Lord fill the Temple.

5   Ezekiel 47:1–2, 8–9, 12
     I saw a stream of water coming from the Temple, bringing life to all wherever it flowed.

OTHER

RESPONSORIAL PSALM

One of the following Psalms is chosen:

FOR READING 5,

PSALM 45   *Psalm 45:2–3, 5–6, 8–9 response v 5*

The waters of a river give joy to God's city,
the holy place where the Most High dwells.

FOR READING 1 OR 3

PSALM 83   *Psalm 83:3–5, 10–11 response v 2, alternative response Apocalypse 21:3*

How lovely is your dwelling place,
Lord, God of hosts

or

Here God lives among men.

FOR READING 2 OR 4

1 CHRONICLES 29   *1 Chronicles 29:10–12 response v 13*

We praise your glorious name, O Lord.

SECOND READING

One of the following readings is chosen:

1   1 Corinthians 3:9–11, 16–17
    You are the temple of God.

2   Ephesians 2:19–22
    All grow into one holy temple in the Lord.

3   Hebrews 12:18–19, 22–24
    You have come to Mount Zion and to the city of the living God.

4   1 Peter 2:4–9
    So that you too may be living stones making a spiritual house.

GOSPEL ACCLAMATION

The Lectionary notes that the pairings of each Gospel Acclamations with Gospel readings are suggestions only. Any other suitable pairing may be used, having regard to the pastoral needs of the occasion.

FOR GOSPEL 1   *Matthew 16:18*

Alleluia, alleluia!
You are Peter and on this rock I will build my Church.
And the gates of the underworld can never hold out against it.
Alleluia!

FOR GOSPEL 2   *cf Matthew 7:8*

Alleluia, alleluia!
In my house, says the Lord,
the one who asks always receives;
the one who searches always finds;
the one who knocks will always have the door opened to him.
Alleluia!

FOR GOSPEL 3   *2 Chronicles 7:16*

Alleluia, alleluia!
I have chosen and consecrated this house, says the Lord,
that my name may remain in it for all time.
Alleluia!

FOR GOSPEL 4   *Isaiah 66:1*

Alleluia, alleluia!
With heaven my throne
and earth my footstool,
what house could you build me? says the Lord.
Alleluia!

or   *Ezekiel 37:27*

Alleluia, alleluia!
I shall make my home among them, says the Lord;
I will be their God,
they shall be my people
Alleluia!

GOSPEL

One of the following readings is chosen:

1   Matthew 16:13–19

> *You are Peter. I will give you the keys*
> *of the kingdom of heaven.*

2   Luke 19:1–10

> *Today salvation has come to this house.*

3   John 2:13–22

> *He was speaking of the sanctuary*
> *that was his body.*

4   John 4:19–24

> *True worshippers will worship the Father*
> *in spirit and truth.*

▷ page 11

The Profession of Faith is said.

PRAYER OVER THE OFFERINGS

Recalling the day when you were pleased
to fill your house with glory and holiness, O Lord,
we pray that you may make of us
a sacrificial offering always acceptable to you.
Through Christ our Lord.   **Amen.**

▷ page 15

PREFACE

THE MYSTERY OF THE TEMPLE OF GOD, WHICH IS THE CHURCH.

Priest: The Lord be with you.
People: **And with your spirit.**

Priest: Lift up your hearts.
People: **We lift them up to the Lord.**

Priest: Let us give thanks to the Lord our God.
People: **It is right and just.**

Priest: It is truly right and just, our duty and our salvation,
always and everywhere to give you thanks,
Lord, holy Father, almighty and eternal God,
through Christ our Lord.

For in this visible house that you have let us build
and where you never cease to show favour

OTHER

to the family on pilgrimage to you in this place,
you wonderfully manifest and accomplish
the mystery of your communion with us.
Here you build up for yourself the temple that we are
and cause your Church, spread throughout the world,
to grow ever more and more as the Lord's own Body,
till she reaches her fullness in the vision of peace,
the heavenly city of Jerusalem.

And so, with the countless ranks of the blessed,
in the temple of your glory we praise you,
we bless you, and proclaim your greatness, as we acclaim:

All: **Holy, Holy, Holy Lord God of hosts...**

COMMUNION ANTIPHON   cf 1 Corinthians 3:16–17

You are the temple of God, and the Spirit of God dwells in you.
The temple of God, which you are, is holy.   ▷ page 59

PRAYER AFTER COMMUNION

May the people consecrated to you, O Lord, we pray,
receive the fruits and joy of your blessing,
that the festive homage
they have offered you today in the body
may redound upon them as a spiritual gift.
Through Christ our Lord.   **Amen.**   ▷ page 59

BLESSING AT THE END OF MASS

Priest: May God, the Lord of heaven and earth,
            who has gathered you today
            in memory of the dedication of this church,
            make you abound in heavenly blessings.
All: **Amen.**

Priest: And may he, who has willed that all his scattered children
            be gathered together in his Son,
            grant that you may become his temple
            and the dwelling place of the Holy Spirit.
All: **Amen.**

Priest: Thus, may you be made thoroughly clean,
            so that God may dwell within you
            and you may possess with all the Saints
            the inheritance of eternal happiness.
All: **Amen.**

Priest: And may the blessing of almighty God,
            the Father, and the Son, ✠ and the Holy Spirit,
            come down on you and remain with you for ever.
All: **Amen.**

RCIA — RITE OF ACCEPTANCE

RITE OF CHRISTIAN INITIATION OF ADULTS
RITE OF ACCEPTANCE INTO THE ORDER OF CATECHUMENS

The Introductory Rites of the Mass are replaced by the act of Receiving the Candidates.

RECEIVING THE CANDIDATES

The candidates, their sponsors and a group of the faithful gather outside the church or at the church door (or elsewhere suitable to this rite).

The assembly may sing a Psalm or appropriate song.

GREETING

The Priest greets the candidates in a friendly manner. He speaks to them, their sponsors and all present about their journey of faith to this point.

He invites the sponsors and candidates to come forward.
As they take their places before the Priest, an appropriate song may be sung
(for example Psalm 62:1–8).

OPENING DIALOGUE

The candidates may be introduced to the assembly, or their names called out. The Priest then asks the candidates their intentions

In asking the candidates about their intentions celebrant may use other words than those provided the and may let them answer in their own words for example, to the first question,

'What do you ask of the Church of God?' or 'What do you desire?' or 'For what reason have you come?',

he may receive such answers as 'The grace of Christ' or 'Entrance into the Church' or 'Eternal life' or other suitable responses. The celebrant then phrases his next question according to the answer received.

Priest:	What do you ask of God's Church?
Candidate:	**Faith.**

Priest:	What does faith offer you?
Candidate:	**Eternal life.**

CANDIDATES' FIRST ACCEPTANCE OF THE GOSPEL

The Priest addresses the candidates and then asks them about their acceptance of the Gospel. His question may end in these or similar words:

Priest:	…Are you prepared to begin this journey under the guidance of Christ?
Candidates:	**I am.**

AFFIRMATION BY THE SPONSORS AND THE ASSEMBLY

The Priest then asks the sponsors and the assembly to commit themselves to support the candidates. He uses these or similar words:

Priest: Sponsors, you now present these candidates to us; are you, and all who are gathered here with us, ready to help these candidates find and follow Christ?

All: **We are.**

Then the Priest says:

Priest: Father of mercy,
            we thank you for these your servants.
            You have sought and summoned them in many ways
            and they have turned to seek you.

            You have called them today
            and they have answered in your presence:
            we praise you, Lord, and we bless you.

All sing or say:

All: **We praise you, Lord, and we bless you.**

SIGNING OF THE CANDIDATES WITH THE CROSS

The catechists or sponsors sign the catechumens on the forehead as the Priest says:

Priest: N., receive the cross on your forehead.
            It is Christ himself who now strengthens you
            with this sign of his love.
            Learn to know him and follow him.

All say or sing this, or another suitable acclamation:

All: **Glory and praise to you, Lord Jesus Christ!**

Other parts of the body may also be signed with the Sign of the Cross. The catechists or sponsors sign the catechumens on the appropriate part of the body as the Priest says each set of words.

Priest: Receive the sign of the cross on your ears,
            that you may hear the voice of the Lord.

All: **Glory and praise to you, Lord Jesus Christ!**

Priest: Receive the sign of the cross on your eyes,
            that you may see the glory of the Lord.

All: **Glory and praise to you, Lord Jesus Christ!**

Priest: Receive the sign of the cross on your lips,
            that you may respond to the word of God.

All: **Glory and praise to you, Lord Jesus Christ!**

Priest: Receive the sign of the cross on your heart,
            that Christ may dwell there by faith.

All: **Glory and praise to you, Lord Jesus Christ!**

Priest: Receive the sign of the cross on your shoulders,
            that you may bear the gentle yolk of Christ.
All: **Glory and praise to you, Lord Jesus Christ!**

Then the celebrant alone makes the sign of the cross over all the candidates at once:

Priest: I sign you with the sign of eternal life
                    in the name of the Father, and of the Son ✠
                    and of the Holy Spirit.
Catechumens: **Amen.**

CONCLUDING PRAYER

Let us pray.   *or*

Lord,   Almighty God,
we have signed these catechumens   by the cross and resurrection of your Son
with the sign of Christ's cross.   you have given life to your people.
Protect them by its power,   Your servants have received the sign of
so that, faithful to the grace which has   the cross:
    begun in them,   make them living proof of its saving power
they may keep your commandments   and help them to persevere in the footsteps
and come to the glory of rebirth in baptism.   of Christ.
We ask this through Christ our Lord.   We ask this through Christ our Lord.

Amen.   **Amen.**

INVITATION TO THE CELEBRATION OF THE WORD OF GOD

The Priest invites the catechumens and their sponsors to enter the church, using these or similar words:

Priest: N. and N., come into the church,
            to share with us at the table of God's word.

The catechumens and their sponsors enter the church to take their places among the assembly.

*During the entry an appropriate song is sung, or the following antiphon may be used
with Psalm 33:2, 3, 6, 9, 10, 11,16.*

Ant.   Come, my children, and listen to me;
        I will teach you the fear of the Lord.

LITURGY OF THE WORD

INSTRUCTION

*After the catechumens have taken their places among the assembly, the Priest speaks to them helping them
understand the dignity of God's word which is proclaimed and heard in the church.*

The Lectionary is carried in procession and placed with honour on the ambo, where it may be incensed.

READINGS

*The readings may be chosen from any of the readings of the Lectionary for Mass that are suited to the new
catechumens.*

OTHER

HOMILY

A homily follows that explains the readings.

PRESENTATION OF A BIBLE *(Optional)*

A book containing the gospels may be given to the catechumens by the celebrant; a cross may also be given, unless this has already been done as one of the additional rites.

INTERCESSIONS FOR THE CATECHUMENS

Each intercession for the catechumens concludes:

Let us pray to the Lord
Lord, hear our prayer

If the Prayer of the Faithful is to be omitted, intercessions for the Church and the whole world are added to the intercessions for the catechumens.

PRAYER OVER THE CATECHUMENS

After the intercessions, the celebrant, with hands outstretched over the catechumens, says one of the following prayers.

Let us pray.
[God of our forebears and] God of all creation,
we ask you to look favourably on your servants *N.* and *N.*;
make them fervent in spirit,
joyful in hope,
and always ready to serve your name.
Lead them, Lord, to the baptism of new birth,
so that, living a fruitful life in the company of your faithful,
they may receive the eternal reward that you promise.
We ask this in the name of Jesus the Lord. **Amen.**

or

Almighty God,
source of all creation,
you have made us in your image.
Welcome with love those who come before you today.
They have listened among us to the word of Christ;
by its power renew them
and by your grace refashion them,
so that in time they may assume the full likeness of Christ,
who lives and reigns for ever and ever. **Amen.**

DISMISSAL OF THE CATECHUMENS

If the eucharist is to be celebrated, the catechumens are normally dismissed at this point by use of option A; if the catechumens are to stay for the celebration of the eucharist, option B is used; if the eucharist is not to be celebrated, the entire assembly is dismissed by use of option C.

A   *The celebrant recalls briefly the great joy with which the catechumens have just been received and urges them to live according to the word of God they have just heard. After the dismissal formulary, the group of catechumens goes out but does not disperse. With the help of some of the faithful, the catechumens remain together to share their joy and spiritual experiences.*

Priest: Catechumens, go in peace,
                     and may the Lord remain with you always.
Catechumens: **Thanks be to God.**

Similar words may be used, for example:

Priest: My dear friends,
            this community now sends you forth
            to reflect more deeply on the word of God which you have shared with us today.
            Be assured of our loving support and prayers for you.
            We look forward to the day when you will share fully in the Lord's Table.

B   *If for serious reasons the catechumens cannot leave and must remain with the baptized, they are to be instructed that though they are present at the eucharist, they cannot take part in it as the baptized do. They may be reminded of this by the celebrant in these or similar words.*

Priest: Although you cannot yet participate fully in the Lord's eucharist,
            stay with us as a sign of our hope
            that all God's children will eat and drink with the Lord
            and work with his Spirit to re-create the face of the earth.

C   *The celebrant dismisses those present, using these or similar words.*

Priest: Go in peace, and may the Lord remain with you always.
All: **Thanks be to God.**

An appropriate song may conclude the celebration.

▷ *page 13*

PRAYER OF THE FAITHFUL AND PROFESSION OF FAITH

Intercessory prayer is resumed with the usual Prayer of the Faithful for the needs of the Church and the whole world; then, if required, the Profession of Faith is said. But for pastoral reasons, the Prayer of the Faithful and the Profession of Faith may be omitted.

Mass continues in the usual way, using the prayers proper to the day.

> After the celebration of the Rite of Acceptance, the names of the catechumens are to be duly inscribed in the register of catechumens, along with the names of the sponsors and the minister and the date and place of the celebration...
>
> ...Joined to the Church, the catechumens are now part of the household of Christ, since the Church nourishes them with the word of God and by means of liturgical celebrations.

cf Rite of Christian Initiation of Adults n 46–47

MUSIC FOR THE ORDER OF MASS

On occasion, music is not provided for the text which precedes the people's response. In this case a cue is given indicating the last note(s) sung before the response, as in the example opposite:

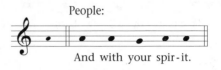

People:

And with your spir-it.

MUSIC

INTRODUCTORY RITES

SIGN OF THE CROSS

All make the Sign of the Cross as the Priest sings:

Priest:

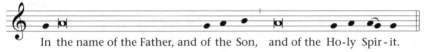

In the name of the Father, and of the Son, and of the Ho-ly Spir-it.

People:

A-men.

GREETING

Priest: The grace of our Lord Jesus Christ,
            and the love of God,
            and the communion of the Holy Spirit
            be with you all.

or

Priest: Grace to you and peace from God our Father
            and the Lord Jesus Christ.

or

Priest: The Lord be with you.

A Bishop will say:

Bishop: Peace be with you.

People:

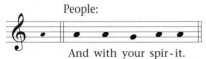

And with your spir-it.

PENITENTIAL ACT
Penitential Act B

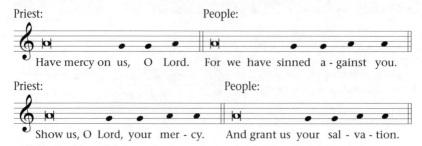

Priest: Have mercy on us, O Lord.
People: For we have sinned a-gainst you.

Priest: Show us, O Lord, your mer-cy.
People: And grant us your sal-va-tion.

Penitential Act C

Priest or minister: You were sent to heal the contrite of heart:

Repeat after the Priest or minister:

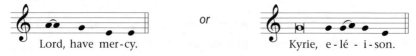

Lord, have mer-cy.   *or*   Kyrie, e-lé-i-son.

Priest or minister: You came to call sinners:

Repeat after the Priest or minister:

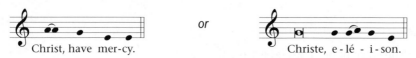

Christ, have mer-cy.   *or*   Christe, e-lé-i-son.

Priest or minister: You are seated at the right hand of the Father
                              to intercede for us:

Repeat after the Priest or minister:

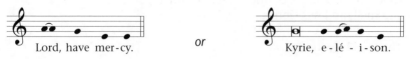

Lord, have mer-cy.   *or*   Kyrie, e-lé-i-son.

ABSOLUTION

The absolution by the Priest follows all of the options above

Priest:

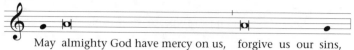

May almighty God have mercy on us, forgive us our sins,

People:

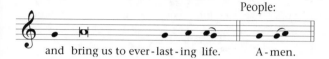

and bring us to ever-last-ing life.   A-men.

KYRIE

V. Lord,   have mer-cy.   R. Lord,   have mer-cy.

V. Christ, have mer-cy.   R. Christ, have mer-cy.

V. Lord,   have mer-cy.   R. Lord,   have mer-cy.

or

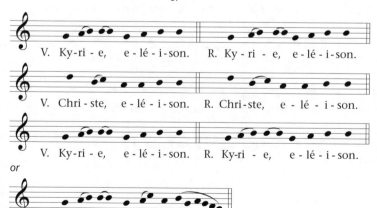

V. Ky-ri - e,   e - lé - i - son.   R. Ky - ri - e,   e - lé - i - son.

V. Chri - ste, e - lé - i - son.   R. Chri-ste,   e - lé - i - son.

V. Ky-ri - e,   e - lé - i - son.   R. Ky-ri - e,   e - lé - i - son.

or

R. Ky - ri - e,   e - lé - i - son.

GLORIA

Glo-ry to God in the high-est, and on earth peace to peo-ple of good will.

We praise you, we bless you, we a - dore you, we glo - ri - fy you,

we give you thanks for your great glo - ry, Lord God, heav - en - ly King,

O God, al - migh - ty Fa - ther. Lord Je - sus Christ,

On-ly Be - got - ten Son, Lord, God, Lamb of God, Son of the Fa - ther,

you take a - way the sins of the world, have mer - cy on us;

you take a - way the sins of the world, re - ceive our prayer;

you are seat - ed at the right hand of the Fa - ther, have mer - cy on us.

For you a - lone are the Ho - ly One, you a - lone are the Lord,

you a - lone are the Most High, Je - sus Christ, with the Ho - ly Spir - it,

in the glo-ry of God the Fa - ther. A - men.

LITURGY OF THE WORD

FIRST READING

Acclamation at the end of the reading.

Reader: People:

The word of the Lord.   Thanks be to God.

SECOND READING

Acclamation at the end of the reading.

Reader: People:

The word of the Lord.   Thanks be to God.

GOSPEL

`ALL STAND`

Dialogue at the beginning of the Gospel.

Deacon / Priest: People:

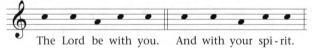

The Lord be with you.   And with your spi‑rit.

Deacon / Priest: People:

A reading from the holy Gospel according to N.   Glory to you, O Lord.

Acclamation at the end of the Gospel.

Deacon / Priest: People:

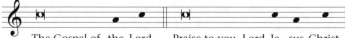

The Gospel of the Lord.   Praise to you, Lord Je‑sus Christ.

`ALL SIT`

PROFESSION OF FAITH

Niceno-Constantinopolitan Creed

in accordance with the Scrip - tures.   He as - cen - ded in - to heav - en

and is seated at the right hand of the Fa - ther.   He will come a - gain in glo - ry

to judge the living and the dead   and his kingdom will have no end.

I be - lieve in the Ho - ly Spir - it,   the Lord, the giv - er of life,

who pro - ceeds from the Father and the Son,   who with the Fa - ther

and the Son   is adored and glo - ri - fied, who has spoken

through the proph - ets.   I be - lieve in one, ho - ly, cath - o - lic

and a - po - sto - lic Church.   I con - fess one bap - tism

for the for - give - ness of sins   and I look for - ward to the

res - ur - rec - tion of the dead   and the life of the world to come.

A - - - men.

214

 LITURGY OF THE EUCHARIST

ORATE, FRATRES

Priest:

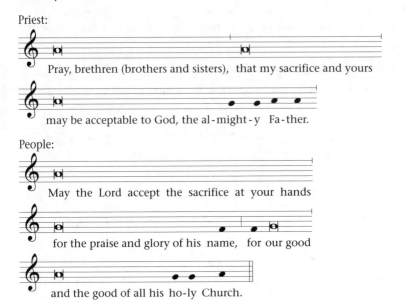

Pray, brethren (brothers and sisters), that my sacrifice and yours

may be acceptable to God, the al-might-y Fa-ther.

People:

May the Lord accept the sacrifice at your hands

for the praise and glory of his name, for our good

and the good of all his ho-ly Church.

PREFACE DIALOGUE

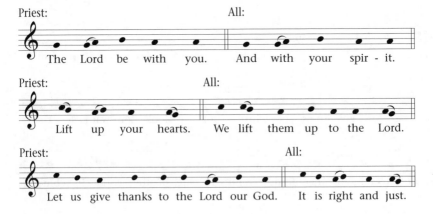

Priest: All:

The Lord be with you. And with your spir-it.

Priest: All:

Lift up your hearts. We lift them up to the Lord.

Priest: All:

Let us give thanks to the Lord our God. It is right and just.

SANCTUS

Ho-ly, Ho-ly, Ho-ly Lord God of hosts. Heav-en and earth are full of your glo-ry. Ho-san-na in the high-est. Bles-sed is he who comes in the name of the Lord. Ho-san-na in the high-est.

or

San-ctus, San-ctus, San-ctus Dó-mi-nus De-us Sá-ba-oth. Ple-ni sunt cae-li et ter-ra gló-ri-a tu-a. Ho-sán-na in ex-cél-sis. Be-ne-dí-ctus qui ven-it in nó-mi-ne Dó-mi-ni. Ho-sán-na in ex-cél-sis.

ALL KNEEL

MEMORIAL ACCLAMATION

Priest:

The mys-ter-y of faith.

Memorial Acclamation A

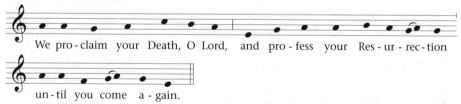

We pro-claim your Death, O Lord, and pro-fess your Res-ur-rec-tion un-til you come a-gain.

Priest:

The mys - ter - y of faith.

Memorial Acclamation B

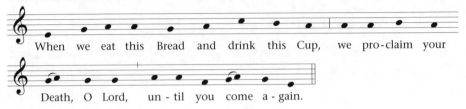

When we eat this Bread and drink this Cup, we pro-claim your

Death, O Lord, un - til you come a - gain.

Memorial Acclamation C

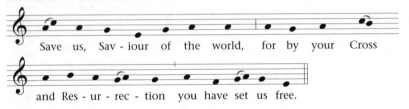

Save us, Sav - iour of the world, for by your Cross

and Res - ur - rec - tion you have set us free.

Memorial Acclamation D *for Ireland only*

My Lord and my God.

DOXOLOGY AND GREAT AMEN

Priest:

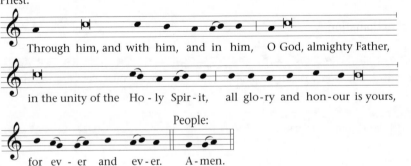

Through him, and with him, and in him, O God, almighty Father,

in the unity of the Ho - ly Spir - it, all glo-ry and hon-our is yours,

People:

for ev - er and ev-er. A-men.

COMMUNION RITE

LORD'S PRAYER

ALL STAND

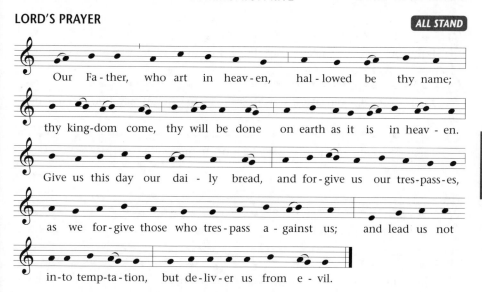

Our Fa-ther, who art in heav-en, hal-lowed be thy name;

thy king-dom come, thy will be done on earth as it is in heav-en.

Give us this day our dai-ly bread, and for-give us our tres-pass-es,

as we for-give those who tres-pass a-gainst us; and lead us not

in-to temp-ta-tion, but de-liv-er us from e-vil.

Priest   Deliver us, Lord, we pray, from every evil,
graciously grant peace in our days,
that, by the help of your mercy,
we may be always free from sin
and safe from all distress,
as we await the blessed hope
and the coming of our Saviour, Jesus Christ.

People:

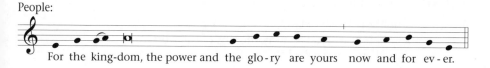

For the king-dom, the power and the glo-ry are yours now and for ev-er.

RITE OF PEACE

Priest: The peace of the Lord be with you always.

People:

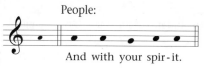

And with your spir-it.

MUSIC

BREAKING OF BREAD

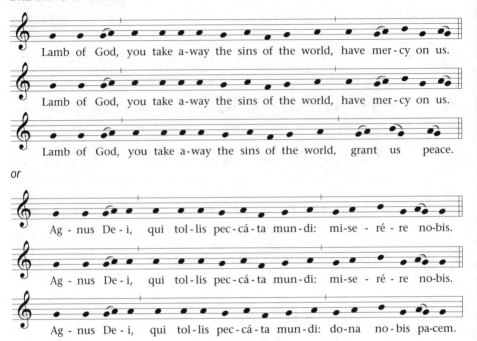

Lamb of God, you take a-way the sins of the world, have mer-cy on us.

Lamb of God, you take a-way the sins of the world, have mer-cy on us.

Lamb of God, you take a-way the sins of the world, grant us peace.

or

Ag - nus De - i,   qui tol-lis pec-cá-ta mun-di: mi-se - ré - re no-bis.

Ag - nus De - i,   qui tol-lis pec-cá-ta mun-di: mi-se - ré - re no-bis.

Ag - nus De - i,   qui tol-lis pec-cá-ta mun-di: do-na   no-bis pa-cem.

The invocation may be repeated several times if the Breaking of the Bread is prolonged.
The final time always ends 'grant us peace' ('dona nobis pacem').

ALL KNEEL

INVITATION TO COMMUNION

Priest   Behold the Lamb of God,
           behold him who takes away the sins of the world.
           Blessed are those called to the…

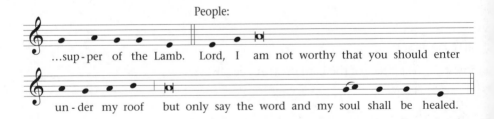

People:

…sup-per of the Lamb. Lord, I am not worthy that you should enter

un - der my roof   but only say the word and my soul shall be healed.

CONCLUDING RITES

BLESSING

Priest: People:

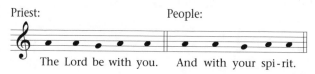

The Lord be with you.   And with your spi-rit.

On certain occasions, the following blessing may be preceded by a solemn blessing or prayer over the people. Then the Priest blesses the people, singing:

MUSIC

Priest: May almighty God bless you:
the Father, and the Son, ✠ and the Holy Spirit.

Priest: People:

...Ho-ly Spi - rit.   A - men.

In a Pontifical Mass, the celebrant receives the mitre and sings:

Bishop: All:

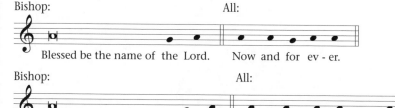

Blessed be the name of the Lord.   Now and for ev - er.

Bishop: All:

Our help is in the name of the Lord.   Who made heav-en and earth.

On certain occasions the following blessing may be preceded by a more solemn blessing or prayer over the people. Then the celebrant receives the pastoral staff, if he uses it, and sings:

Bishop: May almighty God bless you:
making the Sign of the Cross over the people three times, he adds:
the Father, ✠ and the Son, ✠ and the...

Bishop: People:

...Ho-ly Spi - rit.   A - men.

If any liturgical action follows immediately, the rites of dismissal are omitted.

DISMISSAL

Deacon or Priest: Go forth, the Mass is ended.
or   Go and announce the Gospel of the Lord.
or   Go in peace, glorifying the Lord by your life.

Thanks be to God.

or

Deacon or Priest: All:

Go   in   peace.   Thanks be to God.

INDEX

PRAYERS

Prayer before a Crucifix

Behold, O kind and most sweet Jesus,
I cast myself on my knees in your sight,
and with the most fervent desire of my soul,
I pray and beseech you
that you would impress upon my heart
lively sentiments of faith, hope and charity,
with a true repentance for my sins
and a firm desire of amendment,
while with deep affection and grief of soul

I ponder within myself
and mentally contemplate
your five most precious wounds,
having before my eyes
that which David spoke in prophecy of you,
O good Jesus:
'They have pierced my hands and my feet;
they have numbered all my bones.'

On silence

We need to find God, and he cannot be found in noise and restlessness,
God is the friend of silence.
See how nature – trees, flowers, grass – grow in silence;
see the stars, the moon and sun, how they move in silence.
Is not our mission to give God to the poor in the slums?
Not a dead God, but a living, loving God.
The more we receive in silent prayer, the more we can give in our active life.
We need silence to be able to touch souls.
The essential thing is not what we say, but what God says to us and through us.
All our words will be useless unless they come from within –
words which do not give the light of Christ increase the darkness.

Mother Teresa

Salve Regina

Hail, holy Queen, mother of mercy:
hail, our life, our sweetness, and our hope!
To you do we cry,
poor banished children of Eve.
To you do we send up our sighs,
mourning and weeping
in this vale of tears.
Turn then, most gracious advocate,
your eyes of mercy towards us;
and after this our exile,
show to us the blessed fruit of your womb,
    Jesus.
O clement, O loving,
O sweet Virgin Mary.

Pray for us, O holy Mother of God.
That we may be made worthy of the
    promises of Christ.

The Memorare

Remember, O most loving Virgin Mary,
that it is a thing unheard of,
that anyone ever had recourse to your
protection,
implored your help,
or sought your intercession,
and was left forsaken.
Filled therefore with confidence in your
goodness
I fly to you, O Mother, Virgin of virgins.
To you I come, before you I stand,
a sorrowful sinner.
Despise not my poor words, O Mother of
the Word of God,
but graciously hear and grant my prayer.

PRAYERS AFTER COMMUNION

Anima Christi

Soul of Christ, sanctify me.
Body of Christ, save me.
Blood of Christ, inebriate me.
Water from the side of Christ, wash me.
Passion of Christ, strengthen me.
Jesus, hear me.
Hide me in your wounds,
that I may never leave your side
and never let me be parted from you.
From the malicious enemy defend me.

In the hour of my death call me,
and tell me come unto you,
that with your saints I may praise you
through all eternity,
for ever and ever. Amen

O Sacrum Convivium

O Sacred Banquet,
in which Christ is received,
and the memory of his Passion is renewed;
where the soul is filled with grace,
and a pledge of future glory is given to us.

PRAYERS AFTER MASS

Prayer of Saint Ignatius

Teach us, good Lord,
to serve you as you deserve;
to give and not to count the cost;
to fight and not to heed the wounds;
to toil, and not to seek for rest;
to labour and to ask for no reward,
save that of knowing
that we do your will;
through Jesus Christ our Lord.

Jesus, our brother

Dear Lord,
I believe that Holy Communion joins us all
together in union with you and in union
with one another.
As we all received you together at the Holy
Table, let us remember that we are all
members of one family.
Let us help one another and forgive one
another, bearing one another's burdens.
You have said that if we do not love our
neighbour, whom we can see, how can we
love God, whom we cannot see?
Make me careful, therefore, not to despise
anyone, as if they were beneath me; not to
bear a grudge against anyone who may have
done me wrong.
Whenever there is any work to be done for
the good of the parish, make me overcome
my laziness and my pride and give me the
desire to help.
Let me be a good example, not a stumbling
block, to those around me.

Prayer of Saint Francis

Lord, make me an instrument of your peace.
Where there is hatred let me sow peace;
where there is injury, pardon;
where there is doubt, let me sow faith;
where there is despair, let me give hope;
where there is darkness, let me give light;
where there is sadness, let me give joy.
O Divine Master, grant that I may not seek
to be comforted, but to comfort;
to be understood, but to understand;
to be loved, but to love.
For it is in giving that we receive,
it is in forgiving that we are forgiven,
and it is in dying
that we are born to eternal life.

Prayer of St Richard

O dear Lord,
three things I pray:
to see thee more clearly,
love thee more dearly,
and follow thee more nearly,
day by day.

A thought on Thanksgiving

It is very easy to pray to God
when we are in trouble;
even people who do not think
they believe in God
may utter a short prayer in times of crisis.
Fewer people thank God
for the good things which we are given.
Remember how often Jesus said,
'Father, I thank you...'

Etta Gullick